D0500556

THE
ALPS

THE
ALPS

A Human History from
Hannibal to Heidi and Beyond

STEPHEN O'SHEA

W. W. NORTON & COMPANY

Independent Publishers Since 1923

New York • *London*

For information about permission to reproduce selections from this book,
write to Permissions, W. W. Norton & Company, Inc.,
500 Fifth Avenue, New York, NY 10110

For information about special discounts for bulk purchases, please contact
W. W. Norton Special Sales at specialsales@wwnorton.com or 800-233-4830

Manufacturing by Quad Graphics, Fairfield
Book design by Marysarah Quinn
Production manager: Anna Oler

ISBN: 978-0-393-24685-8

W. W. Norton & Company, Inc.
500 Fifth Avenue, New York, N.Y. 10110
www.wwnorton.com

W. W. Norton & Company Ltd.
15 Carlisle Street, London W1D 3BS

1 2 3 4 5 6 7 8 9 0

To my Helpers,

H. Ellison, Dana H., Edward H., Ernst H.

CONTENTS

PREFACE

THE BEST DESCRIPTION OF THE ALPS I've seen comes from a geologist, Richard Fortey, in *Earth: An Intimate History*. Writing of the violent collision of European and African tectonic plates over millennia, he says, "Alpine mountains might be seen as badly made lasagne, crudely layered and buckled in the cooking." The result of a mountain-building process that began about sixty-five million years ago, the Alps form a fearsome, gargantuan intrusion of stone inconveniently located not at the edge but square in the middle of Europe.

I lived almost two decades in Paris, then another few years near Perpignan, in the shadow of the Pyrenees. All the while, I was drawn to Europe's most evocative mountain range, the Alps, again and again. I have overflown them, taken trains through their tunnels, driven over their heart-stopping passes, and skied down their slopes.

There is a temptation to dismiss the Alps as simply a winter wonderland, a backdrop for skiers taking pictures of themselves with stuffed marmots. They are much more than that, and always have been. The Alps impede the passage between northern and southern

Europe. Their size and inaccessibility have made them the source of divisions—in language, cuisine, culture, religion, history, and much more. It is this human geography that interests me most. Their hidden valleys have seen the march of armies since Antiquity, witnessed the clanking of Crusaders and the tramp of pilgrims. Tradesmen have struggled over their passes, as have bishops, emperors, noblewomen, and thieves. Fourteen million people live in the Alps, and many of them cannot talk to one another, so great are the language barriers created by the mountains. *Disruption*, to use a term now in vogue, has been their role in a colorful history.

Before satisfying my curiosity by journeying in their midst, I was unaware that these mountains were the midwife of the Romantic Revolution, that they changed the very way we look at nature, that what was once considered forbidding ineluctably became erotic. The Alps more or less invented tourism, and they ushered in the mania for winter sports. They have inspired artists and criminals. They have also stood as a challenge for people of great courage and intellect. Mountaineering came of age in the Alps, as did the science of geology. They have been the stage for marvelous engineering achievement and the setting for horrible disaster.

Taken together, the various Alpine ranges cover a Kansas-sized 210,000 square kilometers and stretch from France to Slovenia in a 1,200-kilometer arc that is 200 kilometers at its widest. That makes for thousands of peaks—monstrous, medium, and modest—as one proceeds from west to east. There are 1,599 Alpine peaks with an altitude exceeding 2,000 meters. After much head-scratching, I opted to take a route from west to east, from Lake Geneva in Switzerland to Trieste in Italy. This meant that I could engage with the mammoth heights first, while I was still fresh. More important, I decided to concentrate on the high passes of the Alps rather than their high peaks. It is by cresting a pass that one sees the diversity in human geography, learns the different stories told on either side of the height, finds out that what is goofy on one side may be grand on the other. With a high pass, you go through the trees, then they fade away, until you are at a tundra height overlain with snow. Downward you go, around dozens of hairpin turns, and usually you end up in someplace entirely different. You may have passed a national boundary, a "lard line" (pork fat vs. olive oil), a linguistic cleavage (from the Germanic to the Latin or the Slavic), a shift in architecture, or a sudden change in human behavior and custom. To someone who has always been interested in boundaries and differences, the Alpine passes proved irresistible. I am hardly alone in this feeling. Writing in 1904, British mountaineer William Conway observed,

> To climb a peak is to make an expedition, but to cross a pass is to travel. In the one case you normally return to the spot whence you set out; in the other you go from the known to the unknown, from the visible to what is beyond. The peak, which is before you when you set out to climb it, is only explained, not revealed, as you ascend; but every pass is a revelation: it takes you over into another region. You leave one area behind and you enter another; you come down amongst new people and into fresh surroundings. You shut out all that was familiar yesterday and open up another world.

This journey will necessarily be automotive, a vertical road trip for the stout of heart. The ground to be covered is vast—six Alpine countries, tens of thousands of meters up and down, up and down. I do not intend this to be an exhaustive itinerary covering every pass—that is an outright impossibility, given their number. Rather, I will concentrate on those with the most stories to tell. The vistas will be magnificent, scary even, but the insight gained might just be well worth the effort and the fright.

And did I mention that I'm afraid of heights?

A Note on Measurement

The highest mountains of the Alps are called "four-thousanders"—for their metric elevation. Road signage everywhere in the mountains shows kilometers. Signs at the mouth of a tunnel inform you of the distance, in meters, you can expect to be driving in darkness. The Alps are incontestably metric mountains.

Accordingly, throughout this book I have used the metric system. A kilometer is 0.6 mile; thus, 100 kilometers equal 60 miles. The meter is 3.28 feet in length. So, if you insist on getting a foot value for the elevations of peaks and passes, use 3.28 as a multiplier, or 3 and then some. Or just think: slightly longer than a yard.

But I will not abandon our irrational system entirely. Snarled traffic will still *inch* along, a nearby object will still be a few *feet* away. A six-foot-tall man will remain six feet. Consistency is vastly overrated, so in the particulars of daily life I shall revert to the familiar. In this I take my cue from a former leader of the French Communists who, when called out on an inconsistency, used to say, "Such are my contradictions!"

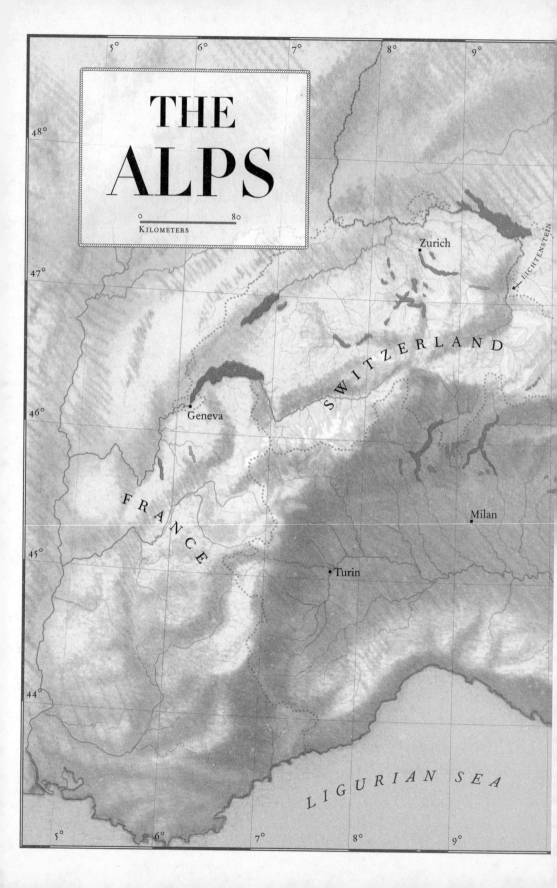

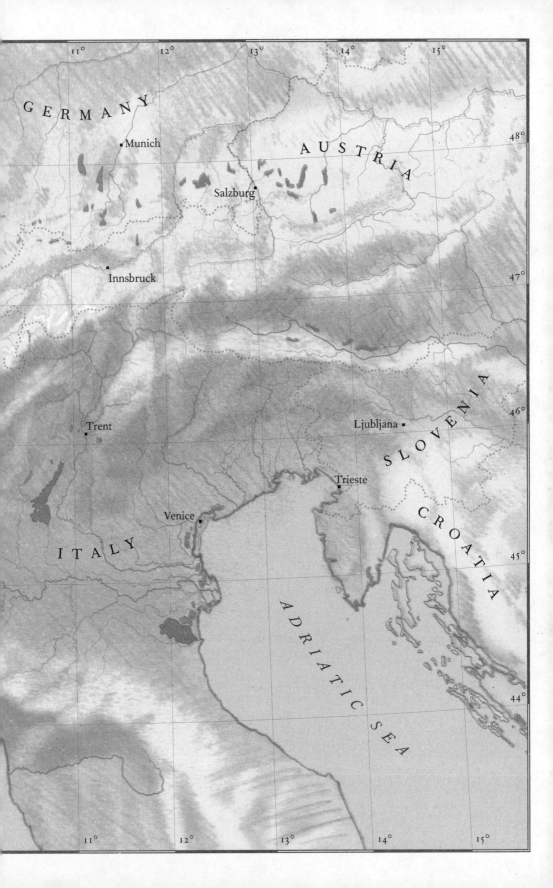

PART ONE

LAKE GENEVA TO
THE GOTTHARD PASS

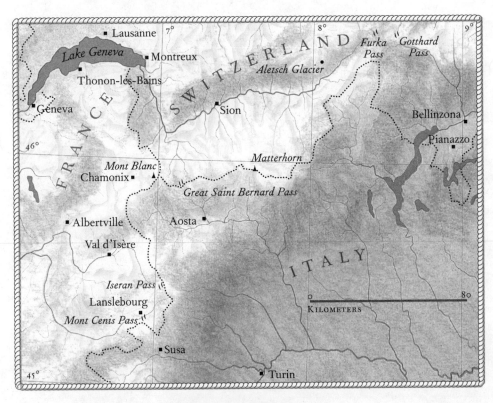

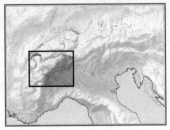

1. Lake Geneva

———— ▫ ————

THE ROAD SOUTH lies before me, the air above it shimmering in the heat. Once past the outskirts of Paris, the woodlands of the Ile-de-France close in, only to be relieved an hour or so later by the vines of Chablis. Farther into Burgundy, fortified farmhouses stand atop the gentle folding of the landscape, sentinels of pastoral plenty since the Middle Ages. The hot day wears on. The vineyards of Beaujolais appear now to my right, whereas beyond the River Saône to my left rise the first foothills of the Jura Mountains. The green hills are harbingers of where I will spend the summer, in a geological bedlam.

The kilometers click past until I'm about an hour north of Lyon. After a quick overnight in a sleepy wine-making town, I leave the north–south expressway for another heading eastward, straight to Switzerland. As the heat of the day has yet to build, I slide the windows down and let the cool morning air flow through the car. The rolling hills and red-roofed houses of the Franche-Comté file past, every public building glimpsed seemingly required to have a huge clock, as if no one here wants to lose track of the time. This strikes me as odd, for the beautiful region seems entirely stuck out of time. Bucolic and peaceful, the Franche-Comté is the kind of France that starry-eyed France-lovers imagine after their second glass of wine.

At last the border arrives. A woman with some sort of Swiss uniform tells me that I have to fork over the equivalent of twenty euros. I comply, and she slaps a sticker on my windshield, allowing me to use Switzerland's expressways for the next twelve calendar months. As my car purrs through the quiet streets of Geneva, heads turn in my direction, almost all of them male, leading me to wonder if I'm in denial about some aspect of my personality. Then I remember that I am at the wheel of a limited-edition, souped-up Renault Mégane Sport, gray with red trim, a muscle car rented for the mountain driving ahead. No one has seen this thing before. When I park by the lakeside, three car-lovers approach, seemingly rising out of the sidewalk, eager to inspect the vehicle.

Geneva is limping through a broiling weekend of late spring. Out in the harbor, the city's famed fountain shoots a stupendous volume of white water more than a hundred meters into the air. Defeated by gravity, the spray falls through the haze of the day into the milky waters below. Those waters, at the western end of the great banana-shaped Lake Geneva (or Lac Léman, as it is called here), then continue on as the Rhône to resume a long journey to the Mediterranean.

Geneva is not a postcard-perfect city. Grand nineteenth-century buildings crowd the shores of its lake, of different shades and hues, like a Paris organized by the color-blind. There is no unity, no coherent civic vista to relieve the eye, just intermittent stretches of architectural beauty. Yet Geneva, the most boring interesting city on the Continent, the spot Fyodor Dostoyevsky dismissed as a "dull, gloomy, Protestant, stupid town," midwife to the Calvinist Reformation, home to do-gooderism past and present—the League of Nations, the Red Cross, the United Nations

High Commissioner for Refugees—Geneva must be where my journey begins. For it was along the shores of Lake Geneva that an aesthetic revolution occurred more than two centuries ago, a revolution in thought that altered how humanity viewed nature. And, more to our purpose, the mountains. What Geneva's worldwide web and its Large Hadron Collider have done to reality, the bygone artists and thinkers and scientists of Lake Geneva did to taste, which is, arguably, reality's stepsister.

On the waterfront, a statue of a woman commands attention through the kinks of scorching air rising from the surrounding cobbles. The regal figure portrayed in bronze is angular, and pretty, although her Scottish creator, sculptor Philip Jackson, has her trying to hide her beauty behind a fan. The monument honors Empress Elisabeth of Austria, murdered near this spot on 10 September 1898, another furnace of a day in Geneva. The sixty-year-old empress was on her way to take a ferry out onto the lake, to escape the torpor. Her Italian anarchist assassin, armed with a sharpened file, had come to Geneva to kill another royal—the Duc d'Orléans—but, upon realizing his intended victim was out of town, settled instead on driving his needle into the heart of Elisabeth—or, as she was universally known, Sisi. To a fawning central Europe, Sisi was a combination of Princess Di and Jackie O, her beauty and many travels cataloged and wondered at. Sisi smoked cigarettes (transgressive, for a woman), wrote poetry (suspect, at court), learned Hungarian (subversive, at best), took lovers (discouraged, unless discreet), and journeyed incognito (scandalous, for a royal).

Her statue stands in the lakeside Rotonde du Mont Blanc, along the Quai du Mont Blanc, near where the Rue du Mont Blanc meets the Pont du Mont Blanc. Yet the sculpture faces northward, inland, staring at the grand old Hôtel Beau-Rivage, where Sisi spent her last night and ate her last meal. The placement of the artwork, erected on the centenary of her demise, is clever: The vain empress turns her back on the famous view out over the lake, as though not wanting to share the spotlight, as though rebelling one last time. And by now it should be clear what that view takes in.

When one turns from the murdered Sisi to look southward over the waters, the true drama of Geneva's location becomes evident. This city on its lovely lake has an operatic hinterland. Here we are not faced with a hilltop castle or a medieval nunnery, as in many places in Europe. Rather, on the far shore from Geneva, in France, rise the Alps, or technically the pre-Alps, in a wall of foothills. They drop to the water as dark green cliffs, seemingly unrelieved by any softening gap or declivity. It appears preposterous that civilized Geneva should share a lake with these untamed heights. Yet were that all that one saw when looking across the waves, the vista would remain striking, but not unforgettable. But as the names of the streets surrounding Sisi make clear, the cliffs opposite presage another presence.

Beyond the green wall, lurking like a permanent cumulus congestus thunderhead, visible even on this haziest of days, stand the summits of the Mont Blanc range, their eternal alabaster mantle of snow rising in superb mockery of the steambath suffered by the humans of Geneva on this day. The mountains are white, but not innocent, and there is no way *not* to see them. To look south from Geneva is to behold a horizon of might and majesty. The mountains—indifferent, superior—seem to block out the sky. Small wonder that they have captured imaginations for centuries.

MOUNTAINS WERE FEARED. Dragons and ogres prowled their summits. They rudely got in the way of travel to important places, like

Rome. They were God's punishment for man's sinfulness. They were use-less. With their avalanches, landslides, and crashing boulders, they were killers. One should climb only as far as the high pastures; almost certain death lay farther up. Mountains were grotesque; the people who lived in their midst were inbred imbeciles, *les crétins des Alpes*, as the French phrase has it. As such, they were suited to their awful habitat. "[T]hese distorted mindless beings," wrote an English traveler in the Alps, "commonly excite one's disgust by their hideous, loathsome, and uncouth appearance, by their obscene gestures, and by their senseless gabbling."

As for mountainous scenery, the tradition of excoriation is just as with-ering. Johann Wolfgang von Goethe's appraisal of the Alps in the 1780s can stand in for dozens of similar denunciations. For Goethe, "These zig-zags and irritating silhouettes and shapeless piles of granite, making the fairest portion of the earth a polar region, cannot be liked by any kindly man." As with so many present-day Germans careering southward at the wheel of a Mercedes, the great man wanted nothing more than to get the mountains behind him and luxuriate in the embrace of Italy.

At about the same time that Goethe was dismissing the mountains, another view of them was coming to the fore. Yes, the view is terrify-ing, went the novel argument, but that is what makes it beautiful, not ugly. Two hundred years ago, a shift in sensibility took hold and became entrenched in our psyche, so much so that lovers in our day beholding Mont Blanc are more likely to give their squeeze a squeeze. They don't turn away from the vista; they wallow in it, savor it, get turned on by it.

This aesthetic change occurred gradually. In the seventeenth and eighteenth centuries, more and more scions of rich aristocratic families, accompanied by a scholarly tour guide known as a cicerone, embarked on the cultural and carnal excursion that came to be called the Grand Tour. Most numerous among these travelers were the British, who took passage at Dover, debarked at Ostend, then proceeded to Paris and Geneva. Their carriages were disassembled at the foot of the Alps, hauled across the Great St. Bernard Pass, then put back together for a journey through the artistic motherlode of Italy: Turin, Florence, then Rome, with multiple side trips, depending on whether the traveler wanted to spend years, rather than months, abroad. Homeward, some would take in the great cities of northern Europe, before ending their tour admiring the collections in the palaces and townhouses of Flanders.

The Grand Tour was a rite of passage, an itinerant finishing school, an occasion to sow wild oats and meet the high-born ladies of Europe, a post-Oxbridge graduate course in civilization and a months-long occasion to polish one's French, then the language of choice among the polite society of Europe. It was only a matter of time before these travelers began to take note of the great anomaly of their journey: the untrammeled, inhuman Alps. As the porters of these young aristocrats grunted under the load of their chaises, hauling them up and over the treacherous mountain passes that would eventually lead to the sunny plains of Lombardy, out came the sketch pads. The vistas were unearthly, uncanny, so at odds with the formal gardens adorning their home estates. Why such chaos? How could God have created it? The Enlightment, then stretching human horizons, had begun touching such young men, or at least those who took their education seriously.

Already in the 1680s, an English cleric named Thomas Burnet had posited that the Alps had been formed *after* the seven days of Creation, thereby explaining the mysterious absence of mountains in Genesis. Burnet's *Sacred Theory of the Earth* caused an unholy stir among the learned classes. Isaac Newton, whose *Principia* on physics (published in the same decade as Burnet's work) would lead Deists to believe in a clockwork universe, fashioned by God then left alone to keep ticking, felt moved to write a lengthy letter to Burnet and suggest that each "day" of Creation could, in fact, encompass a much, much longer period of time than is customarily understood by that word.

Throughout the eighteenth century, biblical literalism wobbled on its pedestal. Although many of the pious believed Creation to have taken place on 24 October 4004 BCE, as calculated by James Ussher, the unfortunately entitled Primate of Ireland, the incremental advances of nascent scientific disciplines could not be ignored. For the Alps, this led to a peculiar hybrid period of science and superstition during the early 1700s. A Swiss scholar, Johann Jakob Scheuchzer, produced finely observed topographic maps of the mountains, yet he still had some of their peaks patrolled by dragons, in whose existence he firmly believed. Similarly, to him and many others, the marine fossils found on the rocky slopes of the mountains were deposited there by the receding waters of the biblical Flood.

Yet the dam could not hold forever. One event, above all others, traumatized the eighteenth-century imagination and led many to distance the divine from nature. Shortly before ten in the morning on 1 November, All Saints' Day, 1755, the great city of Lisbon was flattened by a tremendous earthquake and then swamped by a tsunami. Aftershocks were felt as far away as Britain and Ireland, and the coast of Brazil was buffeted by great waves. But the true tremors of the devastating quake affected a view of the world. Was the clockwork universe a time bomb? Or, if God took an interest in the doings of man, then He surely was possessed of a most ungodly temperament, devastating and destroying all of Catholic Lisbon's churches, witnesses to the greatness of His glory. Worse yet, the Alfama, Lisbon's prostitution district, emerged unscathed.

Gifted minds tried to wrest meaning from the disaster. In Königs-

berg, Prussia (now Kaliningrad, Russia), a thirty-one-year-old doctoral student, Immanuel Kant, fascinated by newspaper accounts
of the cataclysm, published what are commonly thought to be the
founding documents of the science of seismology. From the shores
of Lake Geneva, the habitually caustic Voltaire had the hero of his
novella *Candide* visit Lisbon on the day of the quake, all in the service of shaking him out of his naïve belief in a benevolent God over-
seeing a benign world. The Lisbon catastrophe had laid bare a truth
heretofore only suspected: Our world is a pitiless place, subject to
sudden upheaval independent of any divine design.

The mountains began to make sense. Their awful asymmetry
was not the devil's—or God's—handiwork. They stood as testament to cataclysms of an unthinkably distant past. They were violence frozen, made manifest, the only question being whether their
irruption had been sudden, like the Lisbon earthquake, or a long
process over time. The Enlightment, already a siren song of reason,
would now produce another attraction, a pursuit so widespread and
popular that it eventually came to be the nineteenth century's obsession. Geology, deriving meaning from rock, became the occupation and avocation of thoughtful people throughout Europe. After
Lisbon, there was no turning back the clock; rather, the geologists,
scholarly and amateur, would from now on be the arbiters of time.

But to know the Alps was not necessarily to love them, as curiosity
does not always spell affection.

Enter a new Heloise and Frankenstein's monster.

WHEN I RETURN to my car, someone snaps a picture of me getting into the driver's seat, making me feel like some D-list celebrity

leaving an LA nightclub. Although the air-conditioning systems in Renault vehicles are not as cryogenic as the ones in American cars, relief eventually arrives by the time I leave town. Geneva gives way to the canton of Vaud, a French-speaking area to the east of the city with the infelicitous license-plate abbreviation of VD. And there is a lot of VD about: The shore road is one immense, linear parking lot, as what seems to be the entire populace of the canton heads down to the lake.

The village of Coppet flashes past, its hillside pink chateau famous for hosting salons thrown by the hyperliterate Mme. de Staël. In the opening decade of the nineteenth century, Coppet welcomed the most creative minds of the time. Not only was the hostess from an illustrious family (her Swiss banker father, Jacques Necker, enacted financial reforms in a vain effort to stave off the French Revolution), but Mme. de Staël was also a best-selling author. Her *Corinne*, the story of a poetess swanning scandalously about Italy, made bosoms heave all over the Continent.

Which is an appropriate image at the moment, given the bodies braving the traffic to bounce across the roadway to the water. The handful of kilometers east of Geneva continues in this fashion, as I dodge scores of people determined to beat the heat. When signs for Lausanne, the capital of Vaud, finally appear, all vehicular motion comes to a near-standstill. On the tree-lined Avenue de l'Elysée, we inch past the Olympic Museum. Lausanne is home to one of the world's most succulent gravy trains, the International Olympic Committee, whose pashas travel the planet deciding which will be the next city to host the quadrennial extravaganza.

The sea of pedestrians eddying around my idling Mégane then flows into the lakeside Parc du Denantou, where a carnival midway is going strong, its wrenching rides eliciting shrieks of terror. From my near-stationary vantage point, I can see that the most popular nausea-inducing contraption is called the "Scary Mouse," though it seems to me that the thrill-seekers need not spend their precious Swiss francs for a moment of fright. They need only turn their gaze southward, across the lake, where the vista is, if anything, more fearsome than Geneva's. The lowering dark cliffs of France look taller and more threatening, the snow-capped heights beyond them seeming to stick an icy finger in the eye of God. They are enough to send a shudder down anyone's spine.

Of course, beauty and terror lie in the eye of the beholder, land-scapes being entirely blameless things, the pain or pleasure they inflict entirely the construct of the human mind. We nonscientists see in the natural world attributes that are not, objectively, there. Yet my prob-lem now, as I am determined to sing the praises of those who freed the mountains from their age-old demons, resides in the suspicion that I am not fully convinced, on a visceral level, that these liberators were right. The mountains are scary, as scary as the Scary Mouse, and I'm not sure I can get beyond that.

But, as they say on the ski slopes, "go big or go home." The literary pilgrims who flocked to these shores in the late eighteenth and early nine-teenth centuries had no such qualms. Beautiful Lausanne was a magnet for such visitors, as Edward Gibbon had composed here the final two volumes of his wildly successful *History of the Decline and Fall of the Roman Empire*. The street leading from his house (long since razed) became a warren of booksellers, stocked with the Swiss-published works deemed too seditious in the neighboring absolute monarchies. Yet middle-aged Gibbon may have had another reason to return to the Lausanne of his youth: He had had his heart broken here by the young woman who would later become the mother of Mme. de Staël.

The road eastward turns glorious in the afternoon sunshine. For once, the traveler's gaze is not drawn to the Alps across the lake;

rather, the terraced vineyards on this shore mesmerize. The slopes of the Lavaux chasselas and gamay grapevines are steep, their gray stone retaining walls, first erected by monks a thousand years ago, creating perilous spaces of the horizontal in a plane that is vertical. The colorful châteaux on the green countryside are similarly shored up. It's not hard to see why UNESCO deemed this beauty spot a World Heritage Site.

I reach the resort town of Vevey. A large central square down by the lake seems like the perfect place to stop. I take a quick look at the in-your-face panorama of the Alps across the water, then sit at a café terrace.

"Three francs ninety."

"I beg your pardon?"

"Three francs ninety."

The young waitress, with a long braided ponytail, black against the spotless white of her blouse, looks at me. She has brought me a beer and now stares blankly at the expression of bewilderment on my face.

"Come again?"

"Three francs ninety."

The penny finally drops. She is speaking to me in Swiss French. In the French here (and in that of the Walloons of Belgium), ninety is *nonante*. Similarly, eighty (*huitante* or *octante*) and seventy (*septante*) differ from standard French usage. For those unfamiliar with the distinction, it may come as a surprise to learn that the French language, as spoken in France, Canada, the Caribbean, Africa, and elsewhere, completely loses its mind once the number seventy is reached. Seventy is *soixante-dix*, that is, sixty-ten; seventy-five is sixty-fifteen. But the asylum doors are fully breached when the number eighty arrives. It is *quatre-vingts*, that is to say, four-twenties. Thus, eighty-five is four-twenty-five, and ninety—hewing to this logic—is four-twenty-ten. In 1999, if you wanted to say the year aloud in standard French, you needed most of the afternoon: *mil neuf cent quatre-vingt-dix-neuf,* which gives us, literally, thousand nine hundred four-twenty-ten-nine.

"*Nonante!*" I exclaim as a way of apologizing for my French gaucheness. The waitress remains impassive. As I hand her the coins, I try another tack. I say, "So you're a *Suissesse,*" using the term for a Swiss woman that almost all French-speakers view as one of the silliest words in the language.

She grins appreciatively and responds, "A Suissesse, yes. And proud of it."

She lingers, as if expecting me to say something.

I take a sip of the beer and ask, "Do you like the view of the mountains over there?"

"I love it. Why?"

"I don't know what to think about it," I say hesitantly. I explain my mixed feelings and confess to being a bit frightened by the perspective.

"You are not Swiss, you don't understand," she says with conviction. "We Swiss cannot live without our mountains."

She smiles as she says this, as if to show compassion to an outsider. We both look out at the view.

"Do all of the Swiss feel that way?"

"Of course! We were raised with the Alps."

"You like them even when it snows?"

The smile becomes a laugh. "No, then they become a nuisance."

THE GROUND WAS LAID for the Romantics, the *Zeit* had struck for the *Geist.* As the eighteenth century progressed, the heady brew of nascent nationalism, democratic dreams, and individual self-expression was matched by a bubbling respect for the natural world, quite apart from its new status as something worthy of scientific inquiry. From the growing cities, soon to be blighted by the "dark satanic mills" of the Industrial Revolution, the well-off took to going into the now-unfamiliar countryside in search of the "picturesque"—that is, a scene deemed suited to a painting. The English, in particular, took to their Lake District and the wild Scottish Highlands hunting the picturesque. Many held in their hands a Claude Glass, so named for landscape painter Claude Lorrain. This device was essentially a rearview mirror. When the intrepid traveler confronted a picturesque vista, he would turn his back to it, whip out his Claude Glass, then manipulate it so that its reflecting surface formed an ephemeral, well-composed painting, leaving out all the extraneous sights that might spoil the effect. While turning one's back to the scenery that one is supposedly admiring might seem ridiculous—a series of satirical novels lampooned one Doctor Syntax, a retired vicar besotted with the picturesque—it may be no coincidence that the successor to the Claude Glass, the camera, obliged the photographer to look through a *view*finder.

The Claude Glass, the geologist's hammer, the Grand Tour sketchbooks, the proliferating guidebooks to Switzerland—all conspired to prime the charge of Romanticism in the Alps. The detonation occurred in 1761, when Switzerland's most famous son, Jean-Jacques Rousseau, published *Julie, ou la nouvelle Héloïse* (Julie, or the New Heloise). Originally entitled *Letters from Two Lovers Living in a Small Town at the Foot of the Alps*, the novel streaked across the firmament of eighteenth-century thought like a blazing comet, running into seventy editions in many languages by the year 1800. The book, in short, was a sensation; its reception, ecstatic.

Julie is an epistolary novel, one whose story is told through an exchange of letters. The *Héloïse* of the subtitle refers to Héloïse d'Argenteuil, a brilliant and beautiful scholar of the twelfth century who exuberantly bedded her tutor, Pierre Abélard, then the most influential Scholastic of his day. Their exertions resulted in the birth of a son, whom they named Astrolabe; the castration of Abélard, performed by Héloïse's outraged relatives; and a handful of profoundly passionate and learned letters the two exchanged later in life, after events had forcibly separated them. Fortunately for the fictional Saint-Preux, the tutor and lover of Julie, Rousseau's novel does not stray into the surgical. Instead, Saint-Preux and Julie enthrall one another with declarations and descriptions of their forbidden love (he is a commoner; she, a noble), mixing philosophy, emotion, and the love of the authentic and of nature.

The trysting takes place on the waters and along the shores of Lake Geneva, most notably east of Vevey, in a hamlet called Clarens. The lovers find the mountainous setting purifying, worthy of their unsullied souls. When they get caught out in a storm on the lake, all of Europe swooned in empathetic fright. And when their love is consummated, many readers no doubt took to the privacy of their rooms. *Julie* became an emotional and intellectual landmark, situated in the hearts and minds of aspiring Romantics and, quite concretely, at the foot of the Alps.

I have read *Julie* and can quite sincerely state that it is unreadable. I am not an outlier in holding this opinion: Historian Simon Schama calls it "perhaps the most influential bad book ever written." But it does not matter what gimlet-eyed critics of the twenty-first century think; for Rousseau's contemporaries, his tale captured the aspirations of their time. The moment had come to break free, to realize one's innate goodness, to look upon nature as a friend, to see it as a reflection far profounder than that produced by a Claude Glass.

One can certainly sympathize with the sentiment. Yet when I stand on the lakefront of Clarens, there is still that damned view across the water. The green cliffs form a dark fence protecting the great white monsters touching the sky. The setting is an open invitation to indulge in the pathetic fallacy—i.e., imbuing the natural world with human emotion. Not only did Rousseau find this setting amenable to a change of worldview, but so too did a much later artist, Igor Stravinsky, who composed his epochal *Rite of Spring* in Clarens. To my mind, the latter's violent, discordant hymn to nature, culminating with a young woman dancing herself to death, seems a more apposite work for the site.

Nonetheless, it is Rousseau who clears up any lingering bewilderment about the attractions of inhospitable landscapes. Writing more than two decades after *Julie*, the philosopher explains what it is about mountain scenes that so fascinates him: "I must have torrents, rocks, pines, dead forest, mountains, rugged paths to go up and down, precipices beside me to frighten me, for the odd thing about my liking precipitous places is that they make me giddy, and I enjoy this giddiness, provided that I am safely placed." He could, in fact, be describing the delights of roller coasters, which in many languages are called mountains, usually Russian or American. Rousseau is endorsing thrill-seeking, and where better to feel an enjoyable *frisson* than in the company of a death-inviting drop? As long as one is, in Rousseau's formulation, "safely placed."

Hence the Alps are a source of titillation, or, as Rousseau and his followers preferred to describe it, the Sublime. The Swiss did not popularize the notion; that distinction belongs to an Irishman, Edmund Burke. Although today the patron saint of reactionary scolds, Burke as a young man wrote an influential treatise on the subject of apprehending nature. "The passion caused by the great and sublime in *nature* . . . is astonishment; and astonishment is that state of the soul, in which all its motions are suspended, with some degree of horror," Burke remarked, before going on to say, "Astonishment, as I have said, is the effect of the sublime in its highest degree; the inferior effects are admiration, reverence, and respect."

Burke gave a philosophical stamp of approval to having the vapors; Rousseau pointed out the locale where they might be best experienced—and supplied a Romantic ideology advocating the search for such heightened emotion. As I pass the lakeside town of Montreux, like one of the countless literary pilgrims to have come this way two centuries ago, it occurs to me that my initial reaction on seeing Mont Blanc earlier in the day was useful. Had I not felt that way, I would have been unable to appreciate the next stage of the sublime process: the warm, snuggly embrace of terror.

THE CHILLON CASTLE stands just offshore, perched on a rocky island the same color as its tawny fortifications. It is a multiturreted jewel, a small masterpiece sited in a place of scenic perfection. The castle's landward walls are almost windowless, with watchtowers, sentry walks, and slits for archers that show its role as a jealous guardian of the Via Italica, the age-old trade route linking Burgundy with Lombardy by way of the nearby Great St. Bernard Pass. Lakeward, the façade is punctuated by graceful Gothic windows to take in the view long enjoyed by the ruling family of the region, who regularly summered at Chillon and held feasts in the four great halls of the castle. That view from those halls contrasts the serenity of Lake Geneva and the violence of the Alps, which may account for its status as Switzerland's most visited tourist shrine for generations. In the late nineteenth century, Henry James has the doomed heroine of his novella *Daisy Miller* explore the castle in the company of a confused suitor she has met at nearby Vevey.

As I drift through the halls and dungeons and courtyards, a weird zephyr of fairy voices wafts around the stone walls and staircases. I locate its source: a children's troupe from Moscow is performing a play to celebrate the bicentenary of the establishment of diplomatic ties between Russia and Switzerland. The effect is lovely, a spur to fantasy.

At about the same time those diplomatic ties were knotted, a trio of Rousseau-loving pilgrims toured the castle. Unlike so many others who mooned ineffectually on the shores of the lake, these three were artists of genius: Percy Bysshe Shelley, his future wife Mary Wollstonecraft Shelley, and the clubfooted copulator extraordinaire of his era, Lord Byron. Poems soon issued forth from them celebrating the beauty and melancholy of the area, Byron's *Prisoner of Chillon*, about a monk held captive in the castle, immortalizing the thousand-year-old structure as a redoubt of Romanticism.

In 1816, the weather turned very bad for the English visitors. Several months previously, on the other side of the world, the most powerful volcanic eruption in recorded history—that of Mount Tambora in Indonesia—had launched forty cubic kilometers of debris into the atmosphere. The resulting "Year Without a Summer" brought weeks of torrential rain and terrific electrical storms to the shores of Lake Geneva. Holed up in the villa they shared, the three friends amused themselves by telling each other ghost stories against the phantasmagoric backdrop of tempest, lake, and mountain. Doubtless Byron excelled at scaring the wits out of his friends—"mad, bad and dangerous to know," a former mistress characterized him—and it was he who suggested that each should compose a lengthy tale of horror for their common edification. Of the three, only Mary held up her end of the bargain and the following year produced a manuscript entitled *Frankenstein, or The Modern Prometheus*. No matter whether judged sublime or ridiculous, the novel made the mountains even more of a melodramatic dreamscape.

Much of the early action takes place around Lake Geneva, the haunt of the troubled scientist Victor Frankenstein. After fashioning his hideous monster abroad and then fleeing from it in horror, he returns home to Geneva to find that his creation has preceded him there and murdered his younger brother. Distraught, Frankenstein takes to the mountains—and this is significant—to find solace. Of Shelley's many prose passages devoted to the sublimity of the scientist's surroundings, one in particular stands out as a sort of manifesto for mountain lovers. The narrator is Victor Frankenstein:

> The abrupt sides of vast mountains were before me; the icy
> wall of the glacier overhung me; a few shattered pines were
> scattered around; and the solemn silence of this glorious
> presence-chamber of imperial Nature was broken only by
> the brawling waves, or the fall of some vast fragment, the
> thunder sound of the avalanche, or the cracking reverber-
> ated along the mountains of the accumulated ice, which,
> through the silent working of immutable laws, was ever
> and anon rent and torn, as if it had been but a plaything in
> their hands. These sublime and magnificent scenes afforded
> me the greatest consolation that I was capable of receiving.
> They elevated me from all littleness of feeling; and although

they did not remove my grief, they subdued and tranquil-
lised it. . . . I retired to rest at night; my slumbers, as it were,
waited on and ministered to by the assemblance of grand
shapes which I had contemplated during the day. They con-
gregated round me; the unstained snowy mountain-top, the
glittering pinnacle, the pine woods, and ragged bare ravine;
the eagle, soaring amidst the clouds—they all gathered
round me and bade me be at peace.

Mary Shelley was all of eighteen years old when she wrote those
lines. She, along with her times, had come a long way from Goethe's
"zig-zags and irritating silhouettes and shapeless piles of granite." *Frankenstein*, although published to mixed reviews, instantly garnered popular success and is now regarded as a pioneering work of Gothic and
Romantic literature, as well as an avatar of the science-fiction genre.

I double back from Chillon to take in one last sight in Montreux.
The town is dotted with grand old hotels and art boutiques selling all
manner of bric-a-brac. I head toward the floral lakeside promenade,
through a semipedestrian district, until at last I reach a dead end. An
elderly cop is perched on a stool there, indicating that I must turn into
an indoor parking lot. I frown and wave him over.

"I just want to take a picture of Freddie," I plead.

He considers a moment—his job is obviously to prevent people
like me from littering the waterfront with automobiles—then notices
my muscle car.

Sensing a weakness, I say, "It's a limited edition."

He nods and I spring from the car, leaving him to look at it.

In a few steps, I have rounded a corner and confronted the glowering wall of the Alps across the lake once again. I have company. A

ten-foot-tall statue of Freddie Mercury, the Tanzanian lead singer of Queen, looks out over the same view. He is no Sisi, disdaining the mountains.

Mercury lived for many years in Montreux and recorded his last album, *Made in Heaven*, here. I study the monument. Freddie's left hand grips a mike, while his right forms a fist, pointing skyward defiantly.

I look out at the view, then at the statue. The Alps, then Freddie, then back at the Alps.

It could be the heat, but I have the distinct impression that the singer is egging me on, telling me not to be such a wuss.

I return to the car and bid farewell to the Swiss cop. It is time to drive into the mountains.

2. MONT BLANC

———— ▣ ————

*L*A *ROUTE DES GRANDES ALPES* (Great Alpine Road) was
traced out in the 1930s. It leaves Thonon-les-Bains, a town on
the south shore of Lake Geneva, and winds up and down and up and
down southward seven hundred kilometers or so until reaching the
Mediterranean resort town of Menton, crossing sixteen passes, including all the tallest ones of the French Alps. It is one of the world's great
drives. I shall be traveling only a portion of it, in the Savoy region, but
the passes promise to be very, very high.

Mont Blanc is the destination of this stage of my journey. There
is no way it can be ignored, not even from distant Geneva. In some
ways, its mammoth white dome announces the disruptive vocation of
the Alps, appearing insurmountable, blocking the path for the wayfarer. Mont Blanc and its mountainous siblings merit inspection for
the role they have played in human history, creating divisions and fos-
tering differences. I look forward to exploring the sights and sounds
of the Alps.

Once my hearing returns.

I have just come from a bakery in Thonon-les-Bains, where a French form of speech, the shopkeeper budgerigar, deafened me. This vocal tic occurs in all retail businesses in France. A French saleswoman is expected to talk to her customers in a pitch an octave or two higher than her normal speaking voice. If these customers are female, they then respond in kind. The budgerigar gave a glass-shattering performance at the bakery.

The small shop was crowded with about half a dozen women customers, a stout *boulangère*, and her willowy assistants. Upon crossing the threshold, I was assaulted by what could pass for the soundtrack of Picasso's *Guernica*. It was as if I had somehow stuck my head into a particularly solicitous jet engine. *"Et avec ça, madame?"* *"Et ça sera tout, madame?"* *"Merci, madame. Passez une bonne journée!"* By the time my turn came and I asked for my take-out ham-and-Gruyère sandwich, I was so stunned I could barely catch the polite shriek of reply.

Still, it turns out to be a delicious sandwich. I sit on a very long park bench savoring it—and appreciating the view, as the park is situated on a height overlooking the lake. Opposite, in the distance, I can see Lausanne and the terraced UNESCO vineyards of Lavaux. Beyond them rise the low brown peaks of the Jura, a chain of well-behaved mountains, like the Laurentians of my childhood in Canada. I believe these are what mountains should be, undulations giving visual variety to the horizon, not the horrorshow heights of the Alps hovering at my back. Thonon-les-Bains, I had thought, would be a sort of B-list spa when compared to its famous neighbor, Evian-les-Bains, but its charms are fully on display this morning, and I like it. Mercifully, the ringing in my ears has subsided, and I close my eyes in contentment.

A camera-toting elderly couple in T-shirts and shorts stop to admire the view. The man walks over in my direction and offers a jolly *"Bon appétit!"* At this, he steps up onto the bench and aims his lens at the lake. The bench is very long, about thirty feet or so, yet the man stands so close to me that I can see the follicles of his leg hair. There is, it should be added, no tree or structure obstructing the view from anywhere on the bench, yet there he stands, the threat of leg dandruff landing in my sandwich looming large. I scoot over a couple of butt-widths and resume chewing.

He looks down at me in surprise—or is it disapproval?

I think of the nation the French most like to ridicule. I can't help myself.

"What, are you Belgian?" I ask.

His wife laughs; he does not.

I get up and go to my car. The vehicle's GPS system features another French female speaking style as common as the budgerigar: the whispering model. I put up with her on my first days around Lake Geneva, but I decide I don't want to be bossed around the Alps by a voice sounding like Carla Bruni's. I switch off the device.

Irritation soon gives way to exhilaration. As I head down the Great Alpine Road, I am driving into a heart of green, as tall forested slopes stretch thousands of meters in the air on both sides of the roadway. It's as if the International Style skyscrapers of Sixth Avenue in midtown Manhattan were smothered in ivy—and if Sixth Avenue had a riotous, roaring stream thundering down its middle. At times, the lush foliage obscures the view; at others, especially at bends in the road, a staggering perspective of gigantism assaults the eye. At one point, I behold in wonder what I had not thought possible: a sugarloaf peak that, contrary to its siblings the world over, conjures up menace rather than marvel.

I pull over at a touristy shop advertising a nearby attraction: *Les Gorges du Pont-du-Diable* (The Gorges of Devil's Bridge). I know there are a lot of Devil gorges, bridges, tunnels, peaks, forests, lakes, ridges, and whatnot in this part of the world, but this one well earns its name. A metal and wooden gangplank, with blissfully sturdy handrails, snakes above the angry River Dranse de Morzine, which has carved a deep gash in the scarified limestone. I tread carefully, eyes fixed forward on a maddeningly fearless gay couple, who pause to snap photos of themselves leaning over the void. When these guys stop, I stop. When they move on, I move on. *It's not that I'm afraid of heights*, I just like to watch people in love.

Back in the cozy cocoon of the car, my journey southward leads out of the trees and into grassier slopes punctuated with brutal chevrons of exposed rock. A traffic circle indicates that the town of Morzine has been reached. For the ski world, Morzine is famed for its high-altitude sister resort, Avoriaz, a car-free creation of jet-set entrepreneurs in the 1960s, led by an Olympic ski champion, Jean Vuarnet, who also lent his name to the must-have designer sunglasses. I smile as I pass Morzine, for Avoriaz holds two old memories for me. One, of being in an après-ski bar with a GI on leave who kept bewildering me by his mention of "Alvarez"—until I realized that was how he pronounced "Avoriaz." The other was not my finest moment. At the time, I was married to a young woman who was an expert skier. We spent the day apart in Avoriaz—I, on the baby slopes; she, on the triple black diamonds. We met at the end of the afternoon and decided to ski together, foolish newlyweds that we were. I paid no attention as she led me to ski lifts, leading to other ski lifts—after all, I was in affectionate hands. When we finally turned our skis to the slope, I found myself looking down a cliff. There were so many moguls that descending it would be like skiing down the vertebrae of my GI pal standing at attention. I was furious. And, I'm sorry to say, I lost it. A stream of swearing at the universe at large befouled the clear Alpine air as my bride looked on, appalled at this display of cowardly distemper. When I had finished, she informed me that there was only one way to get off the mountain. Then she turned on her skis and vanished downhill.

My hysteria was not misplaced, I think, while driving through the streets of Morzine. In the nineteenth century, the heyday of hysteria, with Blessed Virgin sightings by real virgins so numerous as to amount almost to a coming-of-age ritual for girls, Morzine stood out for its demonic decade and a half of possessed maidens. Ten-year-old "Peronne T." kicked off the craze in 1857, her convulsions and gibberish aimed at the local priest to be imitated and outdone by dozens of local girls in subsequent years. The then-remote village became something of a tourist attraction—the spectacle of young women pleasuring themselves on altars and in chapels apparently a sight not be missed. On one occasion, a bishop invited in to calm the flock was surrounded by more than fifty hysterics doing their obscene best to let him know that he was not welcome. In many ways, Morzine was the anti-Lourdes—Bernadette Soubirous had her visions in the shadow of the Pyrenees in 1858, the year after Peronne's—for the afflicted Alpine townswomen turned their ire on the Church. There is no sacred grotto in Morzine, no pilgrimage church attracting hundreds of thousands, no nearby airport capable of handling the biggest of jumbo jets—only a very large skeleton in its closet. The phenomenon disappeared in 1873, as mysteriously as it had appeared.

The only other skeleton connected to the town concerns the misfortunes of hometown hero Jean Vuarnet, the skier-turned-entrepreneur whose shades have adorned, among others, the Dude in *The Big Lebowski*, skier Bode Miller, Jake Gyllenhaal in *Everest*, and Daniel Craig as James Bond in *SPECTRE*. Vuarnet's nonbusiness experiences, sadly, proved considerably darker. Sometime in the early 1990s, his wife, Edith (née Bonlieu), another ski champion, and their son, Patrick, secretly became members of the Order of the Solar Temple, a lunatic group of medievalist would-be world-changers based in Switzerland, France, and Quebec. The cult became notorious for its murder-suicide pacts: From 1994 to 1997, seventy-four of its members met their deaths in the three places where it was active. At the winter solstice of 1995, Vuarnet's wife and son died along with fourteen others at a remote campsite in the Alps near Grenoble, the bodies laid out in a star formation on the ground. Vuarnet maintained in the years following that his loved ones were murdered, but uncertainty still hangs over what exactly happened.

The glorious day has turned gray, at least in my mind's eye, and I have no one to blame but myself. Fortunately, the road from Morzine to another ski resort, Les Gets, distracts me from my thoughts by presenting the challenge of negotiating hairpin turns. I get lucky with the first few, though I know there will be hundreds more to humiliate me in the months ahead. As with many things, French and English disagree completely on nomenclature. In this instance, we go for the head, as in hairpin, whereas the French go for the foot, calling them *lacets*, as in shoelaces. Whatever the name—"switchback" is another—I find that taking a right turn is preferable to taking a left one on these downshift-upshift Alpine treats.

However they're characterized, everyone agrees that building hairpins is considerably cheaper than drilling tunnels, hence their ubiquity in mountainous terrain. When a slope is too steep to take directly up and down, it is necessary to wind one's way to the top and bottom, making these 180-degree inducements to whiplash a necessity. They slow traffic, which is a good thing, given the cliff-hanging nature of the roadways, and they are extremely dangerous, which is not so good.

Losing control of the car is always a distinct possibility, especially if the driver has been riding the brakes on a downhill stretch, always the most perilous stage of crossing a pass. Hairpins separate the good drivers from the bad and constitute the most irrefutable argument for the advantages of manual over automatic transmission.

Given the way valleys close off and slopes rise to impede progress, the grinding zigzag is the only way to make forward progress. Alpine locals, especially in France, French-speaking Switzerland, and the Aosta Valley of Italy, made these slopes amusing by inventing an entirely imaginary animal to inhabit them. The *dahu*, a fictitious goat-like being, may have been inspired by a real creature, the chamois, a small horned antelope once a very common sight in the mountains. The dahu differs from the chamois in one notable respect: The legs on one side of its body are shorter than those on the other. This allows for it to stand laterally on steep slopes and move comfortably around a mountain, albeit only in one direction. A dahu with shorter left legs, *laevogyrus dahu* (or *dahu senestrus*, according to which scholar you consult), goes counterclockwise around the mountain; one with shorter right ones, *dextrogyre dahu* (or *dahu desterus*), clockwise. Perhaps still sore at being called *crétins des Alpes* by lowlanders, the Savoyards, in the early days of mass tourism, would sometimes take gullible visitors on dahu hunts. These entailed all-night vigils out in the open, where the would-be trophy hunter had to crouch and hide so as not to be seen by the sharp-eyed dahu.

Of course, the locals would not tell the visitors that the easiest way to capture a dahu does not involve such dedication. It requires two hunters: one with stealth, the other with a bag. The stealthy hunter has only to sneak up on a dahu while his partner remains down at the bottom of the slope holding the bag open. When the quiet hunter gets close to the animal's rear, he should clap loudly, startling the dahu and causing it to turn around suddenly—and thereby lose its balance. It then rolls down the slope into the waiting bag below.

Every schoolchild in the French-speaking Alps knows that this is the way to capture a dahu. When I asked at three different bookstores in France for works on the dahu, I was led by the salesperson, unsmiling and professional, to a shelf devoted to the animal, usually in the children's section. There I perused picture books tracing the dahu as far back as Cro-Magnon times. The dahu was depicted at Lascaux, in Egyptian hieroglyphs, in Renaissance paintings. But, alas, *la chasse au dahu*—the dahu hunt—is a thing of the past. Nowadays, with most tourists hip to the hoax, the dahu is—quite literally—a standing joke.

INEXPLICABLY, the traffic slows to a snail's space. We are near no big city, or even a small town, yet here we are, crawling up hairpins. I look up the slope for an explanation. There he is, leading the procession: the Dutch camper. The scourge of European roads during the hot months, the Dutch camper especially prefers taking his crawling motorcade of like-minded fellows with yellow license plates into the Alps. All who drive southward in the summer know the camper and his much-feared rules of the road: (1) No matter whether the road be straight and flat, always drive at 40 kilometers an hour in an 80 kilometers-an-hour speed zone. If the speed limit is lower or higher, do the math (i.e., divide by two) to determine your Dutch camper speed; (2) Never, *ever* pull off the road for a minute or two to allow the backlog of normal drivers to overtake you and continue their journey with lowered blood pressure. In fact, those other drivers do not exist, because you do not see them.

He is everywhere. Perhaps the camper's ubiquity stems from some well-meaning but disastrous directive dreamed up by the Eurocrats of Brussels. Or perhaps he favors the hardest places to drive—the Alps and the Pyrenees—for the novelty of their non-flatness, so unlike the vertical-free monotony of his homeland. He also seems to travel roads with as many blind curves and as few places to pass as possible—thus, to induce foaming at the mouth in other drivers requires little effort.

To me, it is his obliviousness that mystifies most. The Dutch, to be fair, are the tallest people in the world, and a head floating high in the air often cannot notice the goings-on of us little ones far below. Yet sitting in a car eliminates that height advantage. At the steering wheel, we are all groundlings, but this demotion seems not to faze the Dutch camper. Regardless of how many dozens of cars trail behind in fury, in his mind he and his fellow campers are always all alone, or in convoy, traveling at jogging speed on an empty road leading through a countryside devoid of humanity.

I sigh and realize that I must play along. I open the windows. Cowbells. Somewhere, out on the high meadows, herds of dahu-like animals cling to the slope and graze in peace, their milk (and that of their fellow herbivores elsewhere in the Alps) rendering such delicious cheeses as Gruyère, Comté, Appenzeller, Beaufort, and Emmentaler. These cows, sheep, and goats travel in their grazing habits—down at the bottom of the slopes in the spring, then moving to the upper mountain meadows, in a husbandry technique known as transhumance, to munch on the altogether different flora at higher elevations. This variety of fare leads to a richness in their cheese—sometimes nutty, sometimes fruity, spicy, floral, or buttery. The hard cheese produced is perfect for melting in fondues and raclettes. Among cheese lovers, the Alps constitute the promised land. It is perhaps fitting, then, that these cheese-producing upland meadows—*alps* or *alpages*, as they are known locally—gave the surrounding mountains their name.

A sign appears: *DÉVIATION*. First the Dutch, now the detour. I grumble and turn the wheel. The slow pace of the detoured traffic has lessened my resentment toward the Dutch camper ahead. The secondary road is very narrow, and the climb is steep, so speeding is not an option. As every now and again my rearview mirror kisses a mirror of an oncoming car, I think back to where I live, a small city in New England. There, the drivers are so clueless when gauging the width of their own cars that a street with cars parked on both sides, but with enough room for two cars to pass each other, is a theater of panic, or, worse still, of road-hogging acceleration right down the middle of the street. I've often wished I could transport those drivers to teeny European roads, just to watch their heads explode. But you should be careful what you wish for—although we southbound cars of the ascent have the slope to our right and don't have to worry about being bumped over the cliff, the scene to our left has become aeronautic. We are far, far above the valley floor.

Unbelievably, there is a fork in the road. Arrows point in each direction. One reads *DÉVIATION V.L.*; the other, *DÉVIATION P.L.*. Although fluent in the language, I am not French and thus do not possess a passion for acronyms. *SDF*? A homeless person (*sans domicile fixe*). *TTC*? Taxes included (*toutes taxes comprises*). *IVG*? Abortion (*interruption volontaire de grossesse*). *HLM*? Project/Council housing (*habitation à loyer modéré*). And on and on and on. Reading an acronym-rich French newspaper requires the mind of an Alan Turing, the man who cracked the Enigma code. I brake to contemplate my choice: do I want the VL Detour to the left, or the PL Detour to the right? And what the hell do they mean? Veronica Lake? Peter Lorre? The honk of a horn concentrates my mind and I choose Veronica Lake. There will be no turning back, as there is absolutely nowhere to turn around.

We start the descent. The green pastures deep in the distant valley seem to rock and sway. The road narrows even more. The hairpin turns are now adorned with road signs showing an old-fashioned Klaxon, of the type that blasts "ah-oo-ga." Apparently, we are supposed to honk our horns and hope for the best. This does not inspire confidence.

At a hamlet that is really no more than a woodlot, I turn a corner around some logs and come face to face with a Jaguar bearing plates from the Swiss canton of Neuchâtel. We cannot get past each other. The Suissesse at the wheel smiles angelically and spreads her tanned arms in a gesture of helplessness. Since she has the right of way as the person going uphill, I hit the hazard lights, put the stick in reverse, and gingerly back up around the woodpile. The guy behind me understands and does likewise. Eventually, there is a break in the oncoming line of traffic and we leave the chokehold hamlet behind us. I wonder if the Peter Lorre Detour held a similar trap.

At last we rejoin the Great Alpine Road down in the valley. The happy, verdant town of Cluses spreads before us, surrounded by towering peaks. There are several mega-chalet retirement residences under construction on the steep slopes outside the center of town, leaving one to speculate on the agility of the French elderly. As this is the spectacularly rugged region of Savoy, perhaps spryness has to last well into old age.

A sign flashes past: *MUSÉE DE L'HORLOGERIE ET DU DÉCOLLETAGE.* Once again I am flummoxed. The translation in my head—Museum of Watchmaking and Plunging Necklines—seems an unlikely pairing. I contemplate turning back to investigate, but the Dutch camper has decamped somewhere, so I can now barrel down the broad road running through the valley of the River Arve. On both sides are solid walls of green, punctuated by thin, linear cascades of water, unspooling downward like strands of white lace. The effect would be far lovelier were the floor of the valley not blanketed in furniture factories and workshops.

And a lot of signs use the word *décolletage*. I see EDELWEISS DÉCOLLETAGE *and* ARVE DÉCOLLETAGE competing for the eye in a grimy industrial district, not the type of neighborhood usually associated with a woman's cleavage. Knowing French truck stops to be equipped with wi-fi, I pull into one to seek enlightenment.

Aha! My cell informs me that *décolletage* has a double meaning in French. One conforms to our English adoption of the French word, but the other means "machining," as in the making of precision parts for clockwork mechanisms and the like. The Arve Valley, it turns out, is teeming with machining plants, hence the museum back in Cluses.

Finally, when I round the next bend, there it is, in all its blinding Cyclopean menace, blocking a good portion of the sky. There are eighty-two peaks in the Alps taller than four thousand meters, but this is the tallest of the lot, the monarch, standing at 4,808 meters.

Mont Blanc.

HORACE-BÉNÉDICT DE SAUSSURE was a man on a mission. A native of Geneva, he made pioneering studies in geology and dreamed of standing on the summit of Mont Blanc. As a Genevan, he would have been familiar with the view Sisi turns her back on: the green pre-Alps looming over the lake, and behind them, the ghostly goliath reaching for the sky. Saussure became obsessed with the mountain, sponsoring a reward for anyone with the temerity to make the ascent. In 1760 and the years that followed, flyers were regularly printed up and posted in the villages near the base of the monster, yet the locals did not take up Saussure on his offer. The great scientist from Geneva must be daft, went the reasoning, why in the world would anyone want to do such a thing?

Local interest in the reward perked up as the first trickle of tourists came to the valley in search of the sublime. Hostelries cropped up, businesses blossomed, and the Chamouniards finally took up the vocation that they perform to the present day: mountain guides. Repeated attempts to rise to Saussure's challenge at last began to be made in the 1780s, but it was only on 8 August 1786 that the great white beast was summited. The climbers were Jacques Balmat and Michel-Gabriel Paccard, both locals, who performed the feat with only one overnight bivouac. Balmat was an unlettered fellow, prowling the lower slopes to hunt chamois for their hides and horns and to dig up crystals for the collections of wealthy amateur geologists. Paccard was the town doctor—not a folksy quack but a learned man who published papers in the medical journals of Turin (the Savoy region was then part of an Italian kingdom). But, as the news of the achievement spread across Europe, a funny thing happened on the way to legend.

A writer of some talent from Geneva, Marc-Théodore Bourrit, had it in for Paccard. The animus may have been spurred when the two men unsuccessfully tried for the summit a few years earlier, the expedition having come undone thanks to Bourrit's physical frailty. Whatever its cause, the dislike Bourrit felt for Paccard resulted in the popularization of a story, written by the polemical Genevan, that had the good doctor as a pitiful liability on the historic climb, an inept mountaineer who slowed the exploit and needed repeated rescue by the doughty Balmat. Bourrit may also have been jealous that a fellow bourgeois—Paccard—had made the climb, so he portrayed Balmat in the role of the man of the people, then the hero persona in vogue with the Romantics. The story stuck, and Balmat did little to dispel it. Whether or not the doctor ever spoke to the chamois hunter about this unfortunate fiction may have been complicated by the awkward fact that Paccard married Balmat's sister.

A generation later, when a writer of genius arrived in Savoy, he met up with the then-seventy-year-old Balmat. This was in 1832, five years after Paccard's death, so Balmat had the field to himself (his time would come two years later, when he fell off a cliff prospecting for gold). The writer, Alexandre Dumas *père*, lyrically amplified Balmat's role in the historic climb, calling him "the god of the mountain" and cementing in the European imagination the story of a pathetic Paccard. The truth had to wait until the early twentieth century, after scholars unearthed diaries of eyewitnesses—a crowd had followed the pair's ascent through their long-views—completely debunking the orthodox version of the ascent. Paccard and Balmat had spelled each other, each taking his turn leading the way upward, and the doctor had calmly conducted several scientific experiments on the summit itself. Thus was mountaineering born, in a stew of backbiting and second-guessing that flavors it still.

Saussure finally realized his dream of summiting Mont Blanc, the year following the ascent of Balmat and Paccard. Saussure's huge expedition, laden with numerous scientific instruments and copious amounts of booze, was immortalized in his *Voyages dans les Alpes*. It became the first bible of the new pastime of mountaineering.

Women wasted no time, either, in making their mark on the mountains. First up Mont Blanc, in 1808, was a local girl, Marie Paradis, who later admitted that she had undertaken the climb on a dare, which makes her achievement all the more charming. Unlike Paccard, Paradis did indeed have to be dragged up the final few hundred meters—and by none other than Jacques Balmat. Others followed; an eccentric French noblewoman named Henriette d'Angeville caught the imagination of many for her mix of commonsense innovation (she wore trousers) and flamboyant femininity (her equipment included a compact mirror and cucumber pomade). Her account of her climb also raised eyebrows, as it fairly reeked of Eros. In the weeks before the ascent, Mont Blanc changed in her mind into a "frozen lover." She wrote, after a rain delay: "I was late for my wedding, for my marriage . . . for the delicious hour when I could lie on his summit. Oh! when will it come?" But when she reached the summit, d'Angeville was a blistered wreck, in no mood for any transcendent hanky panky, but made it she had, nonetheless, impressing local guides with her pluck. Back down in the village, d'Angeville met with the pioneer female mountaineer, now an old lady whose lovely Paradis name had been changed to Marie de Mont-Blanc. Although the two women must have had absolutely nothing in common except the summit of Europe's tallest mountain, they shared a snack.

THE AIGUILLE DU MIDI—the Needle of the South—is one of the most celebrated outcroppings of rock in the Alps. The mountain soars to a height of 3,842 meters, on the southern slopes of the Mont Blanc range, and the summit of the Great White One can be seen from its lofty perch. Nearby stands another peak, *Mont Maudit* (Cursed Mount), its name an indication of the lack of affection once accorded these rocky giants by the locals.

In 1955, a lift system was erected to facilitate travel up to the Aiguille's thorny peak, upon which a tourism complex had been constructed. The journey is made in two stages. The first goes up to the Plan de l'Aiguille, a flattening of the slope just above the tree line. From there, visitors board a second gondola for the final ascent.

I cannot say that I enter the far too well-windowed gondola with joy in my heart. About three dozen of us stand silently in expectation, exchanging the equivalent of nervous giggles and empty bravado in six or seven languages. Then with a whoosh we are off, at surprising speed. Almost immediately there come mewls of terror; a teenager is having a meltdown. *"Nein! Nein!"* his father hisses murderously, holding the boy in a viselike grip with his two large Prussian paws. But the kid is having none of it; the mewls become sobs and the tears flow.

Uncomfortable like everyone else within earshot, I unwisely turn around to look out a window. A sea of green, the tops of countless larch trees swim beneath us. Then we traverse a support pillar and the cable car sways back and forth like a drunken pendulum. Sullen muttering greets this movement; for his part, the teenager sounds as if he has just been stabbed. Beads of sweat form on my brow. *It's not that I'm afraid of heights*, I just don't like larch trees.

Seeking relief from any quarter, I turn to a woman I had earlier heard speaking English. I ask her if this is her first time up the mountain. "Good heavens, no!" she says. "We come up here every time we're in Chamonix." What follows is a nonstop soliloquy on her life, her son, her grandchildren—it's as if she's an electric egg-timer and I have just flicked the switch. "We're from Oxfordshire, have you heard of that? . . . My son's a carpenter, does a lot of joinery in the valley . . . lives in Les Contamines. . . . I don't know why. . . . The children should come home for the schools. . . . Nothing like a good English education."

The bath of domesticity calms me, as running it perhaps calms her. I knew in advance that the English would be here in force, but I hadn't quite realized the implications of that. And, according to my sources, they basically own the place. At an Italian pizzeria the night before, my Transylvanian waitress put the number of English proprietors of Chamonix businesses at 80 percent. Then, later, in a Mexican bar, my Swedish server trimmed that to 50 percent. And at the tourist office, a young Irishwoman cut his number by half. Whatever the true figure, they all agreed there were too many foreigners in Chamonix.

A local author, Dominique Potard, in his comic French-language novel confusingly entitled *Welcome to Chamonix*, claims that the ski resort still plays host to the Hundred Years' War. It has long been thus. By the middle of the nineteenth century, more than ten thousand British tourists visited Chamonix annually. Many of them were moved to make the difficult journey by the supremely odd success of Albert Smith, a British charlatan and showman. In the 1850s, Smith had London eating out of his hand. His *Ascent of Mont Blanc*, a sound-and-light extravaganza that was narrated onstage by Smith and featured unfurling slide shows, busty girls in dirndl dresses, exotic animals, and specially commissioned "Alpine" music, played for years to sold-out crowds at the Egyptian Hall in Piccadilly. The ancestor of *The Sound of Music*, Smith's strange, gaslit spectacle fired the imaginations of Victorians itchy to escape the leaden monotony of routine. But not altogether. A canny entrepreneur and committed evangelist named Thomas Cook then created the all-inclusive package tour for such would-be travelers, his promises of an English bill of fare and regular religious services scrupulously kept in the heart of the godless Continent. Starting in 1851, these Cook tourists came in droves, carried along on the new railways, their crisp guidebooks and alpenstock walking sticks clasped in expectant hands, their sights set on bagging the elusive dahu.

The aristocratic veterans of the old Grand Tour were aghast at the sight of these newcomers. Acute class consciousness emerged from a stream of correspondence deploring the middle-class interlopers. One incensed lady, writing to her sister in 1867, was brutal about the brutes, saying that her hotel was "swarming throughout with the most alarming sort of vermin . . . a wretched crowd of limp beings with alpenstocks tipped with chamois horns—such as I never saw before in real life." When the world's first Alpine club opened in 1857, in London, its membership was pointedly reserved for gentlemen. Leslie Stephen, an intellectual mountaineer, was president of the club in the year his first wife* penned that letter about the vermin swarming their hotel. He had a similar view of them: "Although the presence of this species is very annoying, I do not think myself justified in advocating any scheme for their extirpation, such as leaving arsenic about, as is done by some intelligent colonists in parallel cases, or by tempting them into dangerous parts of the mountains. I should be perfectly satisfied if they could be confined to a few penal settlements in the less beautiful valleys."

Yet to ascribe all this hostility to class would be oversimplifying. The Alpine old-timers deplored the newcomers *because* they were newcomers. With a reflexive disdain afflicting all generations in midlife, they thought a secret place known only to a select few had been coarsened by marauding hordes. Things used to be much better, quainter, more authentic . . . the plaint is voiced about every destination on the planet, by every successive generation.

---

* Stephen's second marriage would produce four children, among them two remarkable daughters: Vanessa Bell and Virginia Wolff.

In the Alpine context, a none-too-subtle apartheid was devised to address the problems of nostalgia and class. Clever hoteliers realized that rich Britons were willing to fork over any sum to avoid their countrymen. Thus was born the pricey "palace hotel," with its lackeys, luxuries, and private dining rooms. These last can be explained by the reluctance of the British upper crust to eat in the company of strangers. Unlike the French, whose chefs to the nobility were turfed out onto the street by the Revolution and forced to make their living by experimenting with the Parisian novelty known as the restaurant, the *Downton* diners still preferred the embrace of privacy for the exercise of their mandibles. About the only thing that the Cook tourists and the moneyed elite could agree on was the need for an amenity that would be Britannia's signature contribution to Continental culture: the water closet.

OUR AIRBORNE PLEXIGLASS PRISON arrives at the Plan de l'Aiguille, a treeless expanse of gray rock and dirty snow. The woman from Oxfordshire stops talking, the egg-timer has run its course. I feel tempted to thank her for boring me to distraction, but I fear the compliment might be misunderstood. The second stage, up and up over a white vertical, comes next. From the boarding platform I can see the tourist complex atop the Aiguille, looking toylike and far off. My heart sinks.

Strictly speaking, the system used to carry us up to the Aiguille is known as an aerial tramway. The technology dates back all the way to 1644, when an engineer in Gdansk, Poland, constructed one to move earth over barriers for the construction of a defensive system. That tramway was powered by horses. Some two centuries would have to pass before the device became commonplace, usually in mining districts for transporting ore from higher elevations down to the mill in the valley. People finally got a lift at the turn of the twentieth century—first in Gibraltar, then in Hong Kong. As that century progressed, pylons, cables, and gondolas sprang up like weeds, especially in the Alps when the boom in winter sports came of age. Today, the Germans, Austrians, and Swiss are the experts in constructing these amazing systems.

We get underway with a jolt, and the rock and snow scurry beneath us. Unfortunately, I have done my research on aerial tramways and know of the disasters to which they have been prey. Perhaps the most disgusting occurred in Cavalese, Italy, in 1998, when joyriding US Marine fighter pilots, flying at a lower altitude than permitted, severed a cable and caused a gondola containing twenty people to fall eighty meters to their deaths. I try to forget my reading.

Some multicolored stick figures can be made out on the glaciers and in the gullies in the distance, a handful of the twenty-five thousand climbers who try to summit Mont Blanc annually. Sadly, at least a dozen or so have to be hauled back down to the valley in body bags every year—victims of bad weather, exhaustion, or, more likely, inexperience. I turn from the vista to look at the young man operating the gondola. Last night's Swede in the Mexican cantina told me to watch out for these operators of the second stage of the journey. Given the repeated, punishing changes in oxygen supply, air pressure, altitude, and temperature undergone daily, they usually last only a season before going off their heads, at least temporarily. Our young cable-car guy seems normal enough to me—until I see what he is reading: a French translation of Bret Easton Ellis's *American Psycho*. He is smiling broadly. This does not inspire confidence.

Evidently, relief is not going to come from him, so I turn to the window. Bad idea. An avalanche rumbles down the slope, kicking up clouds of snow and smashing against exposed rock faces. This is not sublime, this is terrifying. Yet the thought of the old Romantic word gives me an idea: Why not test out the theory of the effect of titillation on the libido? I survey my fellow aerial cabin mates. Sure enough, those coupled off are now engaging in the preliminaries of serious primate interaction. As widened eyes stare out at the horror of Mont Blanc, hands stray, bodies press, lips nuzzle lobes, hair is stroked. I'm no longer a sightseer, I'm a voyeur. A young French couple beside me locks pouts, for a good breath or two. They then disengage and behold the rock and ice wall nearing at the end of our ascent.

"Canada in the summertime," he says.

She laughs; I do not.

HIGHLINER. Base Jump. Baselining. Extreme Sliding. Speed Riding. Paragliding. The exhibit in the Aiguille's *Espace Vertical* is devoted to the death-defying variants of present-day mountaineering. These involve young people taking risks that would have horrified the athletic snobs of the British Alpine Club and caused their muttonchops to burst into flame. Tiptoeing along 2.5-centimeter-diameter rope slung between needles of rock, hanging out in hammocks suspended thousands of meters in the air, hurtling into the void with nothing but a billowing suit and a prayer, taking steep slopes headfirst, scuttling around seracs, *running* up and down mountains—such are the images in the Aiguille du Midi's unsettling showroom. The fastest ascent and descent of Mont Blanc took only four hours and fifty-seven minutes, a feat achieved in 2013 by Kílian Jornet, the Catalan superhuman with many world records to his credit. I pause before the pix and the vids—and think that these extreme mountaineers and I are quite possibly from entirely different species.

When I was last in Chamonix—a visit darkened by the news of the Challenger disaster—the complex atop the Aiguille was a fairly undistinguished affair, needing a makeover to escape the 1960s. That need has recently been met, several new attractions having opened, sightseeing terraces built, and constant renovations added to the multistory structure.

One new attraction is a diabolical novelty called *Le Pas dans le Vide* (Step into the Void). Inspired by the Grand Canyon Skywalk, the feature consists of a glass cube jutting out from the uppermost section of the Aiguille's tourist complex. As with the Skywalk, you stare down past your feet at a sheer well of emptiness. And whereas the Skywalk gives you about five hundred meters of dizziness, the drop at Chamonix is well over a kilometer.

My inner debate about whether or not to venture into the cube is silenced when I see it occupied by a pregnant Filipina. She and the fellow I take to be the future father are jumping up and down and squealing in delight. I realize that now I have to go take a look; the only thing stronger than fear is shame. When my turn comes, I gingerly step into the cage and keep my gaze level at the panorama of spiky rock needles and battered white mountaintops, dozens and dozens as far as the eye can see. It occurs to me that the Alps form the water tower of Europe. From this sky-touching chaos of snow and ice stretching as far east as Slovenia, several of the Continent's great rivers—Rhine, Rhône, Po—take their source, as do scores of their tributaries. Without the glacial melt, there would be no risotto, no baguette, no schnitzel, not much of anything except the acres and acres of beets and potatoes that cover so much of northern Europe.

Some singsong Slavic laughter interrupts my thoughts and I turn to see two Poles, to judge from the flag insignias on their fleeces, making their way down the approach corridor to the cube. They cannot walk side by side, as they appear to be vying for the title of fattest man in the European Union. My faith in structural engineering goes only so far, so I vow to be out of the cube before these two guys park the human equivalent of a pickup truck on the glass floor. Quickly, grateful for the excuse of haste, I peer down at the vista beneath my feet. Nothing. There's nothing there, far too much of nothing. If the world's tallest building, the Burj Khalifa, were somehow to be transported here from Dubai, I would still be well over sixty stories above its pinnacle, looking down on the puny strivings of mankind. But the Burj is definitely not here, nothing is—and I feel the familiar twinges of vertigo in my viscera. I make a quick exit.

Once outside, all is well. The weather is beautiful, the only blizzard on the viewing deck coming from an incessant flurry of selfies. The people smiling into their phones differ from their predecessors in that those who long ago wielded a Claude Glass strove to keep themselves out of the picture. The selfie requires the opposite, which may or may not say something about our progress toward the annihilation of a world separate from our screens. Still, the cruel majesty of the panorama cannot help but stir feelings of belittlement, so perhaps the urge to self-aggrandize can be justified here. Of particular menace to the observer, aside from the ghostly height of Mont Blanc nearby, are the Grandes Jorasses, one of the six great north faces of the Alps (the others, from west to east, are Le Petit Dru, the Matterhorn, the Eiger, Piz Badile, and Cima Grande di Lavaredo). Beyond the multispiked behemoth of the Grandes Jorasses in French territory lies—or rather looms—Monte Rosa, which rises more than 4,500 meters above the

plains of Piedmont. This peak, clearly visible from Turin, inspired Leonardo da Vinci briefly to take up the study of mountains.

A thumpa-thumpa-thumpa fills the air. I look up to try to catch a glimpse of the culprit, then realize, with a start, that the sound is coming from beneath me. Leaning over the railing, I can see a helicopter some one hundred meters below, a distinctly odd sensation. Its markings identify it as a Chamonix medevac copter, charged with plucking the imperiled from the snows. I think of the avalanche and the many parties of climbers visible on the ascent in the aerial tramway. The helicopter moves at great speed, carefully giving a flock of leisurely paragliders a wide berth. Unfortunately, the sight of such racing copters is common on the mountain, at all times of year. A first responder named Emmanuel Cauchy, a physician from the mountain rescue unit of the local hospital and an adviser on various action films (including those of James Bond), has mined his experiences to write a series of adventures about one Docteur Vertical, a character as high flying as his creator. His crime stories—smart, sexy whodunits in French—are must-reads for his large following. As of yet, though, Docteur Vertical remains a local hero.

The pleasant giddiness from the thin air has changed into a nagging headache. *Mal di montagna. Höhenkrankheit.* Altitude sickness. I am one of the unlucky to experience the symptoms at non-Himalayan heights: dizziness, pins and needles, and a sense of oncoming nausea, all because of a drop in barometric pressure and a relative scarcity of oxygen. I realize that I must head back down to the valley floor.

HAVING CAUGHT MY BREATH and cleared my head, I take a cog railway from Chamonix back up the western flank of the mountain to view its other main attraction, the *Mer de Glace* (Sea of Ice) glacier, France's largest. The Mer de Glace was so christened in the mid-eighteenth century by English travelers who astounded the locals by their eccentric outlook. One, an amateur Orientalist named Richard Pococke, fresh from journeys in the Middle East, took to dressing as an Ottoman pasha and smoking a hookah under the bemused regard of his mountain guides. Pococke's companion, William Windham, an aristocrat given to drunken fistfights, is credited with giving the great glacier its name. Then a heaving sea of frozen ice spilling down a valley floor almost all the way to the town of Chamonix, the Mer was known for its ghastly crackles and detonations as tons of ice clashed in their slow-motion descent of the mountain. Mary Shelley, who visited in 1816, saw fit that this "most desolate place in the world," as she termed it, should be the setting for Doctor Frankenstein's fateful reunion with the monster he had fashioned. Mary's soon-to-be husband, Percy Bysshe Shelley, after recovering from slipping on the ice and knocking himself out cold, would write "Mont Blanc: Lines Written in the Vale of Chamouni" about the vista.

The trip up the mountain to the hamlet of Montenvers takes about twenty minutes on the train. Opened in 1909, the cog railway uses a third, serrated rail in between the two conventional ones—the locomotive seizes this third rail with a specially designed undercarriage and hauls itself up grades out of the question for a normal train. There are few passengers aboard today. When we arrive, there seems to be no glacier to greet us.

But yes there is. A slurry of gravelly pebbles is hiding a sullen glacier below. Soon it will be out of sight, around a corner, as the ice recedes forty meters every year. A promised Ice Tunnel is closed—

the lift down to the moraine/glacier is out of order. Climate change is triumphing here, as it is in much of the Alps. Glaciers have been halved in size in recent decades and are not expected to survive into the next century. Their disappearance will speed warming further, as the ice reflects sunlight away from the earth. The people of the Alpine countries are worried about the future. As for tourists to the Mer de Glace, the experience is akin to visiting a seaside resort closed for good.

I was forewarned about the tamed ice monster and have come up here to see something else—namely, a scary rock outcropping on the other side of the glacial moraine. The Drus, the big and the small, are the most terrifying mountaineering challenges in this already terrifying range. Le Grand Dru resembles a menhir hoisted on the back of Obélix, if Obélix were a thousand meters tall. It is smooth and relentlessly vertical. Even the spiky Grandes Jorasses, skewering the horizon, look more hospitable than the Petit and Grand Dru.

The Drus are unforgiving. They offer few footholds, little purchase, no mercy. They have been summited, of course—people are crazy—but the ephemeral routes marked out by daredevil climbers are regularly erased by rockfalls. The sheer awfulness of these peaks has inspired many to write of them. The most distinguished in English is James Salter, whose exquisitely wrought novel *Solo Faces*, features a troubled protagonist working out his existential funk by climbing a Dru on his own. Of more global renown is Roger Frison-Roche's *Premier de cordée* (First on the Rope), a stirring story of the confraternity of Chamonix mountain guides. The Grand Dru figures prominently in the adventure tale, particularly in a breathtaking passage where an experienced guide is struck and killed by lightning near its summit. His client, an American who had rashly insisted they continue the ascent despite the worsening weather, promptly loses his mind after the accident. As he is brought back down the mountain by the surviving guide, the addled American is reduced to singing, over and over again, the lyrics to "Ukelele Lady." Thus, generations of French secondary school students, for whom Frison-Roche's 1941 novel was required reading, got their introduction to Chamonix by way of Tin Pan Alley.

The music continues on the way back down in the cog railroad. A few dozen very jolly Belgian retirees belt out Walloon folk songs in the two cars they occupy. Their tour guide, a French government employee charged with promoting the area, falls into conversation with me, as he is evidently not interested in joining in the singalong. He is a fit fellow in middle age, obviously at home in the mountains— and in despair at their degradation.

"Put in your book that Chamonix is situated in the most polluted valley of France," he says. "It's a bottleneck, and the exhaust of the thousands of trucks going into the tunnel every day has nowhere to go. There are a lot of respiratory illnesses in the valley."

The tunnel in question is the Mont Blanc Road Tunnel, an eleven-kilometer affair that links Chamonix with Courmayeur, Italy. In 1999, a catastrophic fire, killing thirty-eight people, closed the tunnel for three years. I ask my new friend about the event.

"Nothing changed. Nothing at all," he says with a shrug. "The next season was as crowded as ever. People acted as if nothing had happened."

"Surely there must have been some effect?"

He smiles ruefully. "Well, yes. The casino almost had to close. The Italians don't have gambling at home and they couldn't get to Chamonix. But other than that, it was business as usual."

He looks out the window, blinking at the passing trees. The Belgians continue their singing. The trees become time-share chalet complexes.

"Do you think there's been too much development here?" I ask.

He nods. "Far too much. And it can't be stopped."

He asks me where I'm going next.

"Savoy, Val d'Isère."

The cog train pulls into the station. He is about to corral his charges when he turns and shakes my hand.

"If you want to see the Alps," he says softly, "go to Switzerland."

3. Iseran Pass and Savoy

———— ▫ ————

O N QUITTING sybaritic Chamonix, one might have the impression that civilization is being left behind. Nothing could be further from the truth. The heart of Savoy, the region to be traversed in the next few days, has been the handmaiden of European culture for centuries. If not as recognized as their cousins—the Italians—for the important role they have played in European history, the Savoyards remain that anomaly, a people who never coalesced into a nation-state in the modern period.

I look forward to exploring it, but first I must deal with another detour. Miraculously, the acronym-crazy French spell things out: *V.L.* is *Véhicules Légers* (literally, "light vehicles"), which go one way; *P.L.* is *Poids Lourds* (literally, "heavyweights"), which go the other. So Veronica Lake is for a car and Peter Lorre is for, well, a lorry, as the British call a truck. The V.L. detour, which leads upward from the town of St. Gervais les Bains, quickly becomes a neurotic noodle of a road, more suited to dahus than miniature muscle cars. Ridiculously, there are speed bumps on the hairpin turns. Motorcyclists fill my rearview mirror, flashing their lights to make me move my sorry rear end over to the right. When I comply, I notice that the overtaking French bikers, alone among all the Harley boys living the dream, let their right foot dangle from the stirrup for a few seconds, as a means of thanking the intimidated motorist. Such a civilized country, *la France*.

And such a strange province, *la Savoie*. Now part of the French republic, for centuries the mountain region punched far above its weight, exercising influence throughout the Continent and beyond. In thirteenth-century England, for example, Savoyard nobles had the run of London, as their incandescently beautiful niece, Eleanor of Provence, wed a besotted King Henry III and proceeded to form one of the most loving royal couples in the history of the English monarchy. Uxorious Henry (Eleanor bore him five children) lavished favor on his Savoyard in-laws, granting one an estate on the north bank of the Thames between Whitehall and the City of London, on which the lucky courtier constructed the sumptuous Savoy Palace, funded by revenues diverted from the local nobility. Naturally, such actions by these fashionable mountain men did not sit well with some—lovely Eleanor was once pelted with refuse when she ventured out onto the river—but by and large the Savoyards are remembered fondly in Britain. Yet the reason for that has nothing to do with the Middle Ages.

Hundreds of years later, the land on which the old Savoy Palace once stood was purchased by Richard D'Oyly Carte, a theatrical impresario. He erected there the Savoy Theatre, the venue in which his protégés, Gilbert and Sullivan, premiered their operettas. With the proceeds from these wildly successful productions, D'Oyly Carte built a hotel, the Savoy, which by the late nineteenth century was recognized as one of the world's most posh. The name of an almost impassable mountain fastness became associated with the acme of sophistication—and lives on in the numerous Savoy Societies, amateur theatrical troupes, the world over. D'Oyly Carte, perhaps in a nod to his hotel's Alpine pedigree, hired as its longtime manager a Swiss, César Ritz, whose name would become as eponymous as the Savoy's for luxury. Under Ritz's stewardship, the dining rooms of the Savoy were a place where society ladies and gentlemen, contrary to their snooty forebears in the palace hotels of the Alps, came for the express purpose of being seen. And, just as important, to be seen eating, for manning the Savoy's ovens was Auguste Escoffier, Europe's foremost chef and the founder of modern French cuisine.

All these refined associations seem improbable, given the ruggedness of the return to the main highway. There seems to be no part of Savoy willing to lie flat. Although the Savoyard nobility gained wealth by levying tolls at the great Alpine passes to and from Italy, the same could not be said of the common folk. This is rough country, scarce in arable land and plentiful in unforgiving rock. Indeed, the detour I have just completed led me atop a ridge far into the sky. One can't feed on scenery, however, so for several centuries many Savoyard youngsters had to migrate north to Paris for a few years, living in boardinghouses run by French Fagins and working hard at menial jobs. The Savoyard chimney sweep became a fixture of the capital, the scrawny boys scrambling up and around the flues of the well-to-do. Their earnings were usually sent to their families back home.

Snow, once the bane of the region, eventually came to its rescue. *L'or blanc* (white gold) caused the Savoy to become blanketed in tony winter resorts, as ski slopes went from being the preserve of the prosperous to the playground of the masses, in much the same way that Thomas Cook's package tourists to the Alps swamped the summering nobility of the nineteenth century. Not all class—and price—distinctions were swept away, however, as the next town I encountered, Megève, amply proves. Its transformation from a sleepy Savoyard hamlet into the first turnkey Alpine ski resort was the brainchild of Baroness Noémie de Rothschild (or Baroness Mimi, as she was called) in the early twentieth century. The story goes that Baroness Mimi, while in St. Moritz, Switzerland, in the 1920s, was aghast at being forced to tolerate the presence of a fellow vacationer, Gustav Krupp, the German industrialist whose munitions had just mowed down a generation of Frenchmen in the Great War. Mimi vowed to establish a "French St. Moritz," where such murderous Huns would not be welcome and where her moneyed friends could empty their wallets patriotically. Thus was born Megève, the resort.

Its success grew. After World War II, the smart set of the French capital regularly descended on the place, with nonstop rounds of partying orchestrated by Jean Cocteau and his coterie. Cocteau called it "Paris's twenty-first arrondissement."* Regulars in the 1950s included Brigitte Bardot, Charles Aznavour, Juliette Gréco, Josephine Baker, and Françoise Sagan. Their hangout, the Hôtel du Mont Blanc's bar, named *Les Enfants Terribles* (after Cocteau's breakout 1929 novel), is still plastered with artwork and frescoes executed by Cocteau.

Times have changed, but not the town's taste for the pricey. The traffic roundabouts have lamp standards adorned with fluttering banners portraying the town's handsome chefs, their Michelin-star ratings dutifully noted beneath their names. The banners look somewhat like online dating profiles, destined for the digestively amo-

---

* To be accurate in the pecking order of all things Parisian, this nickname is more often given to Deauville, a coastal resort in Normandy.

rous. *Après-ski* in Megève apparently entails more than just flirting over mulled wine.

I decide to overnight in Albertville. The town must be quaint, I reason, as it hosted the 1992 Winter Olympics. Those Olympics, the first to be held after the collapse of the Soviet Union and the Warsaw Pact, arrived on the world scene with a sense of expectancy. The long-oppressed nations of eastern Europe appeared now as recently minted democratic entities, and, most important, a newly reunified Germany made its debut on the global stage. Add to this a sense of homecoming. The Winter Olympics, after a sixteen-year hiatus, were coming back to the Alps. The competition is intimately linked with these mountains, the list of resorts to host the Games before Albertville a testament to the role of the Alps in pioneering winter sport: Chamonix (1924), St. Moritz (1928, 1948), Garmisch-Partenkirchen (1936), Cortina d'Ampezzo (1956), Innsbruck (1964, 1976), and Grenoble (1968). The chance for Albertville being a bit odd also influenced my decision—it delivered easily one of the most outlandish Olympic opening ceremonies on record. Performers marched in and out of giant alphorns, aerial devils pranced through the air, and elaborately bedecked couples spun through ballroom-dancing routines as weird electric music filled the arena.

Once again I am dead wrong. Albertville got the Games because of its central location near picturesque winter sports venues—Les Arcs, Courchevel, Les Menuires, Méribel, La Plagne, Pralognan-la-Vanoise, Les Saisies, Tignes, Val d'Isère—and most definitely not its beauty. The visitor is greeted by a ruined and rusting Olympic Hall, once blue and white, its mantle of weeds safe behind a chain-link fence. The heart of the town is not much of an improvement, consisting mainly of a long commercial avenue dotted with optician shops, one-horse cafés, pharmacies, and storefronts displaying remarkably ugly lingerie, the last being the rarest of sights on any French high street.

At dinner, the *salade savoyarde* I eagerly order boasts a brick of fried cheese in batter plopped atop a mountain of bacon bits soaked in a creamy vinaigrette that conceals the wilted lettuce and unripe tomato slices lurking at the bottom. As I walk back to my hotel, I think forlornly of the hunky chefs of Megève.

"Monsieur!"

I look up and see a woman across the street gesturing at me.

"Please, we need men."

She crosses the roadway, her colorful Caribbean garb flowing in the warm evening breeze. I assess the situation. After all, given my resemblance to an elderly Thomas Jefferson having a bad hair day, I hardly seem to be an obvious mark.

She sees what I am thinking, smiles devastatingly, and says, "Men. For dancing."

Within a few seconds, I am led down a side street to a block party. A bearded DJ blares music from a powerful sound system and wine flows from tapped casks. A French kegger, in progress.

The rest of the evening passes giddily. People of every generation come by, to dance, kibitz, and drink. The air warms with the glow of French camaraderie, never much on display in ordinary life but always lurking as a mischief-maker whenever people get together. Laughter is ever present, as are kidding, flirting, and snippets of world-weary wisdom. As an alien being from America, I am welcomed with wide-eyed cordiality. The night wears on and the festive atmosphere remains infectious; perhaps it is no coincidence that the Olympics opening ceremonies here were so memorable. And there is indeed a shortage of men, so my dance card never empties. My part-

ners come in all shapes and sizes, all ages. As I gamely attempt jitter-
bugs, salsas, slows, solos—and we drink—my opinion of Albertville
undergoes a radical revision. The characterless main street is now
hazily remembered as a racy boulevard, the cruddy cafés as literary
salons; even the bad lingerie and the *salade savoyarde* seem now to be
creations of unspeakable beauty. When at last the witching hour rolls
around, the time when rowdiness becomes *tapage nocturne*—disturbing
the peace—the party goes indoors to a bar, but without me. At least
not immediately—I go in and confess to no longer knowing the location of where I'm staying the night, the Hotel Million. Hoots of laughter greet my befuddlement, and a couple from Guadeloupe agrees to
lead me home through the darkened streets. When we part, the young
woman—the one who first accosted me—leans in to give me a kiss on
each cheek.

THE ALBERT in Albertville comes not from Schweitzer or Camus,
but from a king of Sardinia who doubled as a duke of Savoy, a certain Charles Albert who consolidated two towns into one and had the
result named after himself. If this sounds confusing, that's because it
is. Savoy and its aristocratic leaders, whose family lineage stretched
back to the year 1003, specialized in territorial trading. At one point
in the eighteenth century, they inherited the island of Sicily. Scarcely
ten years later, they bartered Sicily for Sardinia, creating an entity
that was only slightly less jerry-rigged. Added to this was their
suzerainty over Piedmont, on the other side of the Alps, with Turin
as their capital.

Events grew progressively more head-scratching as the nineteenth century unfolded. The forces of liberal democracy forced the

House of Savoy to grant parliamentary power to the rising bour-
geoisie, and the impetus of nationalism drove the movement of Italian unification known as the *Risorgimento* (Resurgence). The leaders
of Savoy–Sardinia–Piedmont, especially their ministers, allied themselves with the unifiers and soon became seen as the spearhead of
Italian nationalism. When modern Italy coalesced, the duke of Savoy
became its king.

In the latter half of the nineteenth century, as part of the geopolitical jostling occasioned by the *Risorgimento*, it was crucial to form
alliances of convenience with foreign powers in the struggle to boot
other foreign powers *out* of the Italian boot—and to keep these foreign allies from profiting from the confusion and invading Italy yet
again. Foremost among these outside meddlers was France. So a deal
was struck: In exchange for French military assistance against the Austrians, the duchy of Savoy and the county of Nice would be ceded to
France. A lion of the *Risorgimento*, Giuseppe Garibaldi, born Joseph
Marie Garibaldi, was furious at his allies for giving away his hometown
of Nice (*Nizza*, in Italian). As a sop to international public opinion, ref-
erenda were held—which many observers claimed to be rigged—and
in the 1860s these regions joined France.

Thus it was that the Kingdom of Italy was ruled by the House of
Savoy, even if Savoy was not part of Italy. The battle cry of Italian
soldiers in the Great War was *"Avanti Savoia!"*—which, on reflection, would be similar to American soldiers on the attack in Vietnam
crying, "For Mexico!" The Italo-Savoyard monarchs of the nineteenth and twentieth centuries became similar to their counterparts
elsewhere in Europe—sidelined into ceremonial irrelevance and
living out comic-opera existences. One Savoyard king of Italy was
so short—nicknamed *Re Sciaboletta* (King Little Sword)—that the

minimum height requirements of the Italian army had to be lowered so he could don a uniform and play commander-in-chief. A queen was immortalized by lending her name to a pizza, the Margherita. The new tricolor flag of Italy was immortalized in its red tomato sauce, white mozzarella, and green basil. The Kingdom of Italy was supplanted by a republic after World War II, and the House of Savoy was banished from the peninsula. They have been allowed back in recently, one scion of the line making headlines by fatally shooting a German tourist off the coast of Sardinia, and another, Emanuele Filiberto, by becoming a dreamboat vulgarian of Italian television.

AVANTI SAVOIA! The road south of Albertville becomes an expressway. I fly past factories, warehouses, lumberyards, and box stores for the home handyman. Mountain ranges loom close to both banks of the River Isère, but the pastoral and picturesque have disappeared. This is the lower Tarentaise Valley, an industrial anomaly. Knots of high-tension electrical wires entwine overhead, the offspring of some unglimpsed hydroelectric work supplying juice to Grenoble and Lyon. My skull thrums from last night's excesses, so I decide to exit the motorway in search of a truck stop that serves espresso by the demijohn.

The town of Moûtiers eventually appears, which I know is the signal for me to bear left and continue following the River Isère upstream and eastward. I pass the town's train station, somnolent now, but febrile and frantic in the winter months, for Moûtiers is the gateway to Les Trois Vallées, supposedly the world's largest ski area. The valleys—Saint-Bon, Allues, Belleville—saw much of the action of the 1992 Olympic Games and continue to draw snow lovers with their six hundred kilometers of slopes. A brochure states that the area's 183 ski lifts can hoist 250,000 skiers skyward every hour.

The valley narrows dramatically and the road hugs the meanders of the River Isère. We are in an Alpine heaven, the green meadows with their chalets overlooked by snow-tipped gray mountains. Somewhere to the north, I know, stands the peak of Pierra Menta, a jagged, toothlike summit in the midst of a treeless wilderness. Every March for the past thirty years, a four-day burst of lunacy takes place on these heights. Pairs of racers scale cliffs, ski down glaciers, and pitch camp in the howling winds as part of a cross-country, high-altitude scramble through the clouds. The Pierra Menta event has only two peers in the world of extreme Alpine ski mountaineering: the *Patrouille des Glaciers*, held in the Valais canton of southwestern Switzerland and the *Trofeo Mezzalama*, the arduous, so-called white marathon that takes place on the Italian side of the Monte Rosa massif.

The charming village of Aime comes next. Famous for its Romanesque monastic church (locked today) and historic center, Aime is also the gateway to the Vanoise National Park, mainland France's first and largest. Had it not been designated thus in 1963, the avid developers of the Trois Vallées would have doubtless gobbled up the Vanoise and formed the largest ski area in the solar system.

Aime snoozes peacefully under the hot June sun—the heat wave has continued—although prominent signs for the Born to Burn Motocross suggest otherwise. Fluttering, inexplicably, from a bridge on the outskirts is the blue-and-white flag of Quebec.

The road climbs. The gigantic ski complex to the south is partly hidden by an intermediate mountain, while to the north the roadway is carved into a vertiginous slope far above the flowing blue ribbon of the Isère. In a few pastures near the scarily distant river, I can make out brown dots slowly moving about, most probably the Tarentaise breed of cow whose cheese is so prized by fondue fans. My knuckles whiten on the wheel. *It's not that I'm afraid of heights*, it's just that I like my farm animals at eye level.

Two signs command my attention. One indicates that the towering spike of snow to the right is *Mont Pourri* (Mount Rotten), a competitor with the Cursed Mount of the Mont Blanc massif for the ugliest toponym in the Alps. The other sign shows the usual French graphic for a falling-rock zone, only this time with the unsettling notice, DANGER EXCEPTIONNEL. This does not inspire confidence. My fears are allayed somewhat when the road becomes a ribbon running through a good dozen or so avalanche galleries and tunnels hewn out of the rock. When we emerge back into the sunshine, the sizable town of Bourg-Saint-Maurice heaves into view. Despite its liberal use of flowerpots on lamp standards, the town cannot disguise its role as railhead and poor sister of its fashionable ski-resort neighbors. But it does have a grandiose name. Maurice is the patron saint of Savoy—indeed of the defunct Holy Roman Empire—a black Egyptian general from Thebes of the third century CE who refused to have his legion persecute Christians of the Alps, despite orders from the pagan emperor. Or so the story goes. It all ended very badly for the Theban Legion, of course, but its leader's name lives on in numerous monasteries and towns throughout the region. The most notable is St. Moritz, in Switzerland.

I turn south from Bourg-Saint-Maurice, following the slash of the River Isère. Within minutes, the dam of Tignes can be seen, lying in curving majesty across the gorge below, its massive slab of rusted gray an odd contrast to the dominant green. Beyond it stretches the teal expanse of its reservoir, Lac Chervil, under which the original town of Tignes lies drowned. The new town became, as is only inevitable here, a resort, but its promise of year-round skiing is now compromised by the rapid melting of its glacier, the Grande Motte. Above it all rises the snow-capped Mount Rotten, impervious to such trivial matters as climate change.

I arrive at last at my destination. Val d'Isère, renowned for its wintertime jet-set clientele, awaits inspection.

THE *ESPACE KILLY* encompasses the countryside surrounding Tignes and Val d'Isère. The reference is not to the lethal pastime of France's hunting lobby but to the region's golden boy. In the 1960s, Jean-Claude Killy ripped apart the record books by ripping down mountainsides. In the 1968 Grenoble Winter Olympics, Killy scored an astounding hat trick: gold in the Downhill, the Slalom, and the Giant Slalom. The feat astonished the high-speed ski set of the day; it had been accomplished only once before. In order to shave off a few hundredths of a second on the descent, his innovative technique had him catapulting himself out of the gate, airborne, instead of beginning from a standing start. It worked—not only in Grenoble but also in non-Olympic competitions. Killy was a sensation, a handsome god to the French and to the world at large. But he had clay feet, or rather, a clay stomach—his contraction of a gastroenterological disorder while a French conscript in the Algerian War of Independence in the early 1960s plagued him throughout the decade and may have resulted in his untimely retirement.

To my surprise, Killy's towering presence is not ubiquitous in his hometown. In fact, in the sullen heat of June, I feel no presence. Val d'Isère stretches before me as a ghost town, its hundreds of multistoried Alpine chalets standing shuttered in the sunshine, the only sounds the grind of construction crews building yet more picturesque rentals on the hillsides and the roar of the River Isère channeled beneath the main street. In the sole hotel open in town, I have breakfast the following morning in the company of a group of svelte and buff young adults wolfing down alarming amounts of protein. Given their beauty, I feel like a gnarly thumb on a manicured hand. The proprietress gently informs me at checkout that these exquisite specimens are members of the French national ski team, here to train in the summer snows far above the town, toward the Iseran Pass. I gulp, for this is the first of the many great passes I am to cross. At 2,770 meters, it is the tallest; in fact, the road is the highest pass-clearing stretch of asphalt in the Alps.

The road up into the stratosphere begins innocently. I am soon greeted by the backside of a Dutch camper, but I decide to chill for a bit and enjoy the rush of cooling air flowing through the open windows of the car as we slowly make the ascent. The trees soon shrink to bonsai-size insignificance, then disappear altogether. The trombone-shaped turns give us views of what we are leaving behind, the teal teardrop of Lac Chervil and the lowering spike of Mount Rotten. Thoughtfully, French road builders have neglected to install a guardrail alongside the abyss, presumably so that the views can be unimpeachably terrifying.

The Dutchman swerves slightly to the left and I instantly see the reason. Swarms of cyclists are laboriously pumping at their pedals, barely making headway up the climb, their straining upper thighs as broad and powerful as grasshopper legs. These men and women form, to my mind, a cardiovascular nobility, the thousands who take to the Alps every summer to scale the steep velodromes of the hairpins and to gasp through the thinning air until they reach, after hours of effort, the blessed level ground of the pass. And then the reward: the dizzying, dangerous coast downward to the next valley.

They are inspired, perhaps, by the circus of commercial athleticism that descends on the Pyrenees and the Alps every summer: the Tour de France, a.k.a. *La Grande Boucle* (The Large Loop, or The Big Buckle). Although sketchy in its reputation as a pharmacological proving ground, the Tour is nonetheless an impressive, if not lunatic, spectacle, especially in its mountain stages, those that are labeled *hors catégorie* (beyond categorization) because of their sadistic level of difficulty. The Iseran Pass is one such stage, where scores of sinewy supermen weave in and out of a gaggle of ambulances, police vans, companion cars plastered with advertisements, cameramen riding shotgun on motorcycles, and the shouted encouragements of the thousands who line the roadside, risking life and limb for a glimpse of the greats inching up the slope. Overhead, helicopters clatter incessantly through the clouds of exhaust and dust raised by the raucous procession.

The race is about as bucolic as Times Square. About two decades ago, it passed close to my home in rural southern France, near the Pyrenees. The picturesque road leading from the foothills of those mountains, shaded by tall plane trees, had become a linear campground for thousands of cycling buffs. The men played *boules* or sat in folding plastic chairs with their wives, sipping pastis. There was a distinct holiday feeling in the air, of shared passion, unusual for this lonely but beautiful landscape of peach orchards and vineyards.

The proceedings got underway with the arrival of the advertising caravan, its music blaring through the trees. This exceedingly weird feature of the Tour has been around since the 1930s (the race itself dates from 1903). The caravan consists of dozens and dozens of garishly decorated vehicles, emblazoned with logos or toting outsize anthropomorphic mascots, all in the service of promoting some enterprise or product. The variety of the advertisers astounds: banks, insurance companies, candy makers, bakers of industrial baguettes, mineral-water suppliers, supermarkets, offtrack betting services, and on and on. The students manning these vehicles showered us with commercial samples and branded caps and T-shirts, all tossed toward the outstretched arms of the spectators lining the road three deep.

And then it was gone as suddenly as it had come. We resumed our waiting. The advertising caravan precedes the peloton of riders by about two hours or so. About ninety minutes in, we heard the choppers and regained our places by the roadside. The racers were near.

The first of the police vehicles blew past us, then a couple of satellite trucks. Loud cheering could be heard farther up the roadway, and then, suddenly, the hullabaloo was upon us. Helicopters, cameramen, motorcycles, and then the multicolored packs of riders, sleek and aerodynamic and traveling at great speed on this flat stretch of road. Some of the cyclists were only inches apart, a heart-stopping sight. The leader overall of the race, wearing the coveted yellow jersey, eventually streaked by, which made the excited onlookers redouble their roaring and shouts of encouragement in French, Spanish, and Catalan. People leaned in, as if wanting to touch the speeding gods, but they flashed past, indifferent to the adulation. At last the trailing companion vehicles sped by, and the roadway was again empty, quiet. We then headed to our cars, only to get into a massive traffic jam.

Memories of that distant summer afternoon come to me as I make my way up to the high pass. The Iseran is not the most celebrated of the Alpine stages of the Tour—that honor would go, arguably, to the Alpe d'Huez to the west and to Mont Ventoux at the gates of Provence—but its majesty is undeniable. We pass the Pont St. Charles, a desolate expanse of tundra bracketed on both sides by cold, gray rock walls several hundred meters tall. And then, by some miracle, the dawdling camper in front of me pulls off the road and comes to a halt in a sliver of a turnout. My irritation at the Dutchman turns to admiration, for I do not have the guts to park my vehicle a few centimeters from the void. The camper's disappearance does not mean that I have the road to myself. At irregular intervals, I am overtaken by motorcyclists gunning their engines and rounding the curves at blistering speeds. I notice that the bikers are always organized by nationality. First come the Italians, a few minutes later the Germans, and then the French, the last again dangling their right legs in the Gallic gesture of gratitude for giving way to them.

At a turn called the Tête d'Arolley, there is a sufficiently large and reassuring parking lot for the cowardly. I pull over, skip across the roadway, and head up a hundred meters or so to an orientation table at a scenic lookout. The almost-360-degree panorama boggles the senses. A chaos of snow and gray rock surrounds the viewer in all directions, looking impenetrable and menacing. Or unearthly. I feel that I could be on Mars, so inhospitable is the vista. The table informs me that I am looking at Mont Pourri, the Aiguille du Franchet, the Aiguille du Dôme, the Pointe de la Bailletta, and the Tsanteleina massif. It also informs, in opaque technical language more suited to a French doctoral candidate, that these peaks were formed at entirely different times and that some of the rock has metamorphosed under the enormous seismic pressure. I am, in fact, beholding geologist Richard Fortey's messy lasagne. Difficult as it is to grasp, this panoply of stone, in appearance so stolid and monolithic, is actually a variegated sea of rock in constant, chaotic motion over unimaginable stretches of time. The ranges have been straining up and against each other for millions of years, and continue to do so. The only response can be awe.

The Iseran Pass is visible much farther up, close to a straggling cloud. I had hoped for an Alpine pasture in bloom, alive with gentian and edelweiss, but the approach is a forbidding scree of gravel, with great banks of snow in the upper reaches. The only thing resembling vegetation are the many crisscrossing cables of ski lifts overhead, like lianas awaiting the passage of some high-altitude Tarzan, yodeling as he swings his way home to Switzerland.

The view from the pass itself is unremarkable, as the road goes between two peaks, thus obstructing a wider perspective. A group of Dutch bikers sit on the ground smoking. What is the collective noun for Dutch bikers? I don't know, so I write *tulip* in my notebook. Although one can hardly begrudge them the cheap high of a smoke in the oxygen-deprived air, this particular tulip is astonishingly rude in other ways. The leader of the pack has parked his alpha hog directly in front of the stone marker indicating the name and altitude of the pass. Hikers, cyclists, drivers—none can take the requisite picture of themselves before the milestone. The damned Dutch Harley is in the way. I find this particularly frustrating for the cyclists and hikers; they, after all, expended muscle and grit to get to this point, instead of sitting on their backside—like me—and letting internal combustion do the work.

A few timid entreaties are made to the mute tulip on the ground, but the only response is the creaking of their leather jackets. Being Dutch, it is quite possible that they do not even notice the annoyance they are causing. Strike that—it is not possible, it is certain. Just as we cannot see the heaving and shifting of the mountains, they seem unable to distinguish the movements of their fellow humans. Perplexed, I move a few hundred paces from the standoff and am surprised to see, far below in a snowy vale to the east, a ski lift in operation. Perhaps this is where the demigods with whom I shared breakfast are spending the day.

A deafening roar signals the imminent departure of the sociopathic bikers. By the time I arrive back at the pass marker, iPads are being gleefully retrieved from saddlebags and rucksacks. There is a complicit feeling in the air, a collective post-tulip sigh of relief. I oblige several groups and couples by accepting their proffered devices and taking their pictures, thinking wistfully about how much I admire their youth and vigor. But with one couple, I realize with a start that they are much older than I, perhaps in their late sixties or early seventies, beaming in Day-Glo spandex beside their bicycles. Damn these Europeans!

Chastened and feeling morally and physically flabby, I undertake the descent from the Iseran Pass to the Maurienne Valley. The road is steeper than on the Tarentaise side, the curves more pinched. Intimations of inadequacy are replaced by intimations of mortality, as I repeatedly downshift to make the grade. Going downhill is definitely scarier than going uphill. At points, the roadway is pitched dramatically, so one has the odd impression that the mountains ahead are somehow lying on their sides. And always, there are those overtaking me. A bratwurst of German bikers, a delivery truck, an enraged local—and now even the cyclists, whizzing headlong at tremendous speed. I keep an eye out for Granny and Gramps Day-Glo, praying that they won't pass me. But they do, on a hairpin I take in second gear, racing ahead of my muscle car like golden-age jackrabbits.

It is time to slink out of Savoy.

4. MONT CENIS PASS

———— ▫ ————

HELL HATH NO FURY like a contraried French functionary.
I have arrived in the tourist office of the small town of Lanslebourg in search of information about the pass I am about to cross.
Breakfast was taken at a picturesque village café in the company of
a French biker couple from Colmar, in Alsace, whose early morning
beery bonhomie led me to believe this was a particularly jolly corner
of the country. Lanslebourg disabuses me of that notion.

The two female staffers in the tourist office are whaling on a male
visitor, whose spluttering attempts to get in a word edgewise meet
with failure. Neither whispering model nor shopkeeper budgerigar, their form of discourse is an explosion of indignation perfected
by French public servants. As far as I can gather, the object of their
ire returned to the office to complain that they had directed him to
a crummy restaurant or hotel and to insinuate that they had done so
because a family member or boyfriend owned the place. I consider this
standard operating procedure at tourist offices but am wise enough to
keep my mouth shut. The dread pedantry of the offended functionary

fills the air, with such expressions as *déontologie professionnelle* (ethics) and *règles de bonne conduite* (good behavior) coming fast and furious. The two trill a duet of joyous disdain. Recognizing defeat when I see it, I grab a couple of brochures off the rack and close the door on the scene. My presence has gone entirely unnoticed.

Outside I take a deep breath and examine the great green wall of forested mountains to the east. In only one place does it relent, exhibiting a declivity at the summit ridge in the form of the letter *V*, perhaps a natural hint at the word *via*, or, given the military associations of this gap, a tantalizing suggestion of *victory*. My inner protractor gauges the angle of the *V* to be forty or forty-five degrees, constituting a veritable invitation to marauding armies. The invitation of this pass, the Mont Cenis, and its fellows throughout the great Alpine ranges, has been accepted many times. Carthaginians, Celts, Lombards, Carolingians, Germans, French, Swiss, Huns, Goths, and others sniffing the wealth to be pillaged beyond the southern side of the slopes have been reliably pouring through the mountains since Antiquity. The Alps talk a good game—seeming to mock the wayfarer with their forbidding appearance—but in reality they have collapsed repeatedly like a house of cards before any determined intruder. In the chapter entitled "Concerning the Defence of Hard Passages" of his 1614 *Historie of the World*, Sir Walter Raleigh wrote witheringly, ". . . have the Alpes given way to Armies breaking into Italie? Yea, where shall we finde that ever they kept out one invadour? . . . What shall we say of those mountains which lock up whole regions in such sort, as they leave but one Gate open?"

The most porous of these gates have been, from west to east, Mont Cenis, Great St. Bernard, Simplon, Gotthard, and Brenner. These great passes have seen the ascent and descent of armies, sometimes in the dead of winter, all in the name of conquest and plunder. The loss of men and matériel are a constant in accounts of these passages, yet the tall mountains never made any belligerent leader quail. The common foot soldier is expendable, went the reasoning, so the formidable Alps would take their human toll, but the bulk of the army would survive.

Perhaps the only armed forces to escape this dreary logic were the Swiss. At home on the heights and possessed of a thorough knowledge of their dangers and traps, the Swiss citizen militias marched smartly over the passes and emerged to wreak havoc in the plains below. In the Middle Ages, armed with long and sharp pikes, the Swiss barreled into enemy forces like deadly hedgehogs, seemingly unstoppable. And often, their enemies were enemies in name only—anxious kings and dukes hired them as mercenaries, so fearsome was their efficiency. In *Hamlet*, King Claudius calls out for his "Switzers" to protect him from hostile intruders. Gunpowder eventually put paid to Swiss invulnerability, but their past as fierce pikemen-for-hire lives on in their role as a Swiss Guard defending Vatican City.

One of the most notorious gates of the Alps is the Mont Cenis Pass, which links France's Savoy to Italy's Piedmont. It served nonmilitary purposes as well. As the House of Savoy, first centered in Chambéry (France) then in Turin, controlled lands on both sides of the pass from the eleventh to the nineteenth centuries, Mont Cenis outranked the Great St. Bernard as the busiest traverse of the western Alps, making the Savoyards happy for hundreds of years from the tolls collected from merchants and pilgrims. Of the latter, the Romeward bound followed a route called the Via Francigena over Mont Cenis, their numbers swelling into the tens of thousands during Jubilee years, when throwing coins into the coffers of the Eternal City's churches guaranteed a remission of one's sins. (This lucrative celebration, held every twenty-five years, began in 1300. Its success was so striking that Dante Alighieri chose to set his *Divina Commedia* in the thronged Rome of Holy Week in that year.)

The ascent commences. The road is long and winding but broad and easy. In one pasture, about two dozen black cows rest side by side in the grass at the edge of the asphalt, looking out at my passing vehicle like worldly patrons at a sidewalk café. As I head up through the tall trees, I remember that it was on this slope, not at St. Moritz or at Chamonix, that the passion for winter sports first took hold. As early as 1500, peasants used alder branches, called *arcosses*, tied together to sled down from the pass to Lanslebourg, the town of this morning's irate tourism hostesses. Someone eventually equipped these sledges with chairs (*chaises*) mounted on rudimentary runners, and the five-kilometer descent from the pass could be effected in about ten minutes, thanks to the steering skill of the guides. In 1581, the philosopher Michel de Montaigne made the journey and judged it "interesting," "without danger"—and cheap.

By the 1700s, wealthy English travelers on the Grand Tour came to spend time at Lanslebourg. The novelty of sliding down a steep slope thus predates the development of the ski industry. Aristocrats, delighted at the sensation of safe but titillating speed, sledded down to the town two or three times a day, flashing through the larch trees on a narrow track and yelping with fright at sudden turns. In the pre-railroad age, people had seldom traveled this fast. The locals, equally delighted at this source of easy income, took to honing their sledges to increase speed and making the passage back up to the top less onerous with the help of donkeys and mules. By the mid-eighteenth century, a stop at Lanslebourg had become commonplace, leavening the heavy diet of culture absorption with a week of plain old fun.

But the pass was not, contrary to what Montaigne declared, entirely without danger. In November 1739, the son of British Prime Minister Robert Walpole watched in horror as his lap dog, named Tory, was abducted by a wolf on the Mont Cenis, snatched from alongside his chaise, never to be seen again. One wonders how his traveling companion, Thomas Gray, a poet destined for fame for his "Elegy Written in a Country Churchyard," consoled his heartbroken friend. With a lecture on the brevity of canine life, perhaps.

At last I clear the trees and come to the grassy expanses of the storied pass. Mont Cenis may be said to be the Platonic Ideal of a mountain pass: bare green slopes above, another glorious teal-colored lake below, a modernist pyramidal chapel, crumbling fortresses, and a surrounding panorama of snow-flecked peaks. Three handsome artworks adorn the pass itself, near the sign indicating its altitude of 2,083 meters. These works consist of rectangles of purplish metal anchored against the winds by piles of large stones held fast by mesh. In the upper portions of the rectangles, three parades are shown in silhouette, cut out of the metal: the first, depicting a general riding a rearing elephant followed by a few lesser pachyderms; the second, a short man on horseback wearing a bicorne hat followed by his infantry; the last, a line of speeding cyclists. Of the three, the last two are undisputed. The Tour de France has indeed come this way several times, and Napoleon most definitely did as well—the roadway traversing the pass is his handiwork. In the first decade of the nineteenth century, his engineers came across the old ashes of a tremendous fire thought to have given the place its name: from *Mont des Cendres* (Mount of Ashes), it is but a small step in dialect to Mont Cenis.

The first monument is more problematic: Did the Carthaginian general Hannibal make his famous Alpine crossing at Mont Cenis, en route to further mischief in Italy? Napoleon believed this was the place, and who are the French tourist authorities to doubt the emperor? Others are less sure, and over the years alternate routes have gained favor, the results of lively arguments authored by professional and amateur historians claiming to have divined the definitive answer. One of the strongest rivals to Mont Cenis lies to the north, the Little St. Bernard Pass, which links Bourg-Saint-Maurice to Courmayeur, Italy. We do know that Hannibal spent a night in what is now Albertville before setting off for the mountains with his men, mules, and sixty elephants. Our main sources for this episode of the Second Punic War (i.e., between Carthage and Rome) are Polybius, a scholar writing a generation after the events of 218 BCE, and Livy, a historian writing some two centuries after the fact. Of the two, Polybius is thought the more trustworthy, Livy the livelier. Another important source, Appian of Alexandria, wrote his histories in the second century CE. Unfortunately, none of the three indicate the name of the pass Hannibal used.

Still, the historians tell a gripping story. Setting out from southern Spain, which was then part of an extended empire ruled from Carthage (present-day Tunisia), Hannibal and his men marched northward with the intent of rounding the Mediterranean and invading the Romans in their homeland. Once past Barcelona—which may or may not derive its name from Hannibal's lineage, the Barca dynasty—the Carthaginian general had a fight on his hands. The Iberian forebears of the Catalans were ferocious, and it was only after suffering substantial losses that the Carthaginians were able to subdue the hostile tribes and cross the Pyrenees.

Things went better in what is now southern France. The Carthaginians and their Berber mercenaries—and the elephants—successfully forded the Rhône without being detected. Sensing that the coast was not clear on the way to Italy, Hannibal veered north through Savoy. But when his men got a good look at the Alps, their warrior panache flagged. In a famous passage, Livy puts the following words in Hannibal's mouth as he harangues his men not to fail him after all they've been through together:

> What on earth do you think the Alps are except a collection of high mountains? Perhaps you think they are even higher than the Pyrenees? So what? Nothing on earth can ever reach the sky; no mountain is too high for man to conquer. People actually live in the Alps, for goodness' sake! They till the ground; animals breed and grow fat there. If a small group of natives can cross them, so can an army. Look at these delegates [local allies]—they didn't grow wings and fly here over the top. Even their ancestors were not born here; they came here as immigrant peasants from Italy; they crossed these selfsame Alps in huge migrating hordes, with all their women and children—and lived to tell the tale. What is so difficult then for an army, with nothing to carry but its own equipment?

So off they went, either here at Mont Cenis or somewhere near here. They were guided by local warriors known as Centrones, who Hannibal suspected were up to no good. His instinct proved correct: At a narrowing of the route, more Centrones appeared on a slope above the armies and rolled boulders onto the Carthaginian forces, killing many pack animals. But Hannibal, having foreseen such treachery, had split his army in two, with elephants and pack animals at the front and the mass of armed soldiers in the rear. These latter were ordered to hold back, not to enter the pass. The Centrones were thus lured from their position on the heights to fill the gap between Hannibal's forces. It was then that the hardened Carthaginian soldiery advanced and attacked the locals, engaging in a generalized massacre. By day's end, there were no Centrones to be seen—they had either fled or died.

Now nature took its turn. It was October and the snow began to fly. During the steep descent on the Italian side of the pass, the footing was icily treacherous and many beasts and men fell to their deaths. The debris from a recent landslide then blocked the way. Laboriously, the men worked in shifts to hew a mule track through the rubble. After a day, they had succeeded and made their way with the pack animals to the pastures below the tree line. But the great elephants were simply too big to follow. Another three days of track-widening construction ensued before the exhausted pachyderms could pick their way down the wintry slope. After a pause of several days to regroup, the army, which had been on the march for five months, at last made the descent into the valley of the River Po—and into the historical imagination for the next two thousand years.

The tale of Hannibal's daring crossing added to the allure of ancient Carthage down through the centuries. Gustave Flaubert, enamored of the empire and its customs, set his splendid historical novel, *Salammbô*, in the Carthaginian court of Hannibal's boyhood. Virgil, who lived in the first century BCE and was arguably Rome's greatest poet, opened his epic *Aeneid* with his hero, Aeneas, finding shelter in the Carthaginian court of Queen Dido. The lovely queen falls in love with him, only to commit suicide, heartbroken, when he leaves her city to become the ancestor of the Romans in Italy. The events described in the epic poem have been celebrated in Western culture down to the present day.

Hannibal's fifteen-year stay in Italy consisted of a string of brilliant victories on the fields of battle. His rout of the Romans at Cannae, in southern Italy, is still studied as one of history's most brilliant examples of generalship. Ultimately, the challenge of waging war and occupying territory in the heartland of the Roman Republic, where its allies were thick on the ground and where enemy armies were repeatedly raised to fight him, proved too difficult, even for such a military genius. When the Romans invaded North Africa, he was forced to sail home, where he was uncharacteristically defeated at the Battle of Zama. The Second Punic War was over. It would take a third war, waged two generations later, for the recommendation of a Roman senator, Cato the Elder, to be thoroughly implemented. At the end of every speech in the Senate, whatever its subject, Cato would utter some version of the phrase *Carthago delenda est* (Carthage must be destroyed). In the spring of 146 BCE, the victorious Romans annihilated the city of Carthage, setting fire to it in a blaze that lasted seventeen days and selling its entire population into slavery. Hence our term *Carthaginian peace*, for a victor who shows no mercy to the vanquished.

A less-well-known crossing of Mont Cenis had far greater repercussions than had Hannibal's, for the subsequent actions of the general permanently altered the course of European and subsequent world culture. Despite warnings from his soothsayers, Constantine, the co-emperor of the Roman Empire in charge of Britain, Gaul, and Spain, decided to march on Italy. The year was 312 CE, a time of considerable confusion over who had ultimate authority over the vast empire. Rival factions flourished, civil war loomed. In Constantine's case, this meant going to war against another co-emperor, Maxentius, who also happened to be his brother-in-law. Constantine and his legions crossed the Mont Cenis Pass, handily won a couple of battles in northern Italy, then proceeded on to Rome. Maxentius drew up his legions at Milvio, where a bridge spans the Tiber just north of the city.* On the night prior to the battle, Constantine is said to have seen either a cross in the sky (or in a dream) or the Greek initials X (chi) and P (rho)—the monogram of Christ. This was taken as a sign that the god of the Christians was on his side. Constantine won, Maxentius drowned, and soon the grateful emperor, alone at the top now, ended the persecution of Christians in the empire and legalized the practice of the faith everywhere. Christianity would henceforth flourish under Rome, outlive the empire, and eventually spread around the globe. Perhaps the militantly secular French would have felt queasy memorializing Constantine's epochal crossing of Mont Cenis alongside the safer, faith-free commemorations of Hannibal, Napoleon, and the Tour de France.

In truth, so many armies and conquerors have passed this way— the list also includes Pepin the Short, Charlemagne, Charles the Bald—that Mont Cenis would look more like a scrapyard were every one of its transient generals and troops given their own purple metallic plaque. A small, bidirectional marker hints at the historic centrality of the role of the pass in history: One arrow reads ROME 724 KM.; the other, pointing in the opposite direction, reads PARIS 724 KM. It is sometimes thought that Europe's single-minded devotion to war prior to the founding of the EU usually pits the French against the Germans, or perhaps against the English. What tends to be forgotten is France's long-standing tradition of invading what would become

---

* The *Ponte Milvio* (Milvian Bridge) is Rome's oldest, having first been constructed in the late third century BCE. A more dubious recent distinction credits an Italian novel and subsequent movie with making the bridge the first to introduce Europe to the love-lock craze.

Italy, a national sport of sorts played down the centuries by leaders royal, revolutionary, and imperial. The proliferation of street signs in Paris bearing Italian names owes nothing to an admiration of Italy; rather, they are the names of battle locales, and to reach such places French armies almost invariably took Mont Cenis. Napoleon in particular, his imperial ambition boundless and emulation of old Rome shameless, made Italy his sanguinary playground of choice. His nephew, Napoleon III, took a similar interest in the Italian peninsula, this time to battle a geopolitical rival, the Austrians, who controlled much of Lombardy and the Veneto. His armies crossed Mont Cenis in 1858 and, in the subsequent year, fought the Battle of Solferino in Lombardy, an affair involving a quarter-million soldiers with such a gruesome outcome that a Swiss observer of the agonies of the dying hurried back to his hometown to write the first Geneva Conventions and eventually found the International Red Cross.

It wasn't all bad.

I'VE HAD ENOUGH martial musings for the day and take myself to a weather-beaten café fronting Napoleon's roadway. A bratwurst of German bikers, quaffing dumpster-size steins of lager, occupies most of the outdoor terrace. Their leader nods affably, his resemblance to Gérard Depardieu in his better days uncanny. The others, all very big men, could pass for Hannibal's elephantine companions. I notice that, unlike the tulip at the Iseran Pass, the bratwurst at the Mont Cenis has had the manners to park its hogs far away from any Snapchat-worthy landmarks.

I settle down in the sunshine and feel the gentle breeze in my hair. The day is beautiful. I try to imagine just what this pass has witnessed. The waitress, a smiling elderly woman in a blue polka-dot dress, takes my order. When she comes back with my double espresso and Evian water and spies the French newspaper in my lap, she takes this as a spur to indulge in her country's national sport: complaint.

"We get days in winter that are nicer than this," she says with a sigh. "The skiers come and suntan on the terrace."

I say nothing. The day is so hot that I have remembered to apply sunblock to my insta-burn Irish skin.

"This wind is enough to make you want to cry," she continues. "It's been like this all week."

I remain silent. I have no idea what she's talking about. The weather has been glorious as of late. Just to be polite, I nod. This seems to satisfy her.

A short time later, when she comes to collect the euro coins I have laid on the table, she smiles and asks me where I am headed.

"Susa," I reply. That is the Italian town at the other side of the Mont Cenis.

"Where?"

"Susa," I repeat, gesturing with my hand toward Italy. This does not improve matters.

"What?"

"Susa."

She stares at me blankly. My face must mirror hers.

Then I remember the road signs.

"*Suse*," I say, giving the French name for the town.

"Ah, Suse!" she exclaims, relieved that our relationship has been revived. "Such a lovely town. When my husband was alive, we used to go there often."

At this, she cheerfully scoops up cup, bottle, and glass and returns inside—but not before wishing me "*bonne route*."

I get up to go. A loud roar to my right stops me from crossing the roadway. A line of bright red vintage sports cars comes into view, their drivers leaning on the horns as they pass the marker for the pass. Their license plates show almost all of them to be from the Swiss canton of Neuchâtel. As my knowledge of that locale is limited to its reputation as a former capital of absinthe production, I look to see if any of the convertibles are weaving dangerously. But no, the drivers are all smiling men in their sixties, accompanied by windblown wives letting their scarves trail behind them and waving to the bratwurst and me. We wave back. There must be at least two dozen of them, a remarkable sight.

When the rowdy retirees disappear, I venture across the now-silent road and make my way to a terraced botanical garden near the pyramidal chapel. Exceptionally well laid out, the Alpine beds are today being tended by about a dozen young adults—volunteers, perhaps— as colorfully clad as the blooms they care for. Informational boards tout the richness of Alpine microclimates: The drastic changes in altitude ensure varied flora. Indeed, the Alps have the greatest number of flower varieties of anywhere in Europe.

The reason for this floral supremacy is attributable to changes in elevation. There are distinct ecosystems to be traversed as one climbs a mountain, the elevation attained affecting temperature, barometric pressure, and exposure to ultraviolet light. The Mont Cenis garden, being well above the tree line, naturally has a vocation to show off the blooms of what is called the Alpine tundra, the grass and lichen expanses of the taller elevations, where winters are harsh and summers short. The flowers have adapted to these conditions admirably—red is a common bloom color, as it stores the heat of sunlight—although their fragility has been increased by recent development. The hard snowpack of a ski run is no friend to these hardy yet delicate plants.

Having had a childhood influenced by *The Sound of Music*, I immediately seek out and find the "noble-white" flower—the edelweiss—whose beauty is extolled in an invented folk tune sung by Captain von Trapp. It is too early in the season for the plant to bloom, so all that can be seen are fuzzy green leaves covered in what looks like confectioner's sugar. I think mine is a more charitable description than the one offered by Mark Twain, who in his travels in the Alps said the edelweiss exhibits "the color of bad cigar ashes."

To find the other bloom I want to see, I have to traverse a section of the garden labeled *les plantes qui font mal* (plants that are bad for you). An alpenrose bush, a type of rhododendron that flourishes above the tree line, is in bloom there, its rusty-red flowers looking anything but toxic; still, I decide not to have a taste. Near it, at ground level, is the lovely yellow-and-white Alpine buttercup. Clearly, poison comes in many deceptive garbs.

Of course, many Alpine plants are useful, in cosmetics and as food and medicine. Edelweiss extract has long been used as a cream to arrest the aging of skin and the formation of wrinkles. The root of a weed known as the "cursed thistle" has for centuries provided herders in the high meadows with a pleasant snack, their isolation in this instance being a good thing, as the plant causes flatulence. And the wood sorrel, found in rocky crevices, provides a natural treatment for sore throat, fever, and nausea. As one might imagine, the list goes on and on.

In a few moments, I am before my goal. A clump of blue gentians stands alongside the footpath, almost stemless. In D. H.

Lawrence's poem "Bavarian Gentians," he describes the flowers as "dark darkening the daytime torchlike with the smoking blueness of Pluto's gloom." Unlike my reaction to Twain's edelweiss, this time my inclination is to agree with a famous floral description. The Alpine gentian exhibits a deep, fathomless blueness, so blue as to be almost lewd.

The kaleidoscope is too stunning to be left unrecorded. Out come my smartphone and notepad. Forget-me-not, bird's-eye primrose, black vanilla orchid, snowbell—the native flora of the Alps form a garden of earthly delights. A patch of deep purple beckons. Two species of bellflower, peach-leaved and bearded, are surrounded by clumps of purple lupine, seemingly standing at attention like sentries to protect the more fragile blooms. The afternoon wears on, the colors and fragrances enchant. It is with reluctance that I leave the garden to resume the journey.

I AM SOMEWHERE ELSE. Mont Cenis has become Moncenisio—a change that surely must be unacceptable in the café lady's French worldview. The descent into the Piedmont is distinctly different than the ascent from Savoy. For one, the mountains seem impossibly tall, almost on a Mont Blanc scale. The southern slopes of the Alps are almost always steeper than their northern counterparts, as Italy is part of the African tectonic plate, slamming into the European one. The roadway is forced to narrow, describe many hairpins, plunge at slopes of 10 percent, the greatest I've seen thus far. Clearly, this is a formidable natural frontier, thus it seems only normal that it should give rise to a rupture in culture, that two Latin sisters, the French and the Italians, inhabit either side.

I fall in behind the inevitable Dutch camper, whose slowness gives me time to admire the occasional appearance of old rail tunnels, sturdily buttressed against the rock face. These are the remnants of the Mont Cenis Railway, a technologically innovative means of locomotion developed by British engineer John Barraclough Fell. The Fell system, used here first, relied on a third rail between the two running rails. For going up, horizontal wheels would run along the third rail, ensuring better traction. For going down, brake pads clamped the sides of the third rail. This system is different from the cog or rack railway that superseded it—that type of train, which I rode up to Mer de Glace at Chamonix, relies on a third rail that is a toothed rack rail; the train's third, vertical wheel is a cog wheel that meshes with the rail.

The Mont Cenis Railway is also unusual for how briefly it was in business—from 1868 to 1871—and for the reason behind its construction. It was thought that a conventional rail tunnel under a mountain near the pass would take years to build, and the imperial and entrepreneurial British were impatient to decrease the time it took to get matériel, messages, and men to and from India, now that the Suez Canal had just opened. With the Mont Cenis Railway, the rail trip from Calais in France to Brindisi in Italy (where ships lay at anchor for the rest of journey) would be dramatically shortened. In the event, what dramatically shortened was the time it took to build the conventional rail tunnel through a mountain near Mont Cenis, thanks to improvements in tunneling technology. So the Fell railway, the real-life little engine that could, was made redundant after only four years of operation.

There is a certain irony to some of the graffiti now defacing the old stone bulwarks of the disused Fell system. Again and again, I read: *TAV* = *MAFIE*, which translated and spelled out means,

"High-Speed Train = Corruption."* A rail project, now approved by the French and Italian governments, is destined to link Lyon and Turin by a bullet train, which will entail carving out a new fifty-seven-kilometer-long tunnel under the Alps. No doubt intercity travelers welcome the initiative, but dwellers of Alpine valleys, such as that of Susa, where the train will run, know only too well the pitfalls of development. The first roads and rail lines were welcomed in the nineteenth century, as they opened up isolated areas to the outside world and promoted commerce and tourism. But the limited-access expressways and road tunnels of the twentieth century made the valleys a drive-by landscape; worse still, that landscape, often just a narrow vale between two mountain ranges, was marred by the newcomers, whose high-flying, multipillared viaduct bridges tower over medieval villages and age-old vineyards. The new bullet train that will run through the Susa Valley will doubtless eat up valuable land, require massive earth-moving, and entail widespread use of eminent domain—all for the comfort of business people whizzing past their country cousins at speeds of more than 250 kilometers per hour. And there are lucrative government contracts to be handed out—the estimated cost of the new train connection comes in at twenty-five billion euros—hence, the justifiable suspicion of antidevelopment activists that there will be boundless opportunities for corruption. *Mafie*, indeed.

On the outskirts of Susa, the Dutch camper turns at a sign indicating a road leading to a campsite. I hope, for his sake, that the site is somewhat bucolic. Far too many European campgrounds resemble Walmart parking lots. My destination, the Hotel Stati Uniti, sits

---

* TAV is the Italian acronym for *Treno Alta Velocità*.

opposite the train station—no matter what I do this afternoon, I seem unable to shake trains.

It is often said that the Italians are the French in a good mood. Susa seems to confirm this. There is a definite feeling of theatricality in the air as I stroll its old streets. Young men stop to window-shop as much as the young women do. The whole town seems to be sitting outside. Colorful placemats, on sale at a news kiosk, bear likenesses of Elvis Presley and Pope Francis. Nuns walk by, followed by grave old men in cardigans, their hands clasped behind their backs, as if inspecting their fellow townspeople for signs of excessive frivolity. Death notices are plastered on church doors. And babies are everywhere. One sidewalk café could easily double as a day-care center. People stand around its packed tables, squealing compliments to the *bambini* being dandled and handed around through the fog of perfume and cologne.

"*Dottore, vuole una fantastica giraffa?*" The man addressing me is an African fellow holding a stuffed toy animal. I smile at his use of *dottore*—the jokey Italian form of address—and tell him that, no, I do not want a fantastic giraffe. He salutes me in a mock military manner and then skips off.

The streets turn medieval, then antique. In a park at the edge of the city center, the remains of an old Roman aqueduct and public baths stand in silence amid cypress trees. But the real show-stopper is a triumphal arch decorated with all manner of processional reliefs. It honors the Emperor Augustus and was erected at the very end of the first century BCE by the Celto-Ligurian chieftain of Susa, Marcus Julius Cottius. In exchange for swearing his fealty to Rome, Cottius was made the prefect of the region and, more lastingly, gave his name to the range of the Alps looming on the western horizon, known as the Cottian Alps.

The Cottian Alps, for me, are especially sublime because they trace out what is sometimes referred to as "the lard line." On the north side of the Alps, animal fat is used for cooking; on the south, olive oil. True, the people of Piedmont loved their porkers as much as northern Europeans do, but the culinary revolution occasioned by the unification of Italy is now more or less complete. Whereas the northerners of Italy came out on top economically and culturally when compared to their countrymen in the *Mezzogiorno*, or the south, the sunny southerners took over in matters of the palate. Thus pasta replaced polenta as the carb of choice, and olive oil supplanted animal fat.

I have occasion to revel in this culinary colonialism at dinner that night. A pesto pasta dish—a specialty of neighboring seaside Liguria—comes accompanied by a light garden salad perfectly heightened by olive oil and balsamic vinegar. The creamy, goopy *salade savoyarde* eaten at Albertville the previous week becomes a nightmare consigned harmlessly to the past, when I was fool enough to dally on the wrong side of the lard line.

My companions at the communal table are in agreement with me. Heinz and Irene, from Nuremberg, raise their forks to their mouths sacramentally, savoring each bite as if it were their last. I ask them whether they visit Italy frequently. Heinz interrupts the transubstantiation of his penne to reply, "Yes, as often as we can. They live so much better than us."

I'm inclined to his point of view. We are seated outside, underneath the old arches of a pedestrian arcade, now filled with tables for diners. There is not a hint of an iota of stress, the ambient conversation is convivial and low-key, the men are loose-limbed, the women lovely, the food delicious, the night warm and dry. When my new friends regretfully finish their meal, I ask them what they plan on doing in Susa. Heinz takes out a pen and draws on the paper table-cloth two inverted V's. His forefinger and middle finger "walk" up and down the figures.

"We like to walk up the mountain," he says as he does this. "Then we like to walk down it. That is what we do."

My admiration at his concision is interrupted when a hitherto-unnoticed flat-screen TV placed at one end of the table-filled expanse flickers into life.

"The World Cup," Heinz explains.

Tonight is the kickoff—Spain, the reigning world champion, against the Netherlands.

I ask him who he is pulling for. A pause.

"As a German," he says at last, "I cannot possibly be cheering for the Dutch."

Somehow I instinctively don't want to go there, but any second thoughts about that are forgotten as the air fills with repeated cries of "*Signori!!*" It does not take long to see the source of the chorus of exasperation. Four tall, blond men have taken front-row seats. Two of them have their hands clasped behind their heads, the butterflies of their bent arms obscuring half the screen from view.

They take no notice of the indignant shouts for their attention. They do not hear them. Are they deaf?

Wearily, I get to my feet and walk over to the offending spectators. As I appear to be the only American in the place, I feel obliged to use my native New World lack of manners to break through the logjam of European decorum. And I have figured out by now what awaits.

I tap one of the men on the shoulder. His head whirls in my direction.

"Excuse me," I say, "could you and your friend lower your arms so the rest of us can see the game?"

A look of genuine surprise crosses his features. His companions are similarly thunderstruck. What an unexpected intrusion from a world unimagined!

"I am terribly sorry," he replies. He and his friend comply. "I had no idea. . . ."

His English is perfect, but it has an accent.

Dutch.

5. GREAT ST. BERNARD PASS
AND THE MATTERHORN

———— ▫ ————

"THE HORSE! *Ecce Homo!* They're the same thing!!"

My interlocutor and I are standing in a Turin side street leading to the Piazza Carlo Alberto.* He is a publisher and the proprietor of the city's famed Luxemburg Bookshop, once the haunt of such literary luminaries as Italo Calvino and Primo Levi. The shop is thoroughly international; its warm and welcoming street-level section, overflowing with books, is surmounted by a foreign-language literature selection on the second floor. The shelving is made of dark wood, and there are plenty of nooks and crannies in which to read. A display stand of foreign periodicals constitutes a permanent temptation.

The owner of the Luxemburg is annoyed with me.

"They're not the same thing at all!" I counter, in French. At the outset of our discussion, we determined that my Italian was as challenged as his English, so our absurdist back-and-forth is conducted in a language in which we are both more comfortable.

————

* Carlo Alberto was the king who gave his name to Albertville, France.

The dispute concerns Friedrich Wilhelm Nietzsche. He lived on the Via Carlo Alberto, where he wrote *Ecce Homo*, the philosopher's examination of his life and work. Shortly after completing it, he went mad, for reasons still debated. The police reported that he had a mental breakdown on 3 January 1889. The story goes that his insanity first surfaced when he was traumatized by witnessing in the square the brutal whipping of a horse.

I want to know where the whipping took place. My erudite Italian acquaintance wants to direct me to a plaque on the square. I have just come from it, where I saw that it commemorates the centenary of Nietzsche's birth in the rather revolting language of exalted Fascism then in vogue in the Italy of the 1940s. There was no mention of any horse.

"The horse, the plaque, the same thing . . . ," he repeats gamely, his voice trailing off when faced with the lunacy of the writer before him. I want to mention that my odd insistence stems from knowing the name of Nietzsche to be intimately related to the Alps. He wrote that he loved the view of the mountains to the north of Turin and for many years he summered near St. Moritz. Recent editions of Nietzsche's *Thus Spoke Zarathustra* seem to have required as cover art Caspar David Friedrich's *Wanderer Above the Sea of Fog*, an 1816 canvas depicting a windswept young man with his back to us, walking stick in hand, standing on a precipice and staring down at what can only be called a sublime perspective of cloud and rocky eminences. Is this *Übermensch* terrified by the view, or is he considering it with Olympian disdain? The figure embodies the Romanticism that resulted in the cult of the Alps, and such views are often called "Nietzschean." Then again, that word has been used and mostly abused since the great philosopher's death in 1900, often as a lazy way to describe something or someone extreme. Certainly, the view of the Alps from Turin, like that from Geneva, can evoke sentiments of extremity, of fear of the inhuman ruggedness so close. Whether Nietzsche would approve of using his name for a perspective is something we'll never know.

I never find out about the horse.* We exchange business cards and he says that he'll be interested to see this book when I have finished it. I admire his tact. I continue on the broad streets of Turin, moving through marvelously grandiose squares and past splendid residences from the city's days as host to the self-important House of Savoy. As befits my horse quest, there is no shortage of monumental equestrian statues here.

The place brims with life, not the baby-crazed conviviality of small-town Susa but the carefree cosmopolitanism of big-city Italy. Turin has long been a magnet for travelers, whose opinions of the place vary widely. From the Renaissance onward, the literary have wandered past its imposing façades and passed judgment. Dostoyevsky, reliably cranky, deemed it "very boring" and "odious." Herman Melville thought it "more regular than Philadelphia. Houses all one cut, one color, one height. City seems built by one contractor and paid for by one capitalist." Jean-Jacques Rousseau, like Nietzsche, was enchanted by the city and its environs. As a very young man, he had walked across the Mont Cenis Pass en route to Turin; he had "followed Hannibal over the Alps," as he put it in his *Confessions*. Once in the city, out of money and in need of a place to stay, he was taken in by the clergy and he converted to Catholicism. One of the priests, in a tale told in Rousseau's *Emile*, took him "out of the town on to a high hill above the river Po, whose course we beheld as it

---

* A 2011 Hungarian film, *The Turin Horse*, places the incident outside 8 via Carlo Alberto.

flowed between its fertile banks; in the distance the landscape was crowned by the vast chain of the Alps; the beams of the rising sun already touched the plains and cast across the fields long shadows of trees, hillocks, and houses, and enriched with a thousand gleams of light the fairest picture which the human eye can see."

Rousseau did not know it, but he was describing a vista cinematically. That he did it in Turin is a superb coincidence, as the city is one of the birthplaces of the motion picture. At the turn of the twentieth century, film studios sprang up in the city—Ambrosia, Aquila, and Itala Studios—and Turin's directors began distributing full-length silent features throughout Europe as early as 1914. This prestigious past is memorialized in the city's excellent national cinema museum, housed in one of the strangest buildings in Europe, the *Mole Antonelliana*. Standing 167 meters tall, this brick behemoth—it is the tallest unreinforced brick building in the world—the Mole was originally intended, during its construction in the latter half of the nineteenth century, to house a synagogue for the newly enfranchised Jews of Turin. Relations between the Jewish community and architect Alessandro Antonelli (whose name the building bears) eventually soured, and the city took over the financing of the project, which culminated with erection of a soaring dome and pinnacle. When the Winter Olympics returned to the Alps after Albertville—Turin hosted the 2006 Winter Games—the city used a stylized rendering of the building as its official Olympic logo. The Mole Antonelliana is to Turin what the Eiffel Tower is to Paris. The tallness of the municipal icon is less fitting in Paris, where there is nary a highland in sight, whereas Turin stands close to the towering Alps.

The expressway northward proves the aptness of Turin's logo, for the spiky Alps on the horizon are magnificent, looking like a malevolent white grin. I pull into a gas station to fill my tank. Workmen pour out of a van stopped behind me at the service bay to admire my car. They point to its trapezoidal exhaust pipe below the rear license plate, testament to its testosterone.

My chest involuntarily swells in the reflected glory of my car. After all, we are on the outskirts of Turin, once one of the world's greatest automotive capitals. Fiat is an acronym for *Fabricca Italiana Automobili Torino*, so the bar for making a splash in Torinese car culture is set pretty high. But my status becomes severely deflated when my companions, on asking the price of the car, learn that my muscle Mégane is, in fact, *noleggio*—a rental. Faces fall and questions die in the air.

Hoping to redeem myself, I inform them that there are 265 horses under the hood. I wait to see their mood of disappointment return to worshipful awe, but only a low murmur greets this cock-of-the-walk announcement. One of their number, a thoughtful-looking fellow in late middle age, steps forward and addresses me.

"The car is too powerful," he says, the reproach in his voice palpable. "Too many of our young people are dying on the roads. Because of cars like yours." He gives the Mégane a dismissive gesture, then he and his colleagues clamber back into the van. In the space of a few seconds, I have gone from highway hero to gearhead goat.

THE PLAINS OF THE PIEDMONT give way to the drama of the Aosta Valley. Fabulously tall mountains, some with strangely shaped saddle summits, rise on both sides of the route. The lesser eminences, craggy outcroppings of rock several hundreds of meters in elevation, are crowned with brooding fortresses and castles at almost every turn in the road. These massive piles of hewn stone—Issogne, Verrès,

Ussel, Fénis—carry the freight of history, attesting to a time when the local lords resisted transalpine marauders from what are now France and Switzerland.

The first of the Aostan sentinels to be encountered, Fort Bard, is by far the most solid. Although a castle has sat atop its height for well over a thousand years, Bard is a nineteenth-century construction, its avatar having been razed by an infuriated Napoleon who struggled to get past it on one of his many incursions into Italy. In 1800, the four-hundred-man garrison of the fort held off a forty-thousand-strong French army for two weeks, thereby foiling the emperor's plan to launch a surprise attack on Turin. Rebuilt by the House of Savoy, the fortress is a gray stone monster. Fifty large casemates—apertures for artillery fire—punctuate its northern façade, the direction from which attacks would come. These openings are located in four distinct superstructures that seem to climb up the tall outcropping on which the fort is built. At the summit is a more conventional fortress, it too designed to rain death on an invader via its hundreds of firing slits. All in all, the combined structures count 283 rooms and 323 windows. It looks like a high-rise condo of malevolence. Local government has recently tried to humanize the place by installing a cheerful Alpine museum in the complex—featuring a dahu exhibit—but nothing can really mask its original vocation.

Fort Bard and other subalpine fortresses, stranded on lonely high points, evoke the tense posture of the defender, always awaiting the catastrophic surprise of attack. It is no coincidence that a child of the Alps, Dino Buzzati, twentieth-century journalist, playwright, and novelist, should have fashioned an existential tour de force centered on the fortress mentality. In Buzzati's brilliant 1940 work, *Il deserto dei Tartari* (translated as *The Tartar Steppe*), his protagonist peers for decades over the battlements, waiting for the barbarians to come storming toward him, as he neglects the joys and rewards of normal life in the lowlands he protects. Fort Bard could be Buzzati's fictional Bastiani, so powerful is its effect on the imagination. And its baleful presence remains a catalyst for the creative of all stripes. Two months before I pass it, the cast and crew of *Avengers: Age of Ultron* encamped there, using the fortress as a stand-in for the entirely fanciful country of Sokovia.

I am glad to have the place in my rearview mirror. Yet what rises in front of me is less dystopian than disheartening. The valley stands as a vivid example of infrastructure victimhood. Expressway viaducts, spindly millipedes suspended far in the air, mar the views of the Graian Alps, the chain of mountains first glimpsed at Chamonix and by far the tallest in all of Europe. Foremost among the Aosta Valley's awesome neighbors: Monte Bianco (Mont Blanc), rising 4,808 meters in altitude. The tallest mountain in the Alps, it is also the eleventh tallest in the world in topographical prominence—that is, the distance from base (or lowest contour) to summit, as opposed to its height above sea level. To go from the foot of Mont Blanc to its summit, one has to climb 4,697 meters. To its west rise Monte Rosa, with an altitude of 4,634 meters, making it the second tallest in the Alps, and Monte Cervino (Matterhorn), 4,478 meters in altitude. On the western side of the Aosta Valley rises Monte Gran Paradiso, 4,061 meters in altitude. This last is also the site of a sprawling, sky-high national park, created in the 1920s as a refuge for the fast-disappearing ibex, an Alpine antelope with fantastically long curved horns that once was a common sight throughout the mountains. The conservation initiative succeeded and the animal is no longer endangered—but the same cannot be said of the areas left open to developers.

Yet for all the new blemishes created by the opening up of Aosta to the outside world—the Graian Alps formed a gigantic stockade of stone—an infamous old blemish disappeared: the goiter of cretinism. The curse of this condition especially plagued the isolated mountain villages of the radiating small valleys. The English traveler cited in chapter 1, who deplored the "hideous" appearance of the "*crétins des Alpes*," was, in fact, writing of his experiences in the Aosta region. Caused by a lack of iodine and other minerals in the diet, cretinism—or congenital iodine deficiency syndrome—disappeared with the advent of the railroads, which opened up the fastnesses to different fare from other regions. Seafood, especially, rolled back the tide of cretinism. That is all but a bad memory now, a skeleton in Aosta's closet.

The town itself teems with other memories, many of them connected to its eponym, Augustus. An emperor-was-here triumphal arch greets the traveler entering Aosta's old quarter, soon followed by the *Porta Prætoria*, a huge gray double Roman gateway consisting of six arches. The two central arches are broad and high, obviously designed for carriages and chariots. The four lateral arches are much smaller, destined for foot traffic. The Porta is a massive structure, its outsize blocks— made of a pebble conglomerate known as puddingstone—still a wonder of the builder's art. Once clad in marble, the monument impresses by its size and solidity. Two towers, one distinctly Roman, flank its extremities, making it one of the mightiest remnants of Antiquity on the Italian peninsula. To walk through it is to walk in history. And once past the Porta and in the old town, there are preserved Roman fortifications, a multistoried Roman theater, Roman bridges. For the time traveler, Aosta amply supplies evocative locales for daydreaming.

Of more recent note is the city's rich Christian heritage, remnants of a time near the turn of the first millennium when Aosta, centuries before the Savoyards opened the Mont Cenis Pass to Susa, was the major staging ground for pilgrimages (and invasions) to the south. Ottonian churches, so named for the trio of Ottos to be Holy Roman Emperor around the year 1000, stand cheek by jowl with Aosta's pagan monuments. The city's most famous son, Anselm of Aosta (known more commonly as Anselm of Canterbury), is credited with ushering in the intellectual movement that came to be known as Scholasticism, an attempt to reconcile Reason with Revelation. Anselm has also bedeviled generations of undergraduates with his "ontological argument" for proof of the existence of God.*

Strolling Aosta's animated streets—there is some sort of vintage car show in the main square—reveals that this Italian Alpine town could not be more different than its sister, Susa. The presence of French is everywhere. Historical plaques are in French only; signs in the shops betray a pronounced Gallic tendency. Evidently, the language of nearby Savoy and the Swiss canton of Valais has spilled over the Alps and come to stay. The Aosta Valley—officially called the *Vallée d'Aoste / Valle d'Aosta*—is defiantly bilingual, its status as Italy's tiniest and least populous semiautonomous region wrested from the central government by local patriots following World War II.

Not that their legal nationality is entirely ignored by the Aostans. Flat-screen televisions set up in squares and restaurants pointedly show that both paganism and Christianity have been supplanted by another form of popular religion: soccer. The *ragazzi* (boys) of Italy's national team are playing their first World Cup football match,

---

* Immanuel Kant gave this name to Anselm's argument. Anselm wrote that God is "that than which nothing greater can be conceived." Therefore God exists. [Hint: Existence is greater than nonexistence.] Discuss. You have 1,000 words and one hour.

and their supporters, seemingly the entire town, raise a hullabaloo that echoes down the narrow streets and past the old ruins. As this is the Italian team, there is a lot of fakery of serious injury on the field. And, as this is the arm's-length Italian region of Aosta, there is a lot of mockery of their fellow countrymen.

When, as seems to happen every five minutes, one of the Italian players goes down in a fiery display of fraudulent agony, the air in Aosta is filled with derisive cries of *è morto! è morto!* (He's dead! He's dead!), accompanied by gales of laughter.

IN A MATTER OF MINUTES after leaving Aosta, I am going up, toward the Great St. Bernard Pass. A restaurant flashes by, *Le Lièvre Amoureux* (The Amorous Hare). Then another sign: JAMBON DEPUIS *1789* (Ham since 1789). Clearly, the human geography around here is as unusual as its natural counterpart.

Before me rise several green sentinel mountains, their conifer stands alternating with pastures, where the cows responsible for Aosta's signature fontina cheese graze in peaceful oblivion to their picturesque surroundings. Off to the left, a particularly nasty spike of rock bullies its way through a few wispy clouds. Then a bend in the roadway, and the Mont Blanc massif rises in all its suborbital glory. The villa line is passed, then the tree line.

This is a well-marked road—there are many red-bordered white triangular signs with an exclamation mark in the center. I take this to mean: You won't believe what's coming next! Or what's coming from behind: I am forced to pull over as a Bulgarian in an Audi barrels past me at breakneck speed, in what seems to be an attempt to attain escape velocity and break the bonds of terrestrial gravity. On this road, we are both "going to Switzerland"—European shorthand for seeking assisted suicide—but I think this fellow doesn't need any help.

Mercifully, he quickly disappears from view. I look at my surroundings: to the right, solid guardrails, with hefty blocks of stone linked by sturdy metal poles; to the left, a tawny exposed rock face covered tightly in mesh. The excellent highway engineering cannot hide the fact that we have taken so many hairpins we could open a beauty salon. A pilsener of Czech bikers overtakes me, gunning up the steep pitch to the pass. I now cross a gorge where, thousands of feet up, I can see, sickeningly, where the road leads—into a zigzag of galleries up the flank of the slope, a terrifying Slinky drawn taut. *It's not that I'm afraid of heights*, I just don't like Slinkies. After that, the countryside becomes a mix of hostile gray rock and sullen green lichen. These heights look like slanting moors, windswept and dangerous. Suddenly, in the middle of one upland, there is a rock eminence at least two hundred meters in height from base to summit, looking like a thumb, poised, as if hitching a ride off the fearsome slope. The snow lies thick on the ground now.

After rounding the hitchhiking rock, I reach the Great St. Bernard Pass. A small lake stretches out in the foreground. To my consternation, there are cars everywhere, most of them bearing Swiss or Italian license plates. Do the locals never tire of the pass? I find a place to park and begin walking to the head of the lake, where two eighteenth-century buildings straddle the roadway. From the one on the right comes the sound of liturgical singing; from the other, the barking of dogs. It is a strange canine and churchy call-and-response. My suspicions are confirmed when I see several people of middle age—the men in blue sweaters and overcoats, the women similarly attired, along with their carefully arranged Hermès scarves hiding any hint of flesh—scurrying toward the source of the hymns. These are most definitely bourgeois Euro-Catholics—the blue is a dead giveaway. Blue is the color normally associated with the Virgin Mary, and her cult is alive and well among European Catholics.

I enter the hospice on the right and am immediately greeted by the sulfur of incense. The local mitered bishops are out in force. Today, as luck would have it, is the Feast of St. Bernard, the holy hotelier from Aosta who founded the travelers' hospice in 1034. The mass finishes and the canons of the hospice process out of the baroque chapel, surrounded by ecstatic eucharistic groupies. A youngish Swiss bishop blesses me obligingly. Seeing a woman wearing a name badge, the same bishop takes her hands and squeezes them fondly, then moves off. She looks enraptured. I notice that her badge identifies her as an information officer, so I walk over and introduce myself. I ask her how long the Muslims held the pass before the arrival of St. Bernard. A famous incident of Muslim raiding from the pass occurred in 972, in a town on what is now the Swiss side of the pass. The rapture dies; she looks at me as if I'm furtively fingering her missal. "All kinds of people have come through here," she says sternly, "since the dawn of time, monsieur." With that, she stalks off, her blue cardigan disappearing into the blue crowd.

She is right, of course. The pass has been crossed since well before the time of Augustus, and a rich store of archaeological artifacts is on display in the hospice's handsome museum. The parade has been varied: kings, queens, emperors, saints, bishops, pilgrims, bandits—and countless merchants with their wares of fabrics, tools, arms, spices, metals, even horses. For at least the last thousand years or so, they have usually spent the night at the hospice, which can now house up to 180 visitors at any given time. Since the opening of the Great St. Bernard Road Tunnel under the mountain between Italy and Switzerland, leisure, not commerce, is the main occupation of these wayfarers.

The iconic St. Bernards, the famous rescue dogs, await inspection. The national dog of Switzerland, this canine gentle giant worked itself into Alpine folklore as a heroic first responder, digging its way through avalanches to extract unfortunate travelers. The big animal's shaggy brown-and-white coat, and black snout, are familiar to dog lovers the world over. I pay a small admission fee to their kennel. This may be the only kennel in the world with a sign reading *INTERDIT AUX CHIENS* (No dogs allowed). The St. Bernards lounge in the sun, on the international border, in separate, spacious chain-link enclosures with name signs on them. From left to right are Easy, Karina, Xandy, Kosimo, Bounty, Thalia, Italix, Justin, Zoltan, Phybie, Wenda, Princesse Heidi, and Capons. Across from the kennel, a young woman whose sunglasses hide half her face is grooming a dog with a hairbrush.

"You can pet her," she says affectlessly.

"I . . . I'm not crazy about dogs."

"Oh, too bad."

A silence falls between us, which I eventually fill with a question.

"What's her name?"

The girl answers. I ask her to spell it out, which she does. Jill, a female name not often encountered in French-speaking countries. It is also the name of my ex-wife, the skier who frightened me out of my wits at Avoriaz so many years ago.

I tell the dog attendant about the coincidence.

A hand reaches up and removes the sunglasses. A smile.

"Well, then, you *have* to caress her."

I comply and am rewarded by a wagging tongue. The attendant and I do likewise, falling into a pleasant conversation about her charges.

When I ask her whether the small casks they wore on rescue missions carried beer or brandy—my guidebooks differ on the matter—she scoffs and says that such lore is a tale told to tourists. The dogs never carried casks. Can you imagine an animal bounding up and down in excitement in the snow? Do you think it could stop and offer a drink?

Another day, another illusion shattered. I enter a dog exposition adjacent to the kennel. I learn that there is some mystery as to the origins of the St. Bernard. Some say they came from Upper Assyria thousands of years ago. I'm not in the mood to believe anything more on this day, but I jot it down anyway. More certain is that their first mention at the pass dates back only to 1709. And that the most famous St. Bernard was born in 1800. He has gone down in history as Barry I and is credited with saving more than forty lives during his tenure atop the pass. His heroics stirred public acclaim across Europe, and a statue of Barry I adorns the entrance to the dog cemetery at Asnières in suburban Paris. After his death, he was stuffed and placed in a museum in Switzerland.

Barry I was succeeded by a brace of namesakes, numbered as solemnly as the kings of France, but his era may have been the dogs' heyday. Over generations, the effects of inbreeding made inroads— again, as in any royal line—and by the end of the nineteenth century the animals had to be crossbred with long-haired Newfoundlands. In the twentieth century, they met even further indignity. With the advent of modern mountain rescue units, the rescue dogs became increasingly obsolete. To add insult to injury, they lost their places in rescue helicopters because they took up too much room. The lumbering St. Bernards were replaced by lighter and leaner Belgian and German shepherds. The Great St. Bernard Pass now houses, in fact, a cross between a petting zoo and a puppy farm.

"Want to know where the story of their casks comes from?" The speaker is Jean-Michel, a retiree from the northern French department of Pas-de-Calais. He and his wife sold me the entry ticket to the kennel. They are Catholic volunteers; in exchange for room and board, they will man the holy sites of Christendom for no pay. Last summer they were in Rome; the summer before, Jerusalem. At each place they receive instruction so that they can double as docents. Jean-Michel has spied me taking notes, whetting his hearty appetite for sharing information.

It seems that the cask fable arose in the nineteenth century, when Italian workmen were dispatched to Bern to restore a museum. The story goes that these men ate their lunch every day in a storeroom. In that storeroom stood the stuffed Barry I. But he was stuffed badly. There was an unsightly hole in his throat, putting the workmen off their food. One day one fellow finished his small cask of wine, and, instead of taking it back to his lodgings, he affixed it to Barry's throat so that they wouldn't have to stare at the damned hole any longer. In time, the workmen finished their job and returned to Italy, but the cask remained, as an open invitation to some anonymous fabulist to spread the boozy news.

"At least that's what I've been told," Jean-Michel concludes.

THE ROAD DOWN into Switzerland winds with majesty for a couple of breathtaking kilometers. The snow-covered peaks sway back and forth in the sky, a green valley can be seen on a distant horizon. This, alas, is succeeded by very long stretches of avalanche galleries, structures about as pleasing to the eye as Manhattan's Lincoln Tunnel. After a few minutes, I pass a haggard pair of middle-aged hikers trudging up

toward the pass. No doubt they had thought this would be a bucolic outing, never dreaming they were in for a bath of carbon monoxide.

The galleries give way to a gentle valley in which the old village of Orsières nestles in a pastoral dream. Its roofs are red, its
surroundings green. Up at the pass, I had asked about the Muslims of the Great St. Bernard because of what happened here. In
Orsières in 972, Muslim brigands (or Saracens, as they were then
called) abducted the most important churchman of the day, Mayeul,
Abbot of Cluny, a prelate more influential than any pope or bishop
of the tenth century. Some of the Saracens hustled this prize off to a
cave, while others repaired to the safety of Fraxinet, their Mediterranean stronghold, near present-day St. Tropez. Christendom was
scandalized, especially when the ransom demand was announced.
It was unprecedented extortion, even by medieval standards, but
Cluny, a monastery in Burgundy with many sister houses, was very
rich—a state of affairs that no doubt spurred Mayeul's raptors to
action. Eventually, the fantastic sum of one thousand silver pounds
was handed over and Mayeul was freed. The event soon led the frac-
tious monarchs of the time to bury the hatchet and unite to drive
the Muslims from what would become the Great St. Bernard Pass,
where they are not fondly remembered. The informational brochure
available at the hospice museum contains this less-than-diplomatic
observation: "Once they [the Saracens] became masters of the [pass],
these enemies of Christianity began worship of their own idolatrous
gods. . . ." Not a terribly accurate depiction of fellow monotheists and
one whose intemperate language makes the passage of the 2009 Swiss
referendum banning new minaret construction less of a surprise.

Orsières seems forgetful of its medieval notoriety. If there's a monument to Mayeul here, I do not see it. In fact, I do not see anyone. The

village seems empty of humanity. Enlightenment arrives when a bell tolls dolefully. Across an old wooden bridge stands an ancient church-yard, filled with hundreds of people dressed in their Sunday best. A burial is taking place. I watch from a respectful distance, strangely moved. As the mourners disperse, I ask one friendly-looking woman the identity of the deceased.

"Michel Darbellay," she answers.

"The alpinist?" I ask, stunned.

"Yes."

On this day of coincidences—the dog's name, the Feast of St. Bernard—I have stumbled across the funeral of a man whose exploits I admire. The greatest of these occurred in August 1963, when Dar-bellay made the first solo ascent of the fearsome north face of the Eiger, in central Switzerland. He told his mother that he was leaving for a few days "to collect apricots." A mountain guide for forty years and a photographer of no small talent, Darbellay belongs in the pan-theon of alpinists. I plan on being at the base of the Eiger in a couple of weeks; I shall keep this memory of him in mind when I first behold the famous peak.

The staff at the tourist office, back from Darbellay's funeral, are amused when I ask them about Mayeul of Cluny. They seem never to have heard of their town's distant brush with infamy. Neither have two jolly fellows, Claude and yet another Jean-Michel, encountered a few minutes later on the terrace of a café. The earsplitting sounds of a jackhammer across the street do not deter them from ordering them-selves repeated rounds of rosé.

They explain to me that the terrifying pyramidal peak facing us from the west is Le Catogne, one of the great mountains of the Mont Blanc massif. Behind us rise the Pennine Alps, their tall, snow-covered Grand Combin mountain familiar to the well-heeled habitués of Verbier, the ski resort. Verbier is particularly prized by the British. Royal layabouts and masters of the universe from the City of London have taken the place by storm as of late, investing in posh chalets as if the area were some sort of Alpine Cotswolds. The Swiss government, alarmed by the crypto-colonization of this corner of the Valais canton, imposed a quota system on foreign acquisition of properties there, proof that the creep of millions of pounds sterling had become a stampede. Naturally, local real estate developers were furious.

But the foreigners who most exercise my Swiss café companions are not British. In fact, they are not even a group. They reserve their ire for one foreigner: Napoleon Bonaparte. In 1800, the thousandth anniversary of Charlemagne's crossing of the Great St. Bernard en route to coronation in Rome (and the year Barry I was born), Napoleon passed through this valley on his way to be stymied at Fort Bard. His large army "requisitioned" a cornucopia of supplies—including 21,724 bottles of wine and a mountain of foodstuffs—which Napoleon promised to pay for. Predictably, he never came close to honoring the debt, and my Swiss friends are still sore about it.

"He was just a thief," says Jean-Michel, pointing up toward the Great St. Bernard, "Napoleon and his elephants. . . ."

Clearly, the rosé is taking its toll.

I tell them that I've read that French President François Mitterrand tried to remedy the situation, back in the 1980s.

"Mitterrand, another bad apple!" Claude erupts, his singsong Swiss French turning operatic. "Yes, he came here. And what did he give us? A big fat medal!"

"Maybe it was made of gold?" I counter feebly.

"If it had been gold, Hollande would have come here," Jean-Michel says, referring to current French President François Hollande, "and he would have taken it back!"

"Do you know why?" Claude asks me.

I shake my head.

"Because he's from *Hollande*!"

They burst into laughter at what must be a rehearsed routine of Dutch bashing. Now, I am no fan of Dutch campers, but to imply that as a nation they are cheapskates seems a bit much, coming from guys still miffed about an unpaid two-hundred-year-old debt.

We take our leave of each other—I, returning to the Mégane; they, ordering yet another round of rosé. Within minutes, I am at my writer's-budget hotel in Martigny, once the capital of Roman Helvetia and thus yet another Alpine town with stone memories of Augustus. The place is pleasant enough but has definitely seen better days, its recent urbanism undistinguished. Freed from my responsibilities as a driver, I walk across town and plop down for a glass of wine at the Taverne de la Tour, a place that has been serving fondue since the sixteenth century. Housed on the ground floor of a fine old building, the restaurant interior was brutally renovated into stucco minimalism sometime in the past. The only hint of its age is the arched ceiling held up by ancient pillars, no doubt remnants looted from the town's Roman ruins. Still the place is impressive: Once a hostelry, I read on its menu, past guests included Rousseau, Goethe, Saussure, Madame de Staël, Stendhal, Chateaubriand, Metternich, Lamartine, Byron, James Fenimore Cooper, Dumas *père*, Alfred de Musset, Georges Sand, Franz Liszt, Gustave Flaubert, Charles Dickens, John Ruskin, Richard Wagner, Jules Verne, Guy de Maupassant, and Mark Twain. Not too shabby a list, to be sure. I close my notebook and prepare to leave. An elderly man nearby observes me stashing my writing materials and says, *"Alors, ça pète le feu ou ça pète pas le feu?"* using the expression meaning full of energy and ready to take risks. I assure that I am, indeed, farting fire, which elicits from him a warm smile of approval.

Dinner is taken in a very crowded restaurant where I share a table with a garrulous Swiss businessman. On learning that I live in the United States, he assures me that Switzerland is the best country in the world, the acme of civilization and progress. Why? "We're willing to work and we're willing to pay taxes."

I nod affably and scan the intimidatingly large menu. My companion notices my bewilderment.

"The horse is very good here," he says.

"I beg your pardon?"

"The horse steak. Australian. Best in town."

Thinking of *Ecce Homo*, I heed his advice.

THE NEXT MORNING, my seat-belt sensor refuses to believe that I've buckled up. The warning sound is a pleasant ping, so I can live with it. But I change my mind once the pinging switches to a lacerating wail, much more painful than yesterday's jackhammer in Orsières.

When I pull alongside the Renault garage, I am treated as a hero. The mechanics drop what they're doing and rush out to examine the car.

"It's the latest? This is the first one we've seen."

My chest swells, just as it did outside of Turin. At last, I am a man in full. I nod condescendingly and then explain the problem. Surely these poor chaps will be only too eager to work on my wonderful machine.

One mechanic, a disconcerting lookalike of the young Alain Delon, steps forward and peers into the vehicle. He beckons me to join him. He points downward, into the interior.

"The car thinks that you are not alone."

The others join us and look down at the passenger seat. I have placed there several guidebooks and two heavy laminated road atlases of France and Italy. Admiration turns to chuckling. Once again, I am the gearhead goat. The mechanics head back into the garage.

Chastened and in silence, I drive westward up the valley of the Rhône. This is not the Rhône Valley in which I have been stuck in traffic dozens of times, south of Lyon on the Autoroute du Soleil toward the Med, a broad and majestic valley bounded by walls of green. This Swiss version, where the great river is an onrushing mountain stream headed for Lake Geneva, is barely three kilometers wide, the mountains on both sides almost comically tall. The valley floor is covered in orchards, the lower slopes by vertiginous green vineyards going up and up and up. These yield the refreshing white wine called Fendant de Sion, which was lodged in the literary canon by none other than James Joyce. An avid overindulger of Fendant at his home in Zurich, Joyce likened the wine to the piss of an archduchess, calling it, in *Finnegan's Wake*, "Fanny Urinia." Presumably, the sophisticated wine-makers of the valley know that in American English the moniker is amusing, while in British English it is considerably more hard core. Doubtless the devilish Irishman meant the latter.

The peaks of the Pennine Alps to the south of the valley cannot help but turn thoughts from the nether regions suggested by the vineyards. That does not mean these thoughts are necessarily uplifting, for this stretch of hostile rock and glacier is the setting of a 1925 novel that is a monument to the moody culture of *la Suisse Romande*

(French-speaking Switzerland). In *La grande peur dans la montagne* (Terror on the Mountain), the laconic yet lyrical stylist Charles-Ferdinand Ramuz tells a tale of inevitable disaster, as young villagers ignore the warnings of their elders and take their livestock up to an *alpage*, or mountain pasture, that is reputed to be cursed, a constant of Alpine folklore about inhospitable heights. Bad omens come in quick succession, and the men turn on each other as Nature impassively watches and waits. The prose is a masterwork of description and doom, until the final cataclysm arrives with a brutality worthy of the final pages of *Moby-Dick*. The instant nationwide popularity of the novel suggests that the Swiss were not carried off by the Romanticism of foreign lovers of the Alps. They know how difficult and dangerous their beautiful country is. A likeness of Ramuz adorns the Swiss 200-franc note.

The town of Sion lies before me—as do posters touting a summerlong festival dedicated to Audrey Hepburn. The Belgian-born movie star's association with Switzerland is usually confined to the canton of Vaud: Hepburn resided in a village near Lausanne on the shores of Lake Geneva. I ask the young woman in the tourist office why Sion, the capital of Valais, should pay so much attention to Audrey Hepburn. She looks at me in disbelief and says, "Because she is beautiful."

A walk around the town proves that beauty is no stranger to the place. Castles crown two gentle hillocks, dominating the Rhône Valley, and an old quarter with serpentine streets spreads up a slope. In the threshold of a medieval house stands a bewhiskered Swiss man, felt cap perched atop his head, white shirt tucked into his red shorts, calmly smoking a long yellow pipe in the morning sunshine. The cobbles look clean enough to eat off of.

The lower quarter is another matter. Aside from a monastic book-shop selling Trappist beer, Sion seems to be a wine bar disguised as a town. Although it is far short of noon, the terraces are full of men worshiping their cool glasses of Fendant. The women walking back and forth in front of the cafés, ostensibly running errands, seem to be having a competition to see who can wear the tightest jeans. The garments are so form-fitting that they look to have been painted on every bend and fold of the lower portions of their bodies. I leave the men and women of Sion to play their games.

SOMEHOW I AM NOT SURPRISED by what I see in my rearview mirror as I leave town. Viewed at a distance from the east, the two castle-topped hillocks of Sion exhibit an uncanny resemblance to a woman's breasts. I take a curve in the road and the vision is gone. Sion recedes in memory to be replaced by Sierre, its less pretty sister up the valley. But I do not care about beauty here, I care only about religion. And, as I was raised a Canadian, that religion is ice hockey. I know that one of the heroes of the Montreal Canadiens lies buried in Sierre. Jacques Plante, the goaltender for Montreal during its glory days in the 1950s and 1960s, died in Switzerland in 1986. He was my child-hood idol, and his eminently sensible introduction of the goalie mask to protect his face only heightened the sense of mystery with which I invested him. I never really knew what he looked like.

I ditch the car and lope purposefully to the tourist office. The young man there takes my request in stride. He's heard weirder, no doubt.

"Which cemetery?" he asks, poker-faced.

Seeing my blank look, he adds, "Protestant or Catholic?"

As Plante was from Quebec, there can be only one answer.

The tourist host warms to the task and calls the Catholic cemetery. A long conversation ensues, which entails spelling out the name of the deceased. At last he lowers the cellphone.

"He won't tell you anything."

"Why not?"

The phone returns to his ear and is lowered again.

"Because he's not allowed to."

I must look dumbfounded, because a smile begins creeping across the young fellow's features. At last I ask him, "Is it because of Charlie Chaplin?"

This non sequitur clearly pleases even more. Faced with a growing grin at my lunacy, I hastily explain that Charlie Chaplin's corpse was dug up and held for ransom in 1978. The scandal occurred near Lake Geneva, in Vevey, the town where I chatted with the mountain-loving waitress. Fortunately, Swiss police eventually located the body and it was given a second, more secure burial.

Impressed by my knowledge of Swiss scandal, he takes up the phone and conveys my question. There seems to be a long silence on the other end of the line. Perhaps the gravedigger is impressed, too. A glimmer of hope?

When the phone is lowered, I am informed: "No, it has nothing to do with Charlie Chaplin. But he's willing to tell you that Jacques Plante has been moved to another cemetery."

"Where?" I croak.

The question is repeated into the phone. And the call is ended.

"He's not allowed to say."

My dreams of boyhood dashed by a gravedigging Kafka, I hurriedly leave town, but not before asking where the big change occurs. A few kilometers east of Sierre, I cross a brook named La Ripaille, thereby leaving the land of the Latin for that of the Germanic. I have gone from La Suisse to Schweiz, but I have not in fact crossed a cantonal boundary. Valais is now Wallis.

Out of curiosity, I pull into the first gas station on the other side of La Ripaille. I buy gum at the counter, but it is the newsstand that interests me the most. Astounding. Absolutely all of the publications are in German or Swiss German. Not a trace of the French a mere stone's throw away. Again, as someone raised a Canadian, I am accustomed to bilingualism, but a slow bleeding of English into French, and vice versa, occurs at the meeting of Ontario and Quebec, with signs, newspapers, advertisements, and the like appearing in both languages on either side of the border. Apparently not in multilingual Switzerland.* Here the transition is brutal and uncompromising. Road signs now are exclusively in German. Perhaps the Swiss Federation, formed so that the different peoples of the region would stop their incessant warring with one another, has decided to let the different language groups lick their wounds in peace and quiet, among their own kind.

Whatever the case, in this canton the German-speakers seem to have gotten a raw deal. The verdant valley of the Rhône in Valais eventually becomes a rocky declivity in Wallis, with the river itself now a rush of whitewater. On the north side of the mountain wall, near the village of Susten, at a height of about 150 meters, rises a forest of white satellite dishes pointed in all directions. Are they placed there to detect whether anyone in Wallis is not speaking Swiss German? I learn later that the impressive array owes more to listening than talking. The facility would make Edward Snowden ill: Part of the Swiss military system Onyx, the dishes conduct electronic surveil-

---

* Switzerland's other two official languages are Italian and Romansh.

lance on all and sundry. There are three such sites in Switzerland, constantly monitoring civilian and military communications conducted via satellite, such as faxes, internet traffic, and telephone calls. In 2007, thanks to a leak to a newspaper, it was revealed that Onyx had intercepted a fax from the Egyptian government to its embassy in London confirming the existence of black sites, CIA torture hot spots in eastern Europe. Embarrassed, the Swiss government took those who reported the story to court but eventually lost its case.

I reach a town called Visp, birthplace of one of the most reviled people in the sporting world, Sepp Blatter, longtime head of the insanely corrupt FIFA, the global football federation. In a wonderful turn of phrase, *The Guardian* called him "the most successful non-homicidal dictator of the past century." But I am not here to celebrate chicanery. Visp also marks the turning point for those headed south to its famous neighbor, Zermatt. I leave the Rhône and head into a dreary, kilometers-long tunnel leading to an even narrower valley. The drive is arduous and sinuous, passing industrial outposts and hundreds of holiday chalets. As usual, Swiss highway engineering displays its usual panache of sturdy viaducts and avalanche galleries, but at one point the road builders evidently threw up their hands and gave up. On a multilingual sign, we are warned that we are passing through a NATURE DANGERS AREA, and we will just have to take our chances. It isn't difficult to divine the reason for this: On the west side of the valley, half a mountain face has sheared off and tumbled willy-nilly onto the valley floor near the roadway.

The end of the road is a town called Täsch, where human habitation is dwarfed by automotive imperialism—namely, the type of multistory parking garage usually found at a major international airport. The reason for this ungainly structure in the middle of nowhere lies in Täsch's status as the railhead for the tens of thousands of tourists, climbers, and skiers en route to Zermatt, at the foot of the Matterhorn.

I wait patiently on the platform for the outbound train to arrive back at Täsch. My companions are two Filipina nannies with their charges, towheaded toddlers destined one day to become jet-setters like their parents. At last the red carriages of the train pull into the station and disgorge, on the opposite platform, a suburb of Tokyo. Once this Japanese phalanx has left en masse, bound for a fleet of tour buses in the parking lot, the Filipinas, toddlers, and I board the empty train. Soon we are off.

The cogs do their work, hauling us up steep slopes and then braking us on sudden descents. We seem to be heading into a wilderness, or at least a logging camp, for signs of civilization become scarce, save for the occasional chalet and an intermittently glimpsed road reserved for the locals. We cross a rushing torrent of water. Alas, this unspoiled scenery does not last long. Alighting at Zermatt immediately dispels any idea of approaching an Alpine fastness. The spotless indoor/outdoor railway platform gives way to a thoroughfare lined on both sides with upscale shops hawking jewelry, watches, and designer clothing. We have arrived in a Brigadoon of bling. I mall-walk up the main street, dodging the golf carts driven by municipal employees at vengeful speeds, gawking at the wares on display. Do I really need a $2,000 Swatch? Maybe I do.

My reason for being here—the Matterhorn—lowers somewhere ahead, sheathed in clouds, like a burlesque dancer teasing the tourists staring up at it, past the wall of faux-chalet time shares on the outskirts of town. My disappointment is somewhat allayed when a couple emerges from a chapel, arrayed in their wedding best: she, a ballistically leggy Suissesse perched atop what can only be called Matterhorn stilettos; he, in a bespoke suit, his head crowned by the telltale turban of a Sikh. Both sets of parents are there, posing for pictures, smiling gamely, except for the groom's father, in Sikh garb from head to foot, glowering, obviously not in a *Bend It Like Beckham* mood. The couple, however, seem so happy that it almost hurts to look at them.

Near the chapel in a small square stands the town's museum—or, rather, *hides* the town's museum. It is tucked underground, as if to hush its off-message voice in the surrounding hymn to commerce. The curators seem ruefully aware of Zermatt's idiosyncrasies. On a wall, an oversize bar graph shows the number of lodgings in town over the years; the entry for 1984 is captioned "The building craze continues [the 'money vein']." Elsewhere are evocations of peasant life in the region and a laboratory devoted to the peculiar geological signature of the Matterhorn. Born in the titanic clash of continents millions of years ago, the mountain has the singular characteristic of being a hybrid. Its upper reaches, and its famous summit, are composed of gneisses from the African tectonic plate, whereas the greater part in its lower altitudes is European. Not quite analogous to the wedding party I have just witnessed, but close enough.

The museum's most visited room, fittingly numbered 13, concerns mountaineering, the faded photographs of climbers from the past a moving testament to the spirit of what-the-hell. The innermost room, which has the distinct feel of a shrine, is devoted to Edward Whymper, the first man to summit the Matterhorn. Whymper, an engraver by trade, was dispatched to the Alps in the 1850s to execute stirring renderings of the peaks. He dropped his pencil for the pickax. A human specimen of exceptional agility and bravery, Whymper soon racked up a record of first ascents of dozens of peaks, "bagging" them, as he liked to say. His accomplishments were such that even the genteel snots of the Alpine Club in London were compelled to admit him to their august company.

In the mid-1860s, he turned his attention to the Matterhorn. He tried and failed on eight attempts. Time was pressing. The Italians on the other side of what they call Monte Cervino were organizing a major expedition to bag the peak. In the summer of 1865, in the company of three guides and three British gentlemen, one of whom was no mountaineer, the fearless engraver made a dash for the summit. He reached it on 14 July 1865. His companions may have gone up with a Whymper, but, unfortunately, they went out with a bang. On the descent, perhaps due to some bumbling by the novice climber, the rope snapped and four of the party hurtled hundreds of meters to their death. One of the unfortunates was Michel Croz, a guide from Chamonix; the other three were Britons: Reverend Charles Hudson; the neophyte, Douglas Robert Hadow; and a Scot, Lord Francis Douglas, whose body has never been found. The last two men were aged nineteen and eighteen, respectively. Whymper was the only Briton to have survived.

The English press bayed for his head. The dead had been the flower of the gentry: Why let young gentlemen take such mad risks? Weren't the hounds and the hunt enough? The pretense of scientific inquiry had long since been abandoned in mountaineering circles, Saussure's measuring instruments a distant, oddball memory. Whymper and his ilk were in it for the thrill, and for the glory. Even Queen Victoria weighed in, deploring the loss of life.

A parliamentary investigation cleared Whymper of any wrongdoing. He set about to repair his reputation by penning an outstanding memoir, *Scrambles Among the Alps*, in which he speaks plainly of his great distress at the memory of seeing his companions fall down the mountain. He spoke of many other things of interest also—Whymper is the English traveler cited about the cretins of Aosta—and he used his illustrator's flair to guarantee the work's success. In spite of his appetite for risk, the great daredevil died of natural causes at the age of seventy-one. He is buried in Chamonix.

The Whymper sanctum of the Zermatt museum is remarkable for its religiosity. On one wall, explicitly marked as a reliquary (*Reliquien der Matterhorn—Unglucks v. 14. Juli 1865*), objects belonging to the fatal four are on display: Croz's hat and rosary beads, Hadow's shoe, Douglas's shoe, and Hudson's breviary. Yet the votive object that trumps all others is The Rope. In a glass case in the center of the room, illumined by reverential overhead track lighting, Whymper's severed rope sits on a red cushion. The yellow coil is a few feet long, surprisingly narrow in diameter. But at one end, the rope is splayed into multiple strands, resembling centrifugal fusilli pasta. It is the somber centerpiece of the museum, a relic as worthy of worship as a saint's fibula or, for that matter, the Shroud of Turin.

Out on the surface once again, I squint in the sunshine. Sunshine?! The dance of the seven veils is over, the clouds have vanished. I turn and look for the mountain. I can see nothing but condo chalets, until I notice that a small crowd has gathered in one corner of the square, looking upward. And there it is, the Matterhorn, a stupendous snow-flecked gray tower to the south. It is so steep, so *dru*, that it appears to be an optical illusion fashioned by the gods. Its famed tapering toward the summit seems unearthly, like some sort of extraterrestrial stalagmite. John Ruskin, Britain's foremost arbiter of taste in the nineteenth century and an ardent lover of the Alps, declared that "the effect of this strange Matterhorn upon the imagination is so great that even the greatest philosophers cannot resist it."

I think back on the past few days, about the religious overtones that seem to haunt this range of the Alps. Anselm, St. Bernard, the Saracens, Mayeul, even the religions of soccer, hockey, and the devotion to beauty and Fanny Urinia. And finally Zermatt, the Wailing Wall of mountaineering, with its Whymper's Rope.

I look around me. Everywhere there are people going in and out of shops, garish posters, display windows, mannequins, *stuff*. Why, this is a bazaar, a souk of Western consumerism. And, towering above it all, attracting all regards, is this visitor from another continent, commanding respect and attention. The Matterhorn is, in fact, Europe's minaret.

6. Furka and Gotthard Passes

THE PRETTY AND GRITTY town of Brig seems an unlikely place to have given the world a word for luxury. Yet César Ritz commenced his career here as a sommelier and left it in the 1860s for greener—as in money—pastures. Not that Brig is a pauper—for a millennium and more, the place has profited from its location as the jumping-off point on the route to the Simplon Pass, linking Switzerland and Italy. My route will not take me there today, as I have decided to stay, momentarily, on what I consider to be the wrong side of the lard line. Last night's dinner in Brig proved that assessment right. Although I'm an adventurous diner, the national dish of the Swiss Germans, the *rösti*, left me reeling with its pig-rich sloppy joe of bacon, potatoes, and cream. In this Swiss concoction, Quebec's poutine may have met its match for causing intestinal fisticuffs. Rösti can be many things, but never ritzy. Significantly, the linguistic divide I crossed at the brook called La Ripaille, at the Valais/Wallis boundary, is what the Swiss Germans jokingly term the *Röstigraben* ("the rösti ditch").

Recovered from the digestive apocalypse, I set off toward the uppermost reaches of the Rhône Valley. Or not. The road seems to be heading straight into a mountain, but my faith in Swiss highway engineering is such that I know somehow we will get around it. As usual, there is a lot of roadwork to slow progress. In the Swiss variant, tall red-and-white-striped poles, not unlike the supports of a steeplechase gate, have been erected on both sides of the roadway, warning motorists of construction ahead. There seems to be more of this going on in Switzerland than in France and Italy, even though the Swiss roads appear to be the ones least in need of repair.

The valley contracts, and soon there is room only for road, rail, and river. The white waters of the Rhône thunder loudly in the late morning sun. Unexpectedly, we climb into a high valley. Alpine chalets dot the meadows; snowbound giants block the horizon. I stop at a place called Fiesch. Drifting in the skies above it, dozens of multicolored paragliders catch the shifting air currents, like a shower of rainbow confetti thrown at a gay wedding. Beyond them rises a massive peak called the Eggishorn, which thousands ascend every year for a view of the Aletsch Glacier, Europe's largest, on the other side of the mountain.

I head for the aerial tramway, which, like the one at the Aiguille du Midi, goes up in two stages. As the trees swim beneath us, a young couple holds hands in anticipation of adventure. She, a tiny thing, is saddled with a Babar-size backpack; he, of medium stature, shoulders an even bigger one. They look as if they're going to live in the wilderness for years. The tramway attendant gives them, then me, the once-over; at least he's not reading *American Psycho*. As we near the transfer point, an arresting sight spreads out below: In a very steeply pitched clearing in the conifer forest, cattle are grazing lazily and wandering about, bovine dahus expert in keeping their balance.

The first stage finishes, and the heavily laden couple drift off into the meadows above the tree line. The sole passenger on the second stage, I am now wise enough to keep my gaze locked on the rockface in front of me. On leaving the station, I climb a small incline to the crest of the summit ridge. The view to the north is staggering. Unlike the Mer de Glace, Chamonix's glacier, the Aletsch does not disappoint.

The glacier is an enormous off-white flood, seemingly frozen in time, its ice rippling in hundreds of horizontal striations. It is twenty-three kilometers long and nearly one kilometer thick. The day has turned peculiar. We can reach up and almost touch the long gray cloud above us, yet on its extremities there are shafts of brilliant sun, staging a strange play of ice, snow, and light over such distant peaks as the Eiger and the Matterhorn.

Manic Japanese tourists cavort in the snow. These are not the stolid Tokyo suburbanites seen alighting at the Täsch rail station after a visit to Zermatt. These young people are more hip, sporting strange hats and winsome outerwear adorned with colorful fur balls. One girl has gone far down the slope toward the glacier and is now stuck in a snowdrift up to her waist. She giggles and chatters excitedly to her companions. They laugh and chatter back, then scramble down the ridge to join her. Not certain I want to see how this is going to end, I head to the snack bar on the ridge to get a warming cup of coffee. It is closed from noon to one o'clock so that the employees can eat their lunch. Switzerland.

I return to my vantage point to look out at the glacier, my eyes not believing that such a tremendous mass of ice could be rapidly shrinking, backing up more than a hundred meters a year. Far below, the Japanese frolic just at the edge of the glacier. They are positioned in about the same locale where six hundred naked white people first posed for American photographer Spencer Tunick before heading out onto the ice surface itself. The 2007 shoot was a spectacular stunt intended to raise awareness of global warming and its contribution to the accelerating retreat of Swiss glaciers.

The theme is taken up in a bilingual French/German display in an outbuilding near the Eggishorn cable-car station. It sounds the alarm and underscores Switzerland's particular vulnerability. Twentieth-century temperatures here rose twice as fast as they did elsewhere, and projections show that, by 2050, average Swiss Alpine temperatures are expected to be up 2.5 degrees Celsius in the winter and a whopping 4.5 degrees Celsius in the summer. No wonder the Swiss are alarmed.

It is perhaps fitting then that Eggishorn's other offering concerns therapy, in the form of happy rocks. There is a bowl of them in a jar. Apparently, you are to think of what worries you most and then leave the stone on the mountain. As the instructional poster explains, "Leave your worries behind on the mountain. You can deposit the stones [at Eggishorn] as a symbolic act to leave problems and worries behind you. We promise you that you will return home less burdened and feeling relieved." *It's not that I'm afraid of heights*, but I think "aerial tramway ride downward" and place the rock on the ground.

A young German woman did not get the memo. As the descent gets underway, she stretches out and lies on her back on the hard floor of the gondola, so that she won't see the sickness-making views of the abyss out the window. She affably explains her reasons to her fellow passengers, while her boyfriend, a six-foot-five bodybuilder, tries to cajole her to get up. At last he succeeds. She stands, eyes glued to the floor, but when we rock past a pylon, she freaks out and dives back down, whimpering. I begin to sense a kindred spirit.

In Fiesch, I head for a restaurant that is open during the lunch hour. As I eat my non-rösti salad on the terrace, I witness a constant parade of cars pulling up in front of an upright cylinder of a building and disgorging teenagers dressed to the nines. The boys are half boy-band, half Tarantino antiheroes: black suits, multihued sunglasses, colorful shirts and ties. As for the girls, let us just say that sexual differentiation runs at Mach speed in Fiesch. Whereas hands and face are the only exposed flesh for the boys, the girls are so skimpily clad that they could have posed on the Aletsch Glacier in the naked photo shoot. They also labor under the disadvantage of walking on the stiletto Matterhorn heels first glimpsed in Zermatt, an impairment made worse as the entrance to the cylinder building is up a flight of stairs formed of metallic grates. Invalids of fashion, the wobbling girls have to be helped up the stairs by the sure-footed boys, which may be the whole point of the dress code.

A SLEEK RED TRAIN zips across the flank of a sloping green dale and disappears into an unseen tunnel, like Alice's rabbit vanishing down the hole. The train's destination is impossible to divine, as Switzerland presents a warren—a Swiss cheese—of tunnels, road tunnels, rail tunnels, pedestrian tunnels. Some expressway tunnels have exits that are themselves radiating tunnels. And most cities have long road and rail tunnels running underneath them: To exit town in a car, you simply look for an autobahn green arrow, then take a ramp downward, usually well within the city center. What follows are miles and miles of underground driving. When you finally emerge into the sunshine, the city is ten or fifteen minutes behind you. Alfred Nobel, the inventor of dynamite, may have been Swedish, but he surely belongs on Swiss bank notes.

East of Fiesch, the valley opens somewhat, and chalets and wild-flowers blanket the upland meadows. I roll down the window to be serenaded by cowbells. The unbearably beautiful hamlet of Biel passes by, its church steeple slender, its wooden houses and granges stained a warm dark brown, its surrounding fields covered in a down of Alpine blooms. The valley widens further, so much so that it accommodates an airstrip. But this proves to be the Rhône Valley's last hurrah—the end rises before me, a solid wall of green and gray.

The road climbs and climbs. At first the ascent is as reassuringly sylvan as driving up and over the tree-rich Berkshires of western Massachusetts. But within minutes that metaphor is comprehensively dead. Above the tree line, the bleak and barren Alpine tundra stretches in all directions, especially upward. On one switchback, I peer across a gorge at the rockface opposite and see a road zigzagging back and forth across it like a jagged scar. Oh my God, that is where I am heading.

I round a bend and there, in a gully, stands a forlorn Alpine settlement. This is Gletsch, a rail junction dominated by deserted multistory buildings possessing the air of abandoned orphanages. It is also a road junction—the jagged-scar roadway from which I averted my eyes is not, in fact, where I am headed. That leads to the north, to the Grimsel Pass, which crosses the Bernese Alps. A sign for my destination, the Furka Pass, instructs me to go right at Gletsch and start climbing. I look up and see the roadway up ahead. Jesus! It is far worse than the approach to the Grimsel. Dozens of switchbacks curl up the mountain; worse yet, the distant viaducts over the void are visible, their supporting pillars looking like flimsy toothpicks. I put the car in gear and hit the accelerator. The first road sign I encounter is not in German, French, or Italian; it is in English and reads: THINK! Above the lettering is a horrifying, photoshopped picture of a motorcycle and its rider hurtling over a guardrail toward oblivion. Somehow this is not reassuring.

I continue ascending the mountainside, around hair-raising bends and ever upward. One hundred fifty years ago, this roadway would have been an impossibility, as the Rhône Glacier, the source of the river of the same name, spilled all the way down into Gletsch. It has been retreating at a gallop since then. Every summer, Swiss environmentalists trek to the great ice mass, laden with hundreds of tarpaulins that they spread over the glacier's leading edge to keep the heat out and thus limit the melt. But few predict the glacier's survival into the next century.

A schnitzel of Austrian bikers roars past me on successive hairpins. They don't seem to "think!" One turn yields a surprise, an old five-story structure perched at the edge of the void, with a sign reading HOTEL BELVEDERE. This easily could have been the template for Wes Anderson's *The Grand Budapest Hotel*. There are, of course, others of its ilk scattered around the dizzying heights of Switzerland, grand hotels located in the most unlikely places, restaurants in the clouds. The most famous is the Rigi Kulm, high above Lake Lucerne in the center of the country. Mark Twain, in *A Tramp Abroad*, wrote amusingly of his stay there. In *Tartarin sur les Alpes*, French humorist Alphonse Daudet had his blowhard Provençal hero, Tartarin, undergo serial misadventures while lodged at the Rigi Kulm.

I pass a parked tour bus at a widening in the road, then round a hairpin in the ascent toward the Hotel Belvedere. On my right, a truly ancient couple struggle uphill with their rolling luggage. They look so old they could be Minoans. I brake and gesture for them to hop in my car for the final hundred meters. A great scowl forms on the face of the venerable gent, and he waves me on with an impressively hostile fist. These two are apparently *very* independent tourists.

A little way up, stopped at the next turn. I can see the doughty couple a long way down the slope, but it is the hotel, specifically this view of it, that interests me most. In the movie *Goldfinger*, this is the shot that opens the memorable chase sequence over the Furka Pass. Auric Goldfinger's vintage yellow Rolls-Royce, with Oddjob at the wheel, tootles past the Hotel Belvedere, soon to be followed by James Bond in a silver Aston Martin, then Tilly Masterson in a white Ford Mustang. Tilly is the sister of the naked girl suffocated by gold paint, the film's iconic image. Tilly and Bond, not knowing they are on the same side, then engage in the famous cat-and-mouse race across the Furka.

I am not feeling very Bondian as the journey into the sky continues. This pass is truly treacherous, of the type I had been dreading when I first left Geneva. Off to the left, across a gorge, a fearsome white limestone cliff appears, its particularity a peek-a-boo waterfall. A great mass of water surges from a spot near the top and then disappears, only to spring up again a hundred meters lower and thirty meters to the right before disappearing again and then reappearing in another unlikely location. The roar of the cascade deafens.

I say I am heading into the sky, but now the sky is heading toward me. On a slope to the right, a cloud comes pouring downward, its tendrils of white mist seeking every nook and cranny in the rockface. Soon it is upon me, and my panic turns to relief—the whiteness is gentle and I can see at least fifteen meters ahead of me. It turns out that this mist was a baptism, a welcoming, for within seconds I am atop the Furka Pass. To my amazement, there are no bikers to be seen—no tulip, bratwurst, pilsener, or schnitzel. My only companions are two Swiss guys with mountain bikes, standing at the sign marking the pass and giving its elevation, 2,429 meters. I walk over to them, applauding, and they execute theatrical bows. They hand me their iPad. I take their picture and wish them a *"gute Fahrt,"* the amusing German equivalent of *Bon voyage*. Soon I am alone in the cloud.

I get underway and the descent begins. In a way I am thankful for the mist, because I can't see the scary views. *It's not that I'm afraid of heights*, I just happen to like fog. Alas, the cloud and I soon part company and a horrific vista of yawning emptiness appears on the right. Far across the void is a solid wall of green, striped vertically by the white bands of narrow waterfalls. It is impossibly tall. I grip the wheel as though my life depended on it—the pathetic ankle-high guardrail couldn't stop a tricycle, much less an automobile. I am swearing under my breath as the road narrows to one lane and I take a tight downhill turn.

I come face-to-face with a bright yellow bus, as yellow as Goldfinger's Rolls. This is one of the PostBus passenger fleet that goes everywhere in Switzerland, giving a famed three-tone horn honk at obstacles such as me. The driver and I sit in silent contemplation of one another for a moment. He has the right of way—he is driving a PostBus, he is going uphill, and he is a helluva lot bigger than I am. I nod in defeat and then consider my options: I can back around the turn, up a steep slope until the road widens, or I can clear the way by driving off the damned cliff. I choose the former. I put the car in reverse and very gingerly begin backing up around the bend; the bus follows me closely, as though the driver is curious about whether I will survive. Less than a meter from my passenger-side door is a drop of a kilometer. In a touch of absurdity, I pass a sign unnoticed on the way down. It advertises some stupid golf course somewhere. Will this be the last thing I ever read? Sweating profusely, I finally arrive at a spot where the oncoming PostBus can pass. The driver waves at me. I do not wave back.

I HAVE NOW LEFT Valais/Wallis for the canton of Uri, one of the original three cantons—the others are Schwyz and Unterwalden—to confederate in 1291 and form the embryo of Switzerland.* Uri is the home canton of William Tell, the lodestar of Swiss nationalism. Tell, who many historians believe to be in the same league of verisimilitude as Rumpelstiltskin, supposedly defied a dastardly Austrian governor by refusing to pay him homage. The outraged official ordered Tell, locally famous for his strength and marksmanship, to shoot an apple off the head of the Swiss hero's young son. Tell's crossbow did not falter—and was used some time later to assassinate the governor and spark a rebellion against the Austrian overlords. The old tale obviously holds its attractions for the patriotic—and for the Romantic. Friedrich von Schiller's 1804 play about Tell found success throughout Europe, and Gioacchino Rossini's opera based on the play contains one of the musical canon's most beloved codas, which many first came to know as the theme for *The Lone Ranger*.

The lovely town of Andermatt is no stranger to William Tell trinkets, even if Altdorf, some thirty-five kilometers north into the mountains, is celebrated as the site of the apple shoot. On Andermatt's boomerang-shaped main street, the ground floors of almost all of its handsome wooden houses contain shops or restaurants open year-round, as the town doubles as a ski resort. The mountains surrounding

---

* Contemporary Switzerland has twenty-six cantons.

it are festooned with the cables of ski lifts and arrays of snowmakers looking like oversized howitzers. The slopes are also pierced by the rabbit holes of road and rail tunnels.

Andermatt is situated on the River Reuss, a tributary of the Rhine's drainage basin. By crossing the Furka Pass, I have traversed yet another boundary, the watershed separating the Mediterranean, into which the Rhône flows, from the North Sea, the Rhine's destination. The town also lies on the route to the Gotthard Pass, which marks the boundary between the Germanic and Latin peoples—or, as we know it is called in Switzerland, the rösti ditch. The Gotthard route proper may be said to start a few kilometers downstream the River Reuss in the Schöllenen Gorge, a deep and wild declivity that frustrated travel for many centuries. In the sixteenth century, a stone bridge was built to span the gorge, and, in this fanciful land of William Tell, a legend was also built to explain its erection. The construction of the *Teufels-brücke* (Devil's Bridge) was undertaken by the Devil, at the request of shepherds fed up with fording the dangerous Reuss with their flocks. As payment for performing this task, the Devil demanded the soul of the first one to cross the bridge. The shepherds agreed and work got underway. When the bridge was completed, the Devil waited expectantly. The Swiss peasants then pushed a goat onto the bridge. The Devil could have its soul, as agreed. They had kept up their end of the bargain.

After admiring the old stone bridge—and crossing its modern companion—I traverse Andermatt once again, before heading for the mountains to the south. The road is beautiful and becalming, cosseted by greenery, the opposite of the route from hell over the Furka. Above the tree line, the landscape is one of rock, grass, and snow. One high valley introduces another; the third encountered is a painterly combination of snow and hard gray gneiss illuminated by slashes of amber sunlight to compose a type of Alpine Cézanne. The road widens considerably, so I pull over to take some notes. Outside my passenger door, a bratwurst of German bikers walks by. I look toward where they're heading, along a lakeshore to a complex of buildings about a hundred meters distant. I realize with a start that this is the Gotthard (or St. Gotthard) Pass.

Somewhere in those high valleys I crossed several boundaries, including another watershed. The rivers and streams I passed after crossing the Furka flowed into the North Sea; now they flow into the Adriatic. Another rösti ditch was cleared; I have stayed in Switzerland, but I have gone from Schweiz to Svizzera, from the canton of Uri to the canton of Ticino. But it is still the same country, as attested by the stubbornly unilingual signage—only the language has changed. I buy an entrance ticket to the *Museo Nazionale San Gottardo*. The Alps are remarkable linguistic tricksters—in the space of a few kilometers, a whole cultural outlook shifts. If language can be said to shape our worldview—and I believe it does—then the mountains create worlds around themselves. I have just gone from the Germanic to the Latin, in a matter of minutes. No doubt the Swiss are used to this head-snapping abruptness of change, but those of us from other countries can only marvel at it.

Gotthard of Hildesheim was a tenth-century German bishop who subsequently became the patron saint of traveling merchants. Whether this category includes traveling salesmen is unclear. The museum calls the Gotthard the "King of Alpine Passes," for its centuries-old economic, cultural, political, and military role in linking such important centers as Basel and Zurich to Milan and Venice. Thankfully, the curators lay no claim to Hannibal, as do so many other Alpine passes. The Gotthard boosters promote instead Alexander Vasilyevich Suvorov, a tsarist general who daringly led his troops across the pass in the winter of 1799 and drove the armies of the French Revolution from their encampments in Uri (back at the Devil's Bridge, a monument to Suvorov celebrates this exploit). The museum, in a very entertaining slide show, tells the story of the Devil and the goat, then adds that another devil came to plague the region. A portrait of Napoleon flashes up on the screen. Apparently, the Corsican has few fans in Switzerland, where he annexed cantons and made them *départements* of France and just generally waged war incessantly. Elsewhere there is an exhibit celebrating the yellow diligences (stagecoaches) and later coaches of the PostBus system, which I pointedly ignore out of solidarity with my once-shattered nerves. Finally, in a rueful admission reminiscent of the Zermatt museum's evocation of rampant real estate development, the guardians of the Gotthard exhort the visitor to explore Ticino and "admire what's left of this beautiful countryside." I am also put in mind of the tour guide in Chamonix, who deplored the pollution of his beloved valley.

Once back outside, I feel like General Suvorov. Snow is blowing hard through a cold fog. The cloud is not the friendly misty mantle encountered on the Furka but rather a thick white blanket obliterating visibility. Rather reluctantly, I have to admit that *this* is what crossing a pass should be—an ordeal endured for the privilege of going somewhere new and unfamiliar. Paying one's Alpine dues, so to speak. I abandon my plan to visit the cheese cellar housed in the Gotthard's old stables, for my unworn fleece sits uselessly at the bottom of my backpack in the car.

I eventually dig it out and put it on, then turn on the heat in the Mégane. This is ridiculous. I wait for the cloud to pass. And wait some more. Unless it's my imagination, the conditions seem to be getting worse. Finally, my impatience to go down into the valley and enjoy the benefits of being on the right side of the lard line gets the better of me.

Descending a mountain road in the middle of a cold, cottony cloud is an exercise in masochism. Salvation soon comes in the form of a sloping tunnel, entered a few kilometers from the pass. It is a fairly long affair; when I exit it, the cloud sits harmlessly overhead. This is, and is not, a good thing. On the valley floor now visible far below, I can see an airstrip. This does not reassure—the only time I have seen a similar view was when I was actually in an airplane.

At last the descent ends and I travel along the valley floor of the River Ticino. The farm buildings here are distinctly Italianate. On arriving at the canton's capital city, Bellinzona, the impression of being in Lombardy is overpowering. Perfume fills the air and smart-looking men stroll stylishly down the spotless sidewalks, obvious practitioners of the cult of *la bella figura*.

The city seduces the eye. Although its sister cities in Ticino— Lugano and Locarno—are better known, Bellinzona possesses a grace enhanced by exuberant public art in its squares and streets. I walk past a group of figurative statues with huge phalluses. A group of Italian cheerleaders, complete with pom-poms and short purple skirts, are taking pictures of themselves in front of the statues.

Bellinzona's enduring attraction—one that merits its inclusion in UNESCO's World Heritage list—lies in its necklace of medieval structures built on the town's hilltops. The place possesses no fewer than three medieval castles (each now thoughtfully housing an excellent restaurant), built when the dukes of Milan feared the marauding depredations of the hard men from Uri and Schwyz. In the Middle Ages, the Swiss were more or less invincible, their hedgehog of pikes feared throughout Europe. The largest of the three castles, aptly named Castelgrande, is a two-towered behemoth attached to a crenellated fortification more than a kilometer long. To view it, to walk along the battlements, is to understand what a rough neighborhood this was in the fourteenth century. It hardly needs to be added that in the ceaseless back-and-forth between the Lombards and the Swiss, the latter eventually came out on top. Ticino may look like Lombardy, but it is emphatically not the same place.

ANOTHER BOUNDARY AWAITS. In this journey of lard line, rösti ditch, linguistic switch, and watershed, a far more fundamental border is about to be crossed.

The boundary is the Insubric Line, the most important fault line in Europe. It is where the African and European tectonic plates meet, where they smashed into each other millions of years ago, where the Alps were born. This is to oversimplify, perhaps, for there were several collisions and upheavals in the very distant past, many creating "nappes," great sheets of rocks that slid over their predecessors on the earth's surface. Geologist Richard Fortey, who gave us the lasagne analogy in his *Earth: An Intimate History*, cites historian Mott Greene, who compared the movement of these rocky nappes to a tablecloth on a smooth tabletop: "If you should place your hand flat on the table and push forward, the cloth will begin to rise into folds. Push more and the folds will flop over (forward) and the rearmost fold will progressively override those before it, producing a stack of folds." These stacks are, in essence, the Alps, a geological puzzle that took centuries to work out.

Fortey takes his readers to the place that initiated the process. The fault line lies in the steep Morrobia Valley, below the village of

Pianazzo and south of Bellinzona. The geologist, on his way down to the Insubric Line in the company of his daughter, takes pains to clarify the collision so long ago.

> The *principle* of the Alps being squeezed out inexorably between the moving mass of Africa and obdurate Europe is correct enough. However, the margins of both "sides" were not one single piece of continent—like the jaws of a wood-worker's vice [vise]. Rather, both the African and European edges comprised several smaller pieces that behaved with considerable independence. A better analogy than a vice is to think instead of two huge ice sheets jostling in the sea, with pieces fragmented from either edge grinding together or free-floating by turn as the gulf between the larger sheets waxes and wanes.

As Fortey descends the north slope of the Morrobia, he notices that the exposed plates of mica, formed by tremendous squeezing and heating, stand vertical, forced into that posture by the lateral pressure of the collision. At the valley floor, where an old bridge spans a rushing brook, he and his daughter lean over to inspect the rocks visible through the clear water. They are entirely different, what he calls green schists. Stranger yet, they stand not vertical but horizontal, at right angles to the rock on the northern slope. This then is the place where Africa meets Europe. Father and daughter find a place on the riverbank where the Insubric Line appears on dry land. She poses with her feet on either side of the fault and Fortey snaps a picture. "I can imagine the photograph, by then fading slightly, puzzling one of our descendants—why the legs akimbo on a leafy path somewhere that seems without particular distinction?" he writes. "What would they say if they realized that the curious posture straddled a significant fraction of the world?"

It is hard to comprehend the violence of mountain formation. At Switzerland's San Bernardino Pass, there are rocks on the surface that once lay over a hundred kilometers within the earth. The vertical displacement caused by the events at the Insubric Line is thought to be nineteen kilometers. At a scenic overlook on my way up to the Iseran Pass, I characterized the mountainous panorama as a sea of rock, a metaphor that turns out to be not far off the mark. The seething movements continue, sometimes resulting in seismic catastrophe. Add to this the insidious work of millions of years of erosion—the tall peaks we see now might have stretched much farther in the air, thousands of meters taller. Several times they were engulfed in ice. The gentle mountains that predate the Alps by at least a hundred million years— the Vosges, Jura, and Appalachians—stand in mute testament to the punishing effects of water, wind, snow, and ice over incalculable stretches of time. We cannot get our heads around such eons. In an arresting comment in his study of geology entitled *Basin and Range*, John McPhee writes: "Consider the Earth's history as the old measure of the English yard, the distance from the King's nose to the tip of his outstretched hand. One stroke of a nail file on his middle finger erases human history."

I drive out of Bellinzona to find the village of Pianazzo and the Insubric Line. The capital's hinterland is covered with industrial buildings and construction sites. I begin to understand what the guardians of the Gotthard meant when they spoke of "what's left of this beautiful countryside." Happily, Pianazzo is remote enough to retain some of its natural charms. It is a higgledy-piggledy collection of medieval and modern, many of the homes of recent construction as holiday retreats. The doors and shutters are closed in the midday heat as I squint into the sunshine, hoping to see someone, anyone in the street.

After wandering aimlessly for about ten minutes in the deserted village, I finally spy a middle-aged couple rounding a corner. I sprint over to them and explain that I am looking for the entrance to the path that leads to the medieval bridge in the Valle Morrobia. Would they know where that is?

No, they wouldn't. They have a holiday rental flat here and plan on staying for just a couple of weeks. When they see my disappointment, they kindly offer to take me to a local man they know.

The door-knocker is dropped loudly on the wood. An elderly woman's head sticks out of a window on an upper floor. The helpful couple calls up and explains my mission. Other heads appear in other windows, some doors open, and people come into the street. My visit seems to be newsworthy.

At last the door of the old woman's house swings open and her husband appears in the threshold. He wears boxer shorts, a blue-gray dressing gown, and fluffy pink slippers. He and the couple exchange information in very rapid-fire Italian.

When he at last turns his attention to me, he says that I must go to the *ponte di ferro*. I explain that I don't want the iron bridge, I'm looking for the *ponte vecchio*, the one that crosses the brook in the Valle Morrobia. He insists on the iron bridge. I shake my head.

Exasperated, he sets off down the street and gestures for me to follow him. I bid goodbye to the helpful couple and catch up with my guide. After walking in silence for a good time, we stop at two recycling bins at the edge of a gorge. A walking path leads past them.

"Why do you want to go into the valley?" he asks.

"To see Africa."

He smiles at this and nods.

"Take the path to the bottom. You'll pass the iron bridge." And with that, his pink slippers head for home.

The path is not too steep, and a canopy of chestnut foliage blocks out the harshness of the sun. I pass a shrine to the Virgin Mary. I pay careful attention to the rocks exposed on my way down. Interspersed amid the traces of mica are elongated stones and pebbles standing vertically, as Fortey reported—proof of the tremendous tectonic pressures exerted on them millions of years ago.

I come to the iron bridge, a sturdy construction over a secondary gorge. The path leads on. Within minutes, I see the medieval bridge, a lovely single span of stone, humpbacked and covered in a soft carpet of green moss. Perhaps fifteen meters beneath it, the crystalline waters of the brook rush past.

I peer down into the waters, look at the bank on the far side. The rocks could hardly be more different. The green stone is layered in a resolutely horizontal fashion.

The brook below follows that fault's path. When I look at the schists of the far bank, I see that I am actually looking at the leading edge of the African tectonic plate. My path down from the village took me along the edge of the European plate. The beautiful old stone bridge joins two continents. I contemplate the scene: The collision of these two plates over time led to the creation of the fantastic heights I have been crossing this summer.

All is peaceful now at this place of great geological upheaval. The only sounds come from songbirds and the soft rush of water.

PART TWO

·□·

HEIDILAND TO
GRINDELWALD

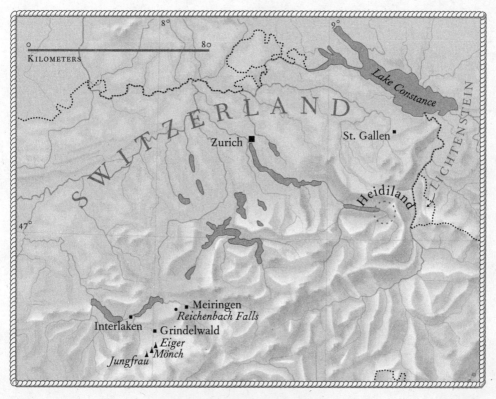

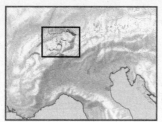

7. HEIDILAND, MEIRINGEN, AND THE EIGER

———— ⊡ ————

THE SMELL OF MANURE is overpowering. I have pulled into a highway rest stop near the small town of Maienfeld, in eastern Switzerland. As a clock strikes the hour, three wooden figures emerge from a belfry atop the restaurant and dance out onto a balcony. Heidi, a boy, and a goat perform several stiff pirouettes as a loudspeaker blares out an anthemlike ditty dedicated to Switzerland's answer to Joan of Arc. A few Swiss seniors, eyes trained on the mechanical spectacle, begin to sing along, delighted at being in the right place at the right time. Clearly, I am entering new territory.

Inside, there are preripped jeans hanging on a revolving clothes rack affixed to the ceiling, as if something had gone terribly wrong at the dry cleaner's. The stores upstairs are called "Kids World" and "Black Out," a juxtaposition that suggests alcoholic parenting. The ground floor of the rest stop, aside from a capacious cafeteria and market, is devoted to all things Heidi, for it was in nearby Maienfeld that the beloved moppet was supposed to have resided. The inevitable souvenir shop abounds with memorabilia, much of it reminiscent of

Hello Kitty fare. This Hello Heidi theme is carried over into how the character is portrayed: Most of the books on display show a round-eyed Heidi drawn in anime style, much like a character in a Hayao Miyazaki movie. It is thus not difficult to guess at the nationality of the tourists to whom these souvenirs are marketed. I also learn at this kitsch treasure trove that there is a Heidiland theme park in the hills above town. I resolve to go there and inspect it, before heading back to the fastness of the mountains.

But first an interlude, a brief holiday of sorts from attacking the high passes of the Alps. A Swiss friend, Ernst, awaits me in St. Gallen, a city near Lake Constance—or Bodensee, as it is called in German. We have known each other since our student-turned-journalist days in the Paris of the 1980s, and St. Gallen is his hometown. On holiday from Hong Kong, where he works for German-language business publications, Ernst has finally persuaded me to visit what he considers the center of the universe. Besides, St. Gallen is just a stone's throw from the Appenzell Alps.

An owlish man in his fifties with a mischievous streak, Ernst proves to be an amusing tour guide. As we stroll the city's squares and streets, taking in the carved medieval and baroque oriel balconies protruding from many of the older buildings, he carefully points out St. Gallen's rich heritage of naked-lady sculptures and bas-reliefs. Many of these figures adorn grand nineteenth-century buildings, testament to the time when the city was an industrial powerhouse. Given all the nudity, it comes as a surprise to learn of St. Gallen's bygone source of wealth: textiles.

Yet the town's claim to fame lies in its monastic library, an exuberant baroque affair that almost hurts the eyes with its decorative excess. The elaborate marquetry floors are complemented by an explosive figurative ceiling showing biblical scenes as they might have been imagined by Cecil B. DeMille. The library's collections of medieval manuscripts made it a center of European learning back when the Dark Ages were pitch black. Some of these manuscripts are written in old Irish, as the avatar of the establishment was a monk from what is now Ulster's County Down. That monk, Gall, came to the area in the seventh century seeking a place to hide out as a hermit. He was accompanied by Colombanus, another Irishman, who would leave his companion behind, cross the Alps, and establish, south of Milan, the venerable monastery in Bobbio, one of the templates for Umberto Eco's fictional library-monastery in *The Name of the Rose*. Gall decided to stay in what would become Switzerland, helped in his search for food and firewood by a remarkably hospitable bear, which then became the holy man's companion for the rest of its life. So too did scores of spiritual seekers, who imperiled Gall's quest for solitude, the fate of so many exceptional hermits in those days. Some seventy years or so after his death in 642, the monastery of St. Gallen was founded.

That its precious collections have survived down to the present day is nothing short of miraculous. The first great trial occurred in the year 926, when the Hungarians were on the move. Wiborada, a female recluse immured in a church wall equipped with a small slot through which food could be given to her, had a vision in which she saw the monastery's seizure, the monks' murder, and the manuscripts' destruction. Informed of the premonition, the abbot took his monks and his books off to the Isle of Reichenau in Lake Constance. Wiborada refused to go, and when the nightmarish onslaught came, she was yanked out of her cubby, raped, and killed. But the manuscripts survived. By all rights, Wiborada should be named the patron saint of literary agents—a profession, to my knowledge, still lacking one.

The library's other moment of jeopardy occurred in the early sixteenth century, when Switzerland rocked with the turmoil of Reformation. The leader of the movement here was Huldrych Zwingli, a charismatic and brilliant thinker. Zwingli, a native of the St. Gallen canton, came to be associated with Zurich, the city in which he preached his revolutionary theology in the 1520s. Like his contemporary and sometime sparring partner Martin Luther (the two men famously disagreed on the presence of Christ in the Eucharist), Zwingli was fed up with the ceremonials and customs of Catholicism, none of which had any grounding in the scriptures. Whereas Luther began his revolt in 1517 by nailing ninety-five theses on the door of a church in Wittenberg in Saxony, Zwingli contrived a much more amusing way to launch his Reformation. In March of 1522, Zwingli and his confederates sat down in the Zurich house of a printer to witness people feasting on sausages, a foodstuff forbidden by the Church during the Lenten fast. The so-called Affair of the Sausages propelled Zwingli to fame, and soon Switzerland saw a steady succession of public theological debates and eventually wars, as different cantons opted for different faiths.

One of Zwingli's principal colleagues, Joachim Vadian, became mayor of St. Gallen in these turbulent years. Whereas in other Reform-minded Swiss cities, the Protestants evicted the monks hated for their corruption, sacked their monasteries, and burned their libraries, nothing happened in St. Gallen. Vadian was a Humanist—and an ardent bibliophile. His prestige and authority must have equaled Zwingli's, for during his tenure no one laid a finger on the monks or their books.

The library's remarkable survival is thus owed to Wiborada, then Vadian.

One of the senior librarians recounts these stories with a certain sly pride. She is a rail-thin young woman with kind, expressive eyes. Where do all the Irish manuscripts come from? Gifts from Irish pilgrims to St. Gallen in the Middle Ages. Do you read old Irish? Yes, of course.

"But my favorite thing," she adds, "are the marginal notations." She explains that the copyists a millennium ago sometimes let their minds wander from the task set before them and wrote down what they were feeling. "One reads, 'My hand aches,'" the librarian recalls. "Another says, 'Tonight is a stormy night so we don't have to be afraid of the Vikings.' And another: 'A blackbird is singing outside my window. Spring is in the air, and here I write to the birdsong of a blackbird.'"

This information silences even the ebullient Ernst.

"I love reading those personal messages," she says quietly. "You feel like you're peering over the monk's shoulder, in the same room as him."

ERNST AND I decide to walk up a mountain, a height he summited many times in his boyhood. It is a glorious Sunday afternoon and the peak in question, the Ebensalp, seems to have attracted a sizable plurality of Switzerland's population. The northernmost of the Alpstein, a range of the Appenzell Alps, its accessibility and ease of ascent have made it popular with the paragliding jump-off-a-mountaintop crowd—scores of them float silently hundreds of meters above us.

The going immediately becomes steep. We begin on a gravel road with a pitch like that of a double black diamond ski slope.

This gives way to a cliff-hugging path, inconveniently littered with boulders. Ernst bounds ahead of me, a suicidal mountain goat, then patiently waits for me to catch up with him, his eyes sparkling behind his round-rimmed glasses as he notices that my legs are visibly shaking.

With the tree line behind us, the path narrows and the drop to our right becomes deeper and deeper. At a particularly dizzying spot, Ernst, who has let me go first, suddenly grabs hold of my shoulders, causing me to shriek in fright. He laughs, I do not.

The way up has been hewn out of the tremendous limestone face of the Ebensalp. A few caves are encountered. The first houses a troglodytic barnyard—chickens and sheep wander about behind a mesh fence. Then comes a remarkable cave restaurant-bar, crowded with hikers sipping beer at the edge of the abyss. We sit beside two German men—one a striking young buck with a well-groomed Labrador on a leash; the other, an older fellow with spiky white hair actively engaged in hitting on his companion. Ernst drily notes that the denizens of the two caves we have seen put him in mind of the long summers of transhumance, when the shepherds led their flocks to the high pastures and then stayed up there with them for months at a time. "It must have been lonely," he muses. "What in the world did they get up to?" I manage not to spit up my beer.

There are more caves to come. One houses a fully furnished Catholic church, the so-called *Wildkirch* (Wild Church) that gave its name to the cave complex—*Wildkirchli*—in the mountain. Ernst explains that the Neanderthals once lived here, followed by Neolithic men, thirty to fifty thousand years ago. The latter would not have seen a yawning valley from their cave dwellings but an immense glacier on which they could venture out to hunt. In the largest of the caves, some eight hundred animal bones were found, which medieval man took to be dragons' teeth. We walk farther into the largest of the caves, which gives onto another chamber through which light shines ahead of us. Here and there on the cave floor stand small cairns of arranged stones, manmade stalagmites. Ernst suggests that these are the work of Switzerland's Tibetan community—Europe's largest—who traded the Himalayas for the Alps when China took over their country in 1960.

We emerge from the cave mouth of the second chamber onto a grassy meadow. On the expanse are three types of mammals: sheep, hikers, and paragliders. We walk over to the last group and watch as the aerial daredevils untangle and arrange the cords of their chutes, pause to catch the breeze, then run and hurl themselves off the cliff, so many multicolored lemmings intent on a good time. Swiss environmentalists have managed to limit the number of places they can pursue their airborne pastime, once it was learned that they frighten the bejesus out of deer, who take them for pterodactyl-like birds of prey.

As this is the country of the Hotel Belvedere and Rigi Kulm, there are of course two restaurants and an inn on the summit. The great mountains of the Alpstein range rise gray and white and fearsome far into the sky. The view southward necessarily commands respect. Or perhaps not. The two restaurant terraces are jammed with Swiss hikers, many of them wolfing down heapings of sausages à la Zwingli when not hoisting giant steins of beer. There is nary a packet of trail mix in sight.

That evening in St. Gallen, we are joined by NoéMie (her spelling, not mine), a Suissesse in her thirties who works in London as a fashion journalist. I pitch an idea to my expat Swiss friends: Why not go to Heidiland tomorrow? Of course you two have never been there— why on earth would you go? But now you have an excuse—me. The invitation is met with skepticism, especially from Ernst, but curiosity wins out in the end.

The following day begins in a seemly fashion. We drive out of St. Gallen and back into the postcard landscape of Appenzell. Rust-colored chalets, rolling green hills, the sounds of cowbells, distant snowcapped mountains—this is Switzerland at its most bucolic. At a pass called Stoss, between the two cantons, I pull over. It was here, in 1405, that the hard mountain men of Appenzell, in revolt against their landlord, the abbot of the St. Gallen monastery, dealt a decisive blow for their freedom. The day was bloody. And rainy. When the troops from St. Gallen stopped at the pass to wipe the mud from their sodden shoes, the Appenzellers launched a surprise attack, slaughtering hundreds who had become separated from their weapons. Ernst, NoéMie, and I head over to the monument commemorating the battle and look out over the scenic perspective of the Rhine Valley. The river flows north here into Lake Constance. Far away to the east rise the heights of the Austrian Alps. The proximity of what was fairly recently a belligerent neighbor is underscored by a collection of defensive bunkers constructed prior to World War II into the hillside below us. This being contemporary Switzerland, the bunkers are now being transformed into vacation rental properties.*

As we are about to cross the road, we pause to let a car pass by. The young man at the wheel is alone, yodeling at the top of his lungs. My Swiss friends burst out laughing as the driver waves to us, his yodeling unbroken. They both swear that they have never seen anything like this before and that, no, this is not some sort of prank staged for my

---

* Near Lake Geneva, a long wall of triangular slabs built as a defensive fortification at the same time is now jokingly known as The Toblerone Line.

benefit, a kind of *Truman Show* for a gullible visitor. A brief seminar on the art of the yodel and the alphorn ensues as we head onto the autobahn in the valley for the quick trip to Maienfeld.

One of the heartlands of Swiss yodeling, I learn, is right here in Appenzell. The peculiar song, alternating between low and falsetto notes loudly produced in rapid succession, carries much farther than a mere shout, especially when aimed at a rockface that serves as an echoing board. The purpose was to convey information from one mountain ridge to another, connecting cowherds from different valleys and telling of local developments, marking liturgical feasts and just generally celebrating life. Predictably, Ernst claims that Swiss yodeling is superior to its Austrian variant. The former is more staccato, edgier, more beautiful, while the Austrian is overly melodic, almost syrupy in its delivery.

"Austrian yodeling sounds nice to me," I say, just to goad.

"Well, it's not," Ernst sniffs. "You don't know what you're talking about."

NoéMie decides it's wise to step in. "Think of yodeling as . . . ," she says, searching for a metaphor, ". . . as the vocal equivalent of smoke signals."

The alphorn is something altogether different. A musical instrument six to eight feet in length, the horn is fashioned, often, from the trunk of a slow-growth fir tree, hollowed out and pared down and polished to smoothness. At one end is the mouthpiece; far away at the other extremity is a bell-shaped aperture, slightly upraised, giving the tubular horn the shape of a very elongated umbrella with a very short handle. The bell rests on the ground, facing upward, while the musician stands at his full height, clasping the monstrosity in both hands and putting his mouth over the blowhole.

The purpose here is not to serenade far-flung neighbors in far-away valleys but to play for the cows. The horn, whose doleful sound carries over great distances, was customarily used to call in the cows from the pastures to come to the stables to be milked. Thus, its loud blasts were usually followed by the tinkling of cowbells. Another purpose of the alphorn, my Swiss friends tell me, was to encourage skittish cows to take the last few steps uphill to the high Alpine meadows where they would spend their summer.

Once past Maienfeld, we head east, up a winding road bordered by high stone walls, to the Kaaba of our pilgrimage. Tour buses disgorging parasol-laden Japanese and Koreans announce that we have arrived. A well-trodden path through a mountain meadow adorned with winsome statuary leads to the goat-cheesy hamlet of Heidiland. A petting zoo awaits inspection, as does a series of chalets, all with a commanding view of the Rhine Valley below and a trio of green shark-toothed mountains to the north, identical in shape and modest height. Erosion has been busy here. An informational plaque tells us that *Heidi* is the third most translated book in history, after the Bible and the Quran.

The heartwarming story, written by Johanna Spyri and first published in 1881, opens when a six-year-old orphan, Heidi, is taken to live with her curmudgeonly grandfather in a mountain pasture far above Maienfeld. Her good-natured charm eventually wins him over, as it does the other mountain folk, including a mischievous goatherd named Peter. After three years of sunny work and play, the young girl is sent to Frankfurt, to be the companion of a sickly child, Clara Sesemann. The country bumpkin gets into a few amusing misadventures in the big city, but the Sesemann family comes to love her, with the exception of their housekeeper, who thinks she's a tiresome brat. While in Frankfurt,

Heidi also learns to read and write, which she promptly uses to understand the Bible and see the light.

Trouble arises when Heidi grows pale and thin, and a ghost begins haunting the Sesemann house. Mr. Sesemann resorts to an all-night vigil and discovers that the ghost is, in fact, Heidi. As a result of her acute homesickness, she has taken to sleepwalking. Clearly, the little Suissesse is very unhappy. Much to Clara's dismay, Heidi is packed off and sent home for her own good.

Once back with her grandfather, Heidi convinces the old man to embrace religion and attend services in the village church in the valley, which he has not visited in years due to a longstanding feud. He is welcomed back with open arms. Spirits buoyed, she exchanges letters with Clara, who misses her old friend. Clara's doctor suggests that as a therapeutic measure, the invalid should spend the following summer with Heidi in the mountains. This Clara does, and the two girls become inseparable. Peter, the goatherd, no longer the center of Heidi's attentions, becomes jealous of the city girl and, in a fit of rage, hurls her wheelchair down the mountain, thus rendering it useless. Clara, desperate, tries to walk on her own and—lo and behold!—manages to do it. The goat's milk and fresh mountain air have worked their wonders. Clara is overjoyed, Heidi is overjoyed, the Sesemann family is overjoyed—and millions and millions of readers the world over are overjoyed.

The three of us approach the entrance of the Heidiland Museum.

"I'm not going," Ernst says. "It's a waste of money."

NoéMie laughs and offers to pay the entrance fee for him.

"I *know* what a Swiss farmhouse looks like," he says, gesturing to a rustic building up a path. "I've been inside lots of them. I'm not going to pay ten francs to see what I already know."

We stand in silence for a moment. Evidently this sudden attack of principled pragmatism is serious. He smiles at me.

I smile back, remembering our Paris café days spent arguing over everything and anything, just for the fun it. I decide not to take the bait.

"Have it your way," I say, and he walks off to the petting zoo to think his thoughts.

NoéMie and I shell out, enter the museum, and are soon perusing dozens of first-edition book covers in as many languages. The eternal Heidiological question—blonde or brunette?—seems to resolve itself in favor of the latter. We see pictures of the author, Johanna Spyri, a rather severe-looking Suissesse who is believed to have written the book in just four weeks. The accompanying information boards make no mention of the recent discovery of a German book published in 1830, whose title translates to *Adelaide, the Girl from the Alps*. In imagery and story line, it is remarkably similar to *Heidi*, and a Spyri expert has conceded that much of it may have been lifted to compose the best-seller.

The exhibits are too derivative, NoéMie and I decide. We resolve to leave the museum and its tedious press clippings to go to the Heidihaus, the rickety chalet that Ernst waved at dismissively when bowing out of our expedition. This farmhouse, we are informed, is where Heidi lived with her cantankerous grandfather. Much of Asia is milling about its entrance, so our pleasure is deferred in favor of a walk around the grounds, serenaded by the Heidi anthem playing over and over again through hidden loudspeakers. We stumble across a "Sri Chimnoy Peace Blossom" plaque, advocating for world peace through horticulture. Similar gardens, the sign says, can be found at Niagara Falls, the Matterhorn, the Russia–Norway border, and Canberra, Australia. On this day and in this place, this list strikes neither of us as strange.

At last the crowd thins and we can enter the sanctum. An electronic turnstile wishes us a *gute Fahrt* as we step into a ground-floor manger and food cellar. We reverently handle the plastic cheese rounds, plastic apples, and plastic potatoes. Upstairs, a mannequin representing Heidi's gruff grandfather sits in a chair, cradling an odd-looking wooden instrument close to his crotch. We both wish Ernst were around to explain what we're looking at. Nearby, in the kitchen, dummies representing Peter and Heidi sit across from each other at a rustic table. In what we assume is a botched attempt to make them look jolly, both have their teeth bared in grimaces. They don't look happy; they look like the homicidal Chucky of horror-film fame. Out come the phones and we snap pictures of ourselves beside the kids as we try to appear just as ferocious.

That, it turns out, is the highlight of our visit to Heidiland. Elsewhere are rooms of unknown purpose filled with tools of unknown use. The chalet is a museum of Swiss mountain life, mercifully nondidactic, without the ghost of an explanation anywhere. The Heidi anthem plays occasionally, punctuated by welcoming messages in German and English, themselves accompanied by a weird tinkle of cocktail music straight out of a 1970s fern bar.

ALONE ONCE AGAIN, I am in the Bernese Oberland, the dramatic mountainous hinterland of the central Swiss canton of Bern. The town of Meiringen sits amid green fields in a valley in the eastern part of the Oberland, seemingly forgotten when compared to its famous neighbors of Interlaken and Grindelwald. Yet the town's renown is global. It claims to have given the world its namesake pastry, the meringue. The shop with bragging rights over the meringue's origin myth still sells the pastries—and they are indeed delicious.

Across the street, about two dozen men of all ages stand on the sidewalk in front of a nondescript building, milling about aimlessly. I am about to ask the café waitress at my hotel whether the building is a brothel—I can think of no other explanation—when the men set off together across the street and form a semicircle before our tables. They thrust their hands in their pockets. What ensues is a heavenly chorus of male voices, drifting in plangent majesty through the evening air. Two fellows, one a plump middle-aged man, the other a lean construction worker, occasionally pierce the melody with falsetto half-yodeling, a hesitant, self-interrupted riff in counterpoint to the surrounding smoothness of polyharmony. The effect is stunning. I remember Ernst telling me at the Stoss Pass, after our encounter with the freelance yodeler, that the Swiss version of the yodel is far more staccato than its Austrian counterpart, which has a tendency to be sentimental and gooey. The choir performs two folk songs and then files into the hotel for its weekly practice session.

"You, the writer! You must sing now!" A woman's voice has come from the far side of the terrace. I look up from my notebook and see that all eyes are upon me.

I shake my head, smiling.

She stands up, a blonde, five-foot-two pillar of impishness.

"You must sing for us!"

Vanquished, I get to my feet and go over to the spot where the singers had placed themselves. I really know only one song, a Clancy Brothers ditty that I sang to each of my daughters in the delivery room just moments after their birth. For each, it was the first time they heard my voice unbuffered by their mother's belly. I clear my throat and dive in:

> *When I was young and had no sense,*
> *I bought a fiddle for eighteen pence . . .*

The amusing song then goes on to recount how the damned fiddle could play only one tune—and then only before daybreak. Best sung in stage Irish, at which I happen to excel, the ditty comes across as a delightful piece of whimsy.

The applause is loud and appreciative. The woman, named Katarina, invites me to sit at her boisterous table. It is her forty-fifth birthday today and she has come here with her mother and friends. I ask her if she learned her excellent English in America.

"I would never go to America," she replies emphatically. "I learned English in Australia."

Beers are ordered and downed. Repeatedly.

Katarina's mother, although in her early eighties, has been taking English lessons. I ask her about her family.

"Katarina has two brothers," she says. "One is fifty-six and one is fifty-eight."

"Fifty-nine," Katarina corrects.

"*Ja*, fifty-nine."

My eyebrows shoot up as I see an opening for payback.

"Tell me," I ask the mother as her daughter looks on, "was Katarina an accident?"

A pause. The old woman looks at Katarina and says with a smile, "Yes. She was a big accident."

Katarina explodes, wide-eyed, "What?! You never told me that!"

But her mother has already turned away to translate our conversation into Swiss German for the others at the table.

The laughter is loud and long, and lasts well into the night.

NOT SO EARLY the next morning, I set out in earnest on my quest to find the spot Arthur Conan Doyle described. Meiringen's other distinction lies in detective fiction, for being the place where two celebrated characters, contemporaneous with and as famous as Heidi, met their deaths, or so it seemed. Sherlock Holmes and Professor James Moriarty had their final fatal encounter at Meiringen.

The author was an avid admirer of Switzerland and one of the pioneers of winter tourism here. He brought his children and his wife, who suffered from tuberculosis, to the spa town of Davos, where the rich and powerful of this world now hold their annual chin wag. An athletic man, Conan Doyle made the acquaintance of two locals who were trying out a new sport, downhill skiing. There had been some skiing in Scandinavia, but none in Switzerland.

As his wife recuperated, Conan Doyle gamely tried to get the hang of the novel pursuit. The people of Davos laughed at the sight of the famous writer—for Holmes was already well loved in Switzerland by the 1890s—repeatedly wiping out on the slopes above town. In March 1894, laughter turned to respect when Conan Doyle and his two Swiss friends climbed from Davos up to a pass 2,400 meters in altitude and then skied down to the neighboring town of Arosa. He wrote an article on the exploit for the monthly *Strand* magazine—where his Holmes stories were published—detailing his experience whizzing down a slope. "You let yourself go," he wrote, "gliding delightfully over the gentle slopes, flying down the steeper ones, taking an occasional cropper, but getting as near to flying as any earthbound man can. In that glorious air it is a delightful experience." The article attracted considerable attention in Britain. "I am convinced," he said prophetically, "that the time will come when hundreds of Englishmen will come to Switzerland for the skiing season. I believe I may be the first, save only two Switzers, to do any mountain work, but I am certain I will not by many thousands be the last."

The previous year, when he and his wife had made a trip to Meiringen, the author had murder on his mind. He wrote to his mother: "I'm thinking of slaying Holmes . . . and wind him up for good and all. He takes my mind from better things." Conan Doyle was heartily sick of Holmes and wanted to move on to other forms of writing. To effect this homicide, he came up with a story entitled "The Final Problem," which opens with Holmes arriving at the home of his sidekick, Dr. John Watson, in a state of extreme agitation. There had been three attempts to murder him that day. Holmes reveals to Watson that he has been on the hunt for a brilliant criminal mastermind, Professor Moriarty, and is just days away from turning him and his many confederates over to the police. This "Napoleon of crime," as Holmes calls him, knows of the detective's plans and will move heaven and earth to kill him.

Holmes asks Watson to accompany him to the Continent to avoid the danger. Watson must follow an elaborate stratagem of evasive action the next day to meet his friend at Victoria Station. But Holmes is not there to greet him—an aging Italian priest takes a seat beside Watson. As the train gets underway, the priest reveals himself to be Holmes in disguise. More important, Holmes spots Moriarty on the platform attempting to get the train to stop. Watson has been followed.

The two men get off at Canterbury and hide behind a pile of luggage as a later train, transporting Moriarty, roars past in pursuit. They take a third train to another port city and board the ferry to Dieppe. They then travel to Strasbourg via Brussels and make their way to Meiringen. Holmes learns that all of Moriarty's gang has been arrested, save for its brilliant leader. The detective fears the worst.

Holmes and Watson spend the night at the Englischer Hof, a Meiringen grand hotel where the innkeeper speaks English. He suggests to the men that the next morning they should take a hike in the mountains to see the Reichenbach Falls, a natural wonder of the region. Fatefully, the Englishmen heed his advice.

The next morning, as Watson and Holmes contemplate the mighty falls, a messenger boy from the hotel runs up to them saying that there is a very ill Englishwoman staying there in need of an English doctor. Watson retraces his steps, leaving Holmes alone. On arriving at the Englischer Hof, Watson discovers the message was a hoax. The innkeeper says it must have been a prank played by the *other* Englishman at the hotel. Watson realizes he has been tricked by Moriarty.

He races back up to the falls but sees neither Holmes nor Moriarty. By looking at the footprints on the muddy trail, he detects signs of a great struggle. There are no footprints leading back down the track. He concludes that the two men must have fought it out and fallen to their deaths in the abyss. He eventually finds a farewell note from Holmes penned in haste. Watson announces to the readers of the *Strand* magazine that Holmes was the wisest man he had ever known.

Readers worldwide have long argued over what exactly happened to Sherlock Holmes here, but the town of Meiringen harbors no doubts. It is not shy about its place of honor in detective lore. The small central square of the town bears a sign in the typography and font familiar to all visitors to London:

BOROUGH OF MEIRINGEN

CONAN DOYLE SQUARE W

Farther on is another sign in the same lettering:

CITY OF WESTMINSTER

BAKER ST.

On a rock in Conan Doyle Square sits a life-size bronze statue of the detective, pensively puffing on his pipe and wearing his signature deerstalker hat. Behind him is the English Church of Meiringen—there were scores of such English churches built in nineteenth-century Switzerland. The church's cellar houses a delightful little museum devoted to all things Holmesian. Its stellar attraction, safe behind a glass wall, is a remarkable full-scale re-creation of Holmes's sitting room at 221B Baker Street, filled with period memorabilia and items mentioned in the stories. We see Victorian armchairs draped with antimacassars, a dining table with a lamp complete with silk shades, the deerstalker cap, Holmes's violin on a chair, Watson's war trophies from the second Afghan war, Holmes's pipe, his magnifying glass, and much more. To one side stands a very rare complete collection of *Strand* magazines. Unlike the creators of Heidiland, the curators of this museum have wisely elected not to people the exhibit with weirdly grinning dummies representing Holmes and Watson.

On my way out of town, I pass what had been the Englischer Hof, the hotel where Holmes and Watson stayed and where Conan Doyle and his wife lodged as he dreamed up his hero's demise. The establishment is now named the Parkhotel du Sauvage. A prominent plaque on its facade reads:

IN THIS HOTEL, CALLED BY SIR ARTHUR CONAN DOYLE
ENGLISCHER HOF
MR. SHERLOCK HOLMES AND DR. WATSON
SPENT THE NIGHT OF 3RD/4TH MAY, 1891.
IT WAS FROM HERE THAT MR. HOLMES LEFT
FOR THE FATAL ENCOUNTER AT THE REICHENBACH FALLS
WITH PROFESSOR MORIARTY, THE NAPOLEON OF CRIME.

I reach the foot of the Reichenbach Falls within minutes, for they are less than a couple of kilometers from town. There, a vintage red funicular awaits boarding, the signs on its slatted wooden seats imploring visitors in several languages not to lean over the side. As we get underway, a Spanish family with two small children proceeds to do just that, much to my dismay. The conductor ignores them.

One hears the falls before seeing them. A deafening roar grows louder and louder as we ascend, the rushing water hidden by a canopy of foliage. At last we arrive at the top and see, from a viewing platform, the falls just about a dozen meters in front of us. It is a tremendous, violent sight, the water cascading from a cliff top to be dashed on green-gray boulders far below. Across the abyss, on the opposite rockface, a small white star adorns a narrow ledge—the spot where Holmes and Moriarty had their showdown. There's barely room for one person on the ledge, let alone two brawling men. Clearly, the gentleman tourist of 1893, who had murder on his mind, found this the ideal place to polish off his famous detective. As Conan Doyle, in a passage of uncommon descriptive power, writes of the falls in "The Final Problem":

It is indeed, a fearful place. The torrent, swollen by the melting snow, plunges into a tremendous abyss, from which the
spray rolls up like the smoke from a burning house. The shaft
into which the river hurls itself is an immense chasm, lined by
glistening coal-black rock, and narrowing into a creaming,
boiling pit of incalculable depth, which brims over and shoots
the stream onward over its jagged lip. The long sweep of green
water roaring forever down, and the thick flickering curtain of
spray hissing forever upward, turn a man giddy with their constant whirl and clamour. We stood near the edge peering down
at the gleam of the breaking water far below us against the
black rocks, and listening to the half-human shout which came
booming up with the spray out of the abyss.

Given that powerful description, one could reasonably assume
that Holmes's demise was definitive. But that would be to assume too
much. Public clamor over Holmes's disappearance eventually led, in
1901, to his reappearance in the novel *The Hound of the Baskervilles*.
Arthur Conan Doyle caved to the pressure of his readers. Holmes had
not fallen to his death; he had been hiding abroad to escape detec-
tion by a confederate of the late Moriarty. The next two decades saw
the publication of dozens of Sherlock Holmes short stories as Conan
Doyle reconciled himself to the brilliance of his creation.

THE DRIVE from Meiringen to Interlaken partakes of breathtaking
beauty, with towering peaks on both sides, then suddenly an aquama-
rine lake surrounded by chalets spilling down deep green hillsides. A
visit to the crown jewel of the Bernese Oberland then requires a left

fishhook turn into a gap so narrow that there's barely room for cars and the gigantic piles of logs and lumber stacked close to the roadway. A series of hairpins leads up into a broader high valley, where, since this is Switzerland, there is a railroad station. Somehow Swiss rail engineers managed to thread the needle of the gap, although how they did this—and where—I did not see.

The valley opens up. There are holiday chalets everywhere. At the town of Grindelwald, with its crescent-shaped main street an impressive string of businesses and banks, there are signs in German, English, French, and Japanese. Construction cranes ring the town. Crowds shuffle along the sidewalks. I pass the Japanese Information Bureau, a privately run purveyor of services, one of which promotes a course in Swiss cheesemaking. Make your own cheese round, then take it home in triumph to Osaka.

Although my daughters informed me on the phone last night that a Grindelwald, namely Gellert Grindelwald, was an evil wizard second in power only to Lord Voldemort, that is not why I have come here. My destination is the Jungfraujoch, home to the most elevated train station in Europe. I cannot even see it for the moment, as a threatening peak blocks it from view. This is the Eiger, the mountain first summited solo in 1963 by Michel Darbellay, the man whose funeral I witnessed in Orsières.

The first stage of the cog-railway journey begins in the valley below Grindelwald. The train moves at remarkable speed up a gentle slope and soon the rumpled green expanse below us is swaying pleasantly and becoming smaller and smaller. The large chalets now appear to be toy houses. Opposite me sits an excited Hindu woman clad in a colorful sari, the *bindi* on her forehead a dark scarlet. She cannot contain herself. "Why, this is perfect!" she exclaims. "Perfect!" Her teenaged son, carrying several thousand dollars' worth of photographic equipment, points his cameras out the train's panoramic windows and fires the shutters like a machine gun.

The train's terminus is Kleine Scheidegg (Little Watershed), a pass where a second train must be boarded to continue the ascent. I alight on the platform and look southward.

This, then, is the Bernese Oberland in all its glory. Towering before me is an Alpine sight as iconic as Mont Blanc or the Matterhorn, a threesome of menace known to mountaineers everywhere. From east to west, I see the Eiger, the Mönch, and the Jungfrau—or, as we would say, the Ogre, the Monk, and the Virgin. These mountains stretch to the heavens, gray rock and white snow in a stirring melodrama of nature. It is no coincidence that composer Richard Wagner came often to Grindelwald and its environs.

The great triangular north face of the Eiger is one of the six great north faces of the Alps (the five others, as mentioned earlier, are Les Grandes Jorasses and Le Petit Dru at Mont Blanc; the Piz Badile and the Matterhorn on the Swiss-Italian border; and the Cima Grande di Lavaredo in the Italian Dolomites).* The Eiger is also the biggest— and the deadliest. Since the 1930s, more than sixty climbers have died trying to get atop it. There is, then, an aura of fear surrounding the mountain. German for north face is *Nordwand*; in German mountaineering circles, the Eiger's face is habitually called the *Mordwand* (the Murder Face). One of its ledges, to take another example, is called the "Death Bivouac." Added to this fearsome reputation is another particularity of the mountain: Its killer rockface, more than 1,800 meters

---

* The three most difficult of these faces—Les Grandes Jorasses, the Matterhorn, and the Eiger—are known in climbing circles as The Trilogy.

from base to apex, can be seen in its entirety from Kleine Scheidegg. Thus, with a pair of powerful binoculars, onlookers could follow the various catastrophes as they unfolded, stick figures falling to their doom or motionless on a ledge, frozen to death. There is, as usual in Switzerland, a luxury hotel at Kleine Scheidegg—Hôtel Bellevue des Alpes—with a terrace conveniently sited for following the progress (or failure) of climbing expeditions. The mountain is a theater.

There is a rail tunnel piercing the Eiger. This is the route of the train that I will take later in the day on the second leg of the journey up to the Jungfrau. In the 1930s, when the race to summit the Eiger was at its deadliest, a gallery leading from the rail tunnel to the rockface was used frequently as a means of egress for rescue parties dispatched to help climbers in trouble.

To understand the frenzy for "bagging" the Eiger's north face, it's crucial to evoke the interwar period in Germany. The 1920s and 1930s saw the flowering of a genre of cinema there, the *Bergfilm* (mountain film). Silents, then talkies, glorified the beauty of mountains and the heroism of those who conquered them in an expressive, exaggerated style. Leni Riefenstahl, for example, got her start in the *Bergfilm*. With the rise of the Nazis, and their bowdlerized interpretation of the Alps and Wagner and Nietzsche, the conquest of mountains became an Aryan duty, a sign of racial superiority, a token of purity far removed from the degeneracy of other Europeans. (The museum in Zermatt screens a clip of an old *Bergfilm* depicting the Matterhorn disaster, *Der Kampf ums Matterhorn*, in which Edward Whymper comes off as a fairly foppish Englishman.) Thus, a mix of nationalism and ideology spurred many Germans and Austrians to be the first up one of the toughest ascents in the Alps.

The contest began in earnest in 1935. Two Bavarian climbers had a crack at the Eiger Nordwand in August of that year. Bad weather forced them to bivouac for four consecutive nights. They froze to death at the Death Bivouac. The following year, ten climbers came from Germany and Austria. One quickly died during a training climb, and the weather closed in, inducing five to abandon any attempt. That left two Bavarians and two Austrians. Theirs was to be the most dramatic catastrophe on the *Mordwand* for thirty years.

They began climbing on 18 July 1936, watched by crowds at Kleine Scheidegg. Considerable progress was made on the first day, but storms moved in on the second, leaving them stuck on the mountain. When a rockfall seriously injured one of the Austrian climbers, the foursome decided that they would have to give up their goal. Unfortunately, however, they had removed the rope from a particularly difficult traverse (thinking, no doubt, they would descend from the summit on the easy western face), so they were forced to abseil (rappel) dangerously down the steep face. They passed the entrance to the gallery of the rail tunnel and told the guard there that they were fine and would get down with no problem.

Then an avalanche hit. One man, unclipped, was swept off the mountain to his death. Another, swinging wildly on his rope, crashed directly into rockface and crushed his skull. The weight of his body caused another climber, to whom he was attached by rope, to die of asphyxiation. That left one survivor, Toni Kurz, dangling in the air, helpless, exhausted. Two courageous Swiss rescuers climbed out of the railroad gallery in the rockface and made their way to the beleaguered young Bavarian. He had been on the mountain, exposed, for four days. The Swiss tied two lengths of rope together and threw it to Kurz. By some malediction of fate, the knot joining the two lengths would not go through Kurz's carabiner (metal clip), so he did not have enough play to make his abseiling descent to the Swiss waiting below, who could not ascend farther because of an overhanging spur of rock. Kurz tried for hours to get the knot through, but his fingers were frozen. One Swiss guide climbed on his colleague's shoulders, reached up with an ice ax and managed to touch the sole of Kurz's crampons. But it was too late. Kurz croaked, "I can't go on any longer," then died. He was twenty-three.

The literature of mountaineering contains many heart-stopping tales of danger courted and overcome. The unlucky Kurz did not live to tell his tale, but other great Alpinists escaped death repeatedly—and some turned out to be accomplished, even philosophical, writers. Their books have fired imaginations for decades. Three of the classic memoirs are (in their English translations), Gaston Rébuffat's *Starlight and Storm: The Conquest of the Great North Faces of the Alps*, Walter Bonatti's *The Mountains of My Life*, and Lionel Terray's *Conquistadors of the Useless: From the Alps to Annapurna and Beyond*. To which a fourth must be added: Heinrich Harrer's *The White Spider: The Classic Account of the Ascent of the Eiger.*

Following the 1936 disaster, another attempt was made in 1937. Two climbers got into trouble on the Eiger but did manage to make their way off the face safe and sound, which ranked as something of an accomplishment. In June of 1938, two Italians promptly died on the rockface. The following month, Harrer, an Austrian, decided to try his luck. In his memoir, he snorts indignantly at the accusation he had Hitlerian motives (the Anschluss had occurred a few months earlier): "Nobody dangled Olympic or other medals before our eyes, nor did we receive any. As to the report we climbed on the orders, or even at the wish, of some personage or other, it is absolutely off the mark."

After about twenty hours into the ascent, Harrer and a fellow Austrian were joined on the north face by two more experienced German climbers. They decided their chances were better if they stuck together. What followed was an epic struggle against the elements, with bivouacs pitched on the edge of the abyss. Observers at Kleine Scheidegg gave them up for dead on several occasions, only to have the clouds clear to reveal the four doggedly inching their way up the rock. At last they reached the White Spider, a starfish-shaped ice cliff near the summit. The weather turned awful, they could hear people who had scaled the easy western slope shouting indistinctly down to them, asking if they needed rescue. Just as progress resumed, Harrer writes:

> The howling of the wind increased, gathering a very strange note—a banging and swishing, a whistling hiss. This wasn't the voice of the storm any more coming down out of wild dance of ice particles and snowflakes, but something quite different. It was an avalanche, and as its harbingers, rocks and fragmented ice!
>
> I snatched my rucksack up over my head, holding it firmly with one hand, while the other gripped the rope which ran up to my companion. I jammed myself against the ice cliff, just as the whole weight of the avalanche struck me. The rattle and hammering of stones on my pack was swallowed up by the clatter and roar of the avalanche. It snatched and clutched at me with fearful strength. Could I possibly survive such pressure? Hardly . . . I was fighting for air, trying above all to prevent my rucksack from being torn away and also to stop the endless stream of rushing snow from building up between me and the ice slope and forcing me out of my footholds.

The avalanche increased in intensity, then abated. All four men had survived, clinging to the White Spider. And, at 3:30 in the afternoon of 24 July 1938, in a howling blizzard, they trudged onto the summit ridge of the Eiger. The news spread quickly around the world.

As the second train heads toward the tunnel bored through the mountain, it is impossible not to think of Harrer and his ilk with a great measure of respect. Or of his successors. Many have since climbed the face—and many have died—all of them drawn by the challenge. The first woman to summit the Eiger via the north face continued Marie Paradis's tradition of female firsts with delightful names. In September 1964, a German woman achieved that distinction: Daisy Voog.

This second train, the Jungfraubahn, is smaller than the first but just as comfortable, and modern and red. Once in the steeply pitched tunnel, we ascend slowly as the cogs strain to do their work. We are inside the Eiger now. Ads for Tissot watches hang like laundry from the ceiling and video screens inform us that the railway celebrated its centenary in 2012. What is not said is that Swiss entrepreneurs one hundred years ago realized that English tourists were crazy enough to pay a fortune to go up to the Jungfrau. And they were right. The train is now a babel of excited visitors, loudspeakers making announcements in eight languages, each followed by the trademarked phrase, in English only, for the locale: "The Top of Europe." We were all given Swiss chocolate after buying our round-trip tickets. It is the most expensive chocolate bar of my life: $185.25.

The train makes its first underground stop at the Eigerwand station. We passengers, a sort of United Nations of Tourism, dutifully troop through the gallery carved out of the rock and behold, through a reassuringly sturdy plexiglass wall, the rocky view from the middle of the north face. It was from this gallery that the valiant attempt to save Toni Kurz was launched—and from which Clint Eastwood was rescued in *The Eiger Sanction*, a 1975 thriller with superb mountaineering scenes marred by a dog's breakfast of a plot down in the valley.

Underway again, the video now turns its attention to a music festival held every year in Grindelwald. This features a Vladimir Putin lookalike singing Elvis Presley's "Suspicious Minds." The performance is riveting. We soon arrive at another underground stop, this time at the Eismeer (Ice Sea) station. The view from this gallery lives up to its billing: The Grindelwald-Fiescher Glacier is a frozen white pandemonium lying between the Mönch and the Jungfrau.

At last we reach the topmost station at the Jungfraujoch. This "Virgin Yoke" is actually a glaciated pass between the Jungfrau and the Mönch—we have traversed the Eiger—although, given its elevation (3,466 meters) and its extreme conditions, not many travelers in the past must have made use of it, as opposed to the other Alpine passes I have visited. Duty trumps the growing sense of giddiness in my head and I take a lift a further hundred meters to the Sphinx, a scientific observatory high in the sky. From its viewing deck, I look down on my old friend, the Aletsch Glacier, flowing east into Wallis/Valais. I can also see scores of tall peaks playing with the clouds—in Switzerland, Italy, France, and Germany. The view is truly stupendous, humbling. I begin to feel less grumpy about the cost of the train ticket.

Once back down at the Jungfraujoch complex, I wander dazedly through various glossy exhibits about Alpine derring-do, one of which, with admirable self-deprecation, deals with the strange business of selling the Alps to tourists. But my real goal is to participate in that absurdity by consuming a chicken tikka masala. Finally I come across it—the Bollywood Restaurant. Alas, there are no seats available, and dozens of Indians outside its doors wait patiently to join their countrymen within. A sign reads:

INDIAN BUFFET

32 EUROS

NO SHARING

The reason for this extraordinary sight stems from Indian cinema. In the 1980s and 1990s, almost all big-budget Bollywood musical romances included what it is called a "Cut to Switzerland" scene. This entailed either a dream sequence or just an unexplained stand-alone transition that had the two romantic leads cavorting in Swiss mountain meadows, with a backdrop of wildflowers and glorious scenery. The filmmakers of Mumbai had once used the Kashmir for this technique, but that area grew too geopolitically dicey—hence the Cut to Switzerland. Once millions of Indians grew familiar with distant Switzerland—in much the same way the Japanese came to know Heidi—the country became a destination of choice for the affluent of the subcontinent. And the Swiss, experts in tourism since the invention of tourism, started to learn how to make curry.

Unable to wait for the buffet, I board the train and leave India behind. Everywhere I go, I seem to bump into fiction. Opposite me this time are three sleepy Gangnam-style Korean kids, plump, sporting colorful shades and hair dyed various hues of red. The video above them shows footage of the famed local hero, Ueli Steck, a speed mountaineer. In 2008, Steck climbed the Eiger's north face solo, in the astounding time of two hours and forty-seven minutes. I watch, fascinated, as the Swiss climber races up rockfaces around the world.

On the second stage of the train journey, my companion is a fellow from County Kilkenny, who, on learning of my Alpine book project, categorically pooh-poohs the idea.

"The mountains, the magic, they've already been done."

"By Mann?" I say, trying to catch his drift.

"Who?"

"Thomas Mann. *The Magic Mountain*."

"No, by Tolkien."

The Irishman turns out to be a full-on druid lover. The rest of the trip down to Grindelwald becomes a disquisition on runes, standing stones, mysterious powers, oracles, and the like. Perhaps, I think as the Celtic seer continues his explanations, my daughters were right after all—Gellert Grindelwald of Harry Potter fame does belong here.

He's sitting beside me.

PART THREE

INNSBRUCK TO
TRIESTE

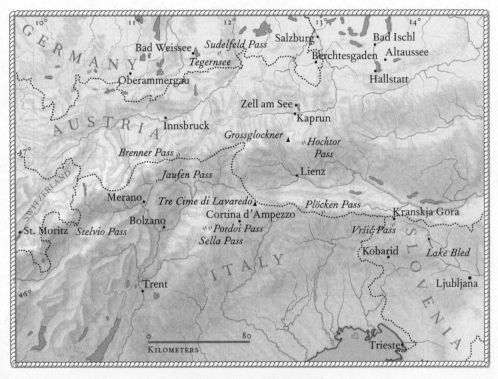

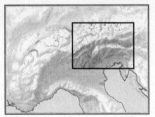

8. FERN AND SUDELFELD PASSES AND BERCHTESGADEN

———— ▫ ————

CUT *AWAY* FROM SWITZERLAND—to Innsbruck, Austria, where the sky has opened and what seems to be a microburst pours down on the old town, as though Zeus or some other mischievous god has just emptied a celestial bucket of water. I take shelter from the deluge at a recessed storefront in the company of about a dozen Japanese people. Most carry a black tote bag emblazoned with a kangaroo road sign with a red slash through it. Large lettering declares: NO KANGAROOS IN AUSTRIA. The language barrier between my companions and me appears insuperable until one smiling old fellow nods at me—I must have been staring at his bag—and says, "Austria, no Australia." This is greeted by an appreciative titter from the others.

When the storm passes, I stroll the gleaming cobbles of Tyrol's capital and admire its collection of sixteenth- and seventeenth-century buildings, a legacy of the days when the city was an important administrative center of the Habsburg holdings in central Europe. A fuller explanation of the kangaroo mystery comes from the owner of a souvenir shop. The Austrians are tired of being mistaken for Australians.

This happens a lot abroad when an Austrian reveals his nationality to a stranger, only then to hear how Sydney is such a beautiful city and how the beaches are the best in the Pacific. Hence the tote bag.

I drive out of the city the next morning. The daylight reveals a remarkable feng shui of mountains. To the north rises the towering screen of the Nordkette range; to the south, a ski jump seems pointed at the heart of the town. Small wonder then that Innsbruck has twice hosted the Winter Olympics, in 1964 and 1976, though the latter one landed in its lap when the city originally chosen, Denver, backed out of its commitment.

The River Inn flows quickly—Innsbruck means "Bridge on the Inn"—through its broad valley on its long route to meet the Danube at Passau, Germany. Another watershed has been crossed, as the waters of the Inn will flow into the Black Sea. Off to the left, a truly massive baroque building rises in differing hues of yellow. This is the Cistercian monastery of Stams, founded in the thirteenth century. One of Tyrol's baroque jewels, Stams also has the distinction of being, I believe, the only monastery anywhere to run a snowboarding school.

It is near Stams where I must turn right and head to the Fern Pass, which leads from Austria's Tyrol toward Germany's Bavaria. Clouds wreathe the middle slopes of the mountains before me like white bandannas. On an isolated hilltop stands a pale neo-Gothic church, its red needlelike spire pointing skyward. The Church of Maria Locherboden attracts pilgrims from all over Tyrol—indeed, from all over Austria. It also overlooks my route, along the trace of the Via Claudia Augusta, which, in Roman days, first saw the march northward of the legions, then the race southward of the barbarians. We motorists and bikers fall somewhere in between.

The road climbs to meet a sudden plateau filled with rolling grass-lands and lovely red-roofed villages. Churches punctuate the landscape in every direction, for these are very Catholic Alps. This Tyrolean dream—the Mieming Plateau—stretches on for several kilometers, the tall mountains to its south and north like lines of stone watchtowers.

Once past the plateau, the Fernstein Castle, a massive turreted stone affair looming over medieval dwellings, nestles in a gorge. Unexpectedly, the road then leads down into an Alpine valley, its par-ticularity three ponies in a field standing stock-still as if flash frozen. After that, the climbing begins in earnest and swaying valleys below grow smaller and smaller as the gray rock of the mountains looms closer. But the road is exceedingly good—it has to be, as long-haul truckers use it—and the Fern Pass arrives in no time. The view to the north is dominated by the fearsome Zugspitze, an angry-looking limestone behemoth standing on the border of Germany and Austria. A triangular massif with spiky summits, its easternmost peak (2,962 meters) is the highest point in Germany. Doubtless, my Irish acquain-tance at Grindelwald would characterize it as the approach to Mor-dor, so sinister is its appearance. I contemplate it in silence as a grilled ham-and-cheese sandwich is placed before me—an event causing an eruption at a neighboring table occupied by four unilingual Britons, who begin desperately gesticulating to the waitress in my direction.

Next I turn westward and watch with relief in the rearview mir-ror as the Zugspitze monster begins shrinking. Between the towns of Reutte and Füssen, I cross into Germany. The aspect of the coun-tryside changes. Scenic rumpled green pastures and gullies compete for attention with nearby forested foothills and the occasional needle peak in the distance. I have been forewarned, but I recognize the land-scape near Füssen immediately. It was here that an iconic movie scene was filmed: Steve McQueen's motorcycle chase in *The Great Escape*. In the sequence, he tries unsuccessfully to jump the double barbed-wire fence to Switzerland, which, of course, does not border Füssen—just as Salzburg, which the von Trapps of *The Sound of Music* leave to climb a mountain and descend the next day into freedom, lies 370 kilometers from Switzerland. No matter, the McQueen countryside has remained beautiful and bucolic a half century on.

Its beauty attracted another admirer, King Ludwig II of Bavaria. In the second half of the nineteenth century, he drained his personal treasury to construct a personal Xanadu here. As a child, dreamy Ludwig liked to play with his cousin Sisi, later to become the empress assassinated on the shores of Lake Geneva. When the prince attained manhood and ascended to the throne, he gave his fantasies free rein. A friend and fanatic of Richard Wagner, he decided to set the compos-er's medieval phantasmagoria in stone. The result was called Schloss Neuschwanstein (New Swan Stone Castle). It is a huge fairy-tale structure perched on a crag with stupendous views. Of the dozen or so rooms completed before Ludwig's death in 1886—the plan called for two hundred rooms—their pastiche of Romanesque, medieval, and Byzantine causes what can only be called architectural indigestion. It is understandable why we borrowed the words *kitsch* and *ersatz* from their language—obviously the Germans got there first.

Neuschwanstein, a place with no context or content, is one of Germany's principal tourist attractions, a Disneyland without the rides. On this day it is thronged, as usual, with visitors, includ-ing me. The wait for the obligatory guided tour is long, giving me ample occasion to wonder what the hell Ludwig was think-ing. He was living in a very dynamic country in a very dynamic time—instead of embracing them, he drifted off into sterile medievalism, a Wagnerian wank. He lived alone—after breaking off his engagement to Sisi's younger sister—and mooned for a time that never was, the very acme of the incurable Romantic. Now thought to have been firmly in the closet—there is no record of mistresses, just a succession of close male friendships—Ludwig enthusiastically dilapidated his fortune on building projects. Linderhof Castle, also in Bavaria, is a French rococo gem built in the style of Louis XV. But it was that French king's predecessor, Louis XIV, who provided the inspiration. Taking his cue from the "Sun King," Ludwig styled himself as the "Moon King." In Linderhof's formal gardens, he ordered built a Venus Grotto, a replication of Capri's Blue Grotto, to which he would be rowed in the moonlight as electric lights—then a novelty—changed the colors of his fantasy cove. He rode around the castle's environs in an eighteenth-century carriage, complete with coachmen in eighteenth-century livery, distributing largesse to a delighted peasantry.

Many other grandiose projects were conceived. A replica of the Palace of Versailles, only larger, was partly completed on an island. But Ludwig's aesthetic ambitions outran his bank account. When, at last, in 1886 he turned to the Bavarian parliament to subsidize his building craze, an uproar ensued. Within days after the lawmakers had him adjudged insane and deposed him, Ludwig was found dead in the waist-deep water of a lake. Coincidence? Although no water was found in his lungs, his demise was deemed a drowning.

The route northward stretches through beautiful farmland, not at all mountainous, but I have miles to go before I sleep. This is, nonetheless, the *Deutsche Alpenstrasse*, as well as the *Romantische Strasse*, but it really is the Excess Strasse. Buttoned-down Austria has given way to blaring Bavaria. The people are louder and they take up more space. The famed "too-muchness" of Germany hits you in the face.

The villages traversed do not pass quietly. One has gigantic wooden carved likenesses of bears and other wildlife waving at the passersby. Another sports sculptures of a truly awful confection: metallic and rusted boxes, like discarded sardine tins for a giant, fenced off by wire mesh. And everywhere, cow statues striped in the red, black, and yellow of the German flag, announcing dairy shops. It's as if the inhabitants of this pastoral paradise were embarrassed by the beauty of their surroundings.

I make a detour to Wieskirche and its pilgrimage Church of the Scourged Savior, a noted rococo masterpiece that apparently no one in the area must miss. From the outside, the church looks white, plain, and unassuming. Inside is another story. To enter this sanctuary is to enter a wedding cake. Every vaulting, wall recess, and workable space has been covered with colorful figurative painting. Elaborate statuary emerges from walls, and brilliant white pillars covered in swirling stucco hold up the kaleidoscopic ceiling. The effect is dizzying. I am brought to my senses at the rear of the nave when a man in his seventies puts his thumb and middle finger into his mouth and emits a high-pitched whistle. Everyone turns to him, looking for the dog. He does it again, angrily—a trim, mean fellow resembling a retired U-boat captain. At the third summons, a flustered matron rushes to join him, nodding meekly. The two dozen of us in the church collectively shake our heads—theirs is not the ideal marriage.

The next stop promises more excess. I enter the narrow valley of the River Ammer. At its southern end, a distinctive mountain stands alone, looking somewhat like an old man with hunched shoulders. This height, called the Kofel, overlooks a supernova of tourism: the town of Oberammergau. There is an Unterammergau nearby, but the poor place is outshone by its world-famous twin. *Gau*, I learn, is an old

German word for an administrative district, now outdated, so the more renowned town could be styled, in English, as Upper Ammershire.

Every ten years, Oberammergau plays host to the *Passionsspiel*, or Passion Play. The tradition dates from the seventeenth century, when the villagers, fearing the plague, promised God to reenact Christ's crucifixion if He would spare their lives. Apparently, God agreed to the deal, and the townspeople have been staging the play ever since. Heavyweight theatrical professionals from Munich descend on the town to lend a hand, and the *Passionsspielhaus*, an enormous theater at the edge of town, regularly sells out years in advance.

As might be imagined, the town itself is a riot of piety and commerce. One of its long-standing specialties is woodcarving, so a profusion of shops selling statuary of all sizes awaits inspection. Whether you're in the market for the Blessed Virgin Mary or for a goofy-looking wooden squirrel, this is the place for you. Adding to the sensory overload is another of the town's particularities, *Lüftlmalerei*— decorative frescoes on the façades of houses and businesses. As this is Bavaria, these artworks are anything but muted. Large, loud, colorful, attention-grabbing, but not without touches of whimsy, these paintings—depicting devotional scenes, peasant life, even fairy tales—give the visitor to Oberammergau the impression of having walked into an open-air graphic novel. We tourists wander about distractedly, bumping into each other. At last I find a café terrace, plop down in a chair, and order a glass of red wine—a way of paying my respect to the host of the *Passionsspiel*.

The town will not be hosting me, though. On learning its hotels are fully booked, I drive around the Kofel and head south to the regional capital, the twin cities of Garmisch-Partenkirchen—or, as they are known to the smart ski set, Gapa. Partenkirchen's Ludwigstrasse—

part of the Via Claudia Augusta—displays a fondness for *Lüftlmalerei* as extravagant as Oberammergau's. I find a pizzeria and take a seat. My waiter, whom I'm surprised to discover is a Neapolitan, explains to me, "Italy is a good place to visit; Germany is a good place to work."

He nods sadly and goes to fetch my pizza. When he returns, I ask him one last question: What is that monstrous mountain on the southern horizon?

"The Zugspitze," he replies.

ON THE WESTERN OUTSKIRTS of Partenkirchen stands an old stadium, built in the muscular art deco style in vogue in the 1930s. In truth, a more accurate description would call it Fascist. In 1936, with Germany then in thrall to Hitlerian madness, Garmisch-Partenkirchen hosted the Winter Olympics (Berlin got the Summer Games of that year). This stadium witnessed the opening and closing ceremonies one snowy February long ago.

The stadium building houses a small museum with an exhibit called "The Dark Side of the Medal." The first thing one sees on entering is a yellow-and-black swastika medallion encircled by the words *JUDEN UNERWÜNSCHT* (Jewry Undesirable, or Jews Not Welcome). These medallions were attached to road signs on many German byways, including in Bavaria. When the head of the International Olympic Committee, a Belgian, visited Garmisch-Partenkirchen prior to the Winter Games, he was upset to see such signs and forced Hitler to have them taken down. (They were put back up after the Games.) He also mentioned seeing road signs at dangerous curves telling Jews that they were exempt from taking precautions, anti-Semitic black humor at its darkest.

The exhibition itself presents photographs from the event, and accompanying texts explain how the Games were hijacked for feel-good pro-Fascism purposes. Not all the athletes were taken in, though: One striking shot shows three distinctly unhappy ski jumpers on the medals podium flanked by an official giving the Nazi salute. A projection room screens "Youth of the World," a Nazi newsreel, coproduced by Paramount and Fox. The film opens with a bucolic evocation of Garmisch-Partenkirchen, before ascending to capture terrifying if not revolutionary (for the 1930s) aerial *Bergfilm* footage taken above the tree line, showing avalanches and forbidding rockfaces. I am put in mind of the scary opening mountain shots of *The Sound of Music*. That idle thought dissipates when we descend through a cloud into the valley and the Olympic stadium. On the reviewing stand in a driving snowstorm is a crowd of dignitaries, among them a chatty Adolf Hitler and a positively giddy Joseph Goebbels. We cut to the parading athletes, most of whom give the Olympic salute, which, in this setting, looks uncomfortably close to a *Sieg Heil* arm stretch. The American delegation, whose passage we do not see, was the only one not to lower its flag before the reviewing stand. Mercifully, we eventually leave the inevitable shots of adoring crowds saluting their Führer to focus on the feats of the athletes. Clearly, this gathering was a militaristic cornucopia of propaganda, a show that should have been a huge embarrassment for the Olympic movement. Not so: Somewhat unbelievably, in 1939— *after* the Nazi annexation of Czechoslovakia and *Kristallnacht*—the IOC awarded the 1940 Winter Olympics to Garmisch-Partenkirchen. They were never held. One wonders whether the grandees of the IOC had any regrets about who lost the war.

I try to cleanse my mind of the images seen in the museum by taking secondary roads westward. I pass a mountain pleasingly called

Wank, then enter a narrow valley with fastidiously arranged haystacks alternating with black, yellow, and red cow statues. At a hamlet named Wallgau, I turn into a tiny road that I have to squint to see on my map. The route follows the northern bank of the River Isar, which will eventually flow through the great city of Munich. The Karwendel Alps tower in limestone majesty on both sides of the silver waters. Great birds of prey soar high above in the thermals and kayakers race down the waterway. There are no cars, no villages, just a kind of pristine natural beauty not usually associated with European landscapes. At last, a settlement is reached: Vorderiss, a collection of wooden houses once favored by King Ludwig on his many hunting expeditions.

The road leads to the Achen Pass. The approach and descent to this low pass is guarded by stands of conifers, so the motorist can drive unperturbed by the views. I am delighted to be passed by a soufflé of French bikers, who again lower their right legs in a gesture of Gallic gratitude when I move over to the right to let them roar by me. What follows is a succession of villages in a mountainous sylvan setting, paradise for hikers and cyclists with the legs of Vegas showgirls. At Wildbad Kreuth, I slow to look at the old spa buildings, knowing that two Russian tsars and one Austrian emperor came here to take the waters. The road then moseys down to the teal expanse of the Tegernsee, one of Bavaria's loveliest Alpine lakes, surrounded by mountains of modest height. The proportions are very pleasing to the eye. Given the aesthetics, it may be no coincidence that the town of Tegernsee, situated on the eastern lakeshore, hosts a *Bergfilm* festival every year.

The major town of the area is Bad Wiessee, a sleepy resort in the midday sun. I wander down a path toward the lake, noting that I am the only white-haired person here—and there are many of us—not

using Nordic walking poles to propel me forward. The otherwise
serene place click-click-clicks like an old-time ticker-tape machine.
I pause in front of a glass display case, celebrating Bad Wiessee's
twin town, Dourdan, in the Ile-de-France near Paris. Pictures of a
French medieval festival—Dourdan has one of the best-preserved
thirteenth-century castles in Europe—wallpaper the backdrop to a
box (empty, one hopes) of *pavés de Dourdan*, the delicious chocolate specialty of the town. Bad Wiessee and Dourdan seem to have
enthusiastically embraced their twinning, first established in 1963
and formed as part of a Continental movement to foster friend-
ship between former adversaries, in particular the French and the
Germans.

Yet Bad Wiessee's lasting notoriety lies not in international relations but in domestic affairs. Or, to be blunt, in intra-German frat-
ricide. The town played host to what has come to be known as The
Night of the Long Knives, which means, alas, that we are back with
the jackbooted fellows of Garmisch-Partenkirchen. In the predawn
hours of 30 June 1934, Hitler, Goebbels, Rudolf Hess, and a detach-
ment of the *Schutzstaffel* (Protective Echelon, or SS) stormed a resort
hotel here and arrested the holidaying leaders of the *Sturm Abteilung*
(Assault Division, or SA), brownshirted storm troopers and street
thugs whose growing influence, independence, and power worried the
Nazi leadership in Berlin—as well as the regular German army and
the country's capitalist elite. The SA's leader, Ernst Röhm, as vicious
a brute as any produced by the Nazi movement, had taken to criti-
cizing Hitler for ignoring the *socialism* in National Socialism. Hitler
personally arrested his old friend—Röhm had been at his side during
the 1923 Beer Hall Putsch in Munich—and had him shot the next day.
Dozens more were later summarily executed, including perceived

enemies who had nothing to do with the SA. Overnight, Germans awoke to the realization that extrajudicial killing by the Nazis would henceforth go unpunished and that the man they had democratically elected their leader the year before was now an absolute dictator. After Bad Wiessee, Germany entered its darkest hours.

I realize with a jolt that today—30 June—is precisely eighty years to the day after the historic occurrence here. The hotel where the drama took place is now shuttered. It closed in 2011, apparently to make way for a casino development that has yet to break ground. I take a few desultory pictures of the banal lakeside chalet complex, vaguely disappointed. What was I expecting? If there is a historical plaque marking the site's infamy, I do not see it.

Yet in a larger sense, it could be argued that Romanticism met its final death here, that what began on the shores of Lake Geneva ended on the shores of the Tegernsee. The diabolical offspring of German Romanticism—the Nazis with their ill-digested Wagner and Nietzsche and their concomitant cult of death—began eating their own at Bad Wiessee. Dr. Frankenstein's monster turned out to be wearing a swastika.

The early proponents of Romanticism—Rousseau, Byron, and many others—would have been aghast at what their aesthetic revolution eventually spawned. In its heyday—the first half of the nineteenth century—Romanticism could be seen as a force for good, liberating imaginations through the embrace of the irrational. Nature was revered, and the past—particularly the Middle Ages—was fondly reinvented. Politically, it fostered the development of national sentiment. Spurred by the Alps and their encouragement of the sublime, Romanticism placed emotion in a bear hug.

Although Romanticism went out of fashion—replaced by Realism, especially in literature—it managed to linger in the imagination. The effect of this lingering could be innocuous, as in the erotic charge still felt on beholding unforgiving mountain scenery. One need only remember the couples clutching and caressing each other in the aerial tramway on its way up to the Aiguille du Midi in Chamonix. Yet the lingering of Romantic sentiment could also be destructive. In Germany, Romanticism in its dotage rotted and turned nasty. All of the aspects listed above—about the movement as a force for good—have their flip side as well. Embracing the irrational can lead to desperately dangerous thinking. Nature can be overidealized, and a reinvented past can be twisted out of recognition to serve a dark purpose. Nationalism, if excessive, can lead to xenophobia and war. And emotion can chase reason out into the wilderness.

It has been argued, most notably by historian Modris Eksteins in his brilliant *Rites of Spring: The Great War and the Birth of the Modern Age* (1989), that the Nazis were quintessential Moderns, enamored of technology and the irrational. The wrecking ball that was World War I caused a lot of nineteenth-century certainties to collapse—to wit, a belief in progress, in God, and in Western cultural superiority. Moral codes came unbuttoned, traditional sexual roles were shaken up, class distinctions faded. Peering into this cauldron, many on the Left divined the evil of capitalism and embraced Communism. On the Right, a curious hybrid emerged, one that plucked inspiration from the past and the future. Romanticism coexisted with the Modern.

For all their autobahns and state-of-the-art aircraft, the Nazis fashioned a resolutely Romantic viewpoint. Susan Sontag observed that the Third Reich was "the grotesque fulfillment—and betrayal—of German Romanticism." A mythologized past for the *Volk* (the nation), consisting of virtuous and pure peasants and laborers, was set in a state of nature polluted only by non-Aryans. The cult of death, so prevalent in Romantic works of art, pervaded Nazi ideology, even down to the death heads on their uniforms. *Bergfilm*, derided as mawkish by bourgeois film critics, made the chest of the Nazi "New Man" swell with pride. And nationalism, Romanticism's political spearhead, took on a demonic dimension under the Nazis, with the nations of eastern Europe thought worthy only of enslavement in an ever-expanding *Lebensraum* (living space) for the German people.

There was no finer observer of the historic subversion of German Romanticism than the late Italian film director Luchino Visconti, as noted in cinema expert David Huckvale's *Visconti and the German Dream*. Visconti's *Ludwig* chronicles the life of Ludwig II, the Romantic builder of Neuschwanstein. It is no coincidence that Adolf Hitler counted himself one of King Ludwig's most ardent admirers. In *The Damned* (1969), Visconti portrays the hellish descent into decadence of a wealthy German family during the Nazi years. In his reimagining of The Night of the Long Knives in the film, hundreds of SA arrive in Bad Wiessee and proceed to get riotously drunk. As the night wears on, a homosexual orgy takes place, while a lone SA in the bar sings the "Liebestod" (love-death) aria from Wagner's opera *Tristan und Isolde*. In the opera, Isolde sings the aria over the body of her dead lover. Thus, in this barroom performance the apex of Romanticism meets its nadir. The SS then arrive, hustle dozens of naked young men into courtyards and dining rooms, and turn their machine guns on them. In point of historical fact, only two men were shot at Bad Wiessee—a senior official found in bed with his eighteen-year-old boy lover—while the rest were herded into the hotel's basement laundry room to await transport to Munich and almost certain death. No matter, in Visconti's vision a worldview is being executed here. However grotesquely distorted that worldview was in its Nazi iteration, it—Romanticism—could be said to have been born and to have died in the mountains.

The Alps giveth and the Alps taketh away.

THE ROAD LEADING AWAY from the Tegernsee promises more Bavarian beauty. At the lake's northern end stands the picturesque village of Gmund. The church here has a sturdy white steeple topped by a black ball, like a pearl onion. I decide that today I will ignore the horror stories of the 1930s and concentrate instead on the pleasures to be found in the meeting of man and mountain. With this in mind, I forgo the temptation to peer at Heinrich Himmler's former house in Gmund. It is in private hands, so any attempt to snap pictures would result only in postcards from the hedge. Besides, there are websites for that.

Still, I can't shake the feeling that I am doing a disservice to my Bavarian hosts, especially given the Nazi associations of my ultimate destination, Berchtesgaden. The Germany that I have visited many times is a welcoming and tolerant place, far removed from a nightmarish past almost beyond the horizon of living memory. And the Germans whom I have met in France and America have all been decent, principled people, vehement in their belief in the primacy of human rights. Why rub their noses in the sins of their forefathers?

Yet mention of the nightmare has to be made, I conclude as I drive westward from the Tegernsee along the *Deutsche Alpenstrasse*. As noted before, a distinct leitmotiv of the Bavarian Alps, vis-à-vis human geography, is excess. Village, church, castle, and king here—

all exhibit a penchant for the overstated and the outlandish. In physical geography, the mountains here are far lower than their terrifically tall cousins in Switzerland and France, but the people living in their valleys and on their slopes are far more exuberant, as if making up for their homeland's Alpine modesty. When that exuberance turns to the dark side, as it did eighty years ago, the result is not mere unpleasantness but utter madness, of a kind we hope never to see again. Nonetheless, it is part of the region's pageant of excess.

From Gmund, the road rises through fields dotted with roofed hayracks. These give way to the outlying foothills of the Mangfall range of the Alps. The road steepens until it reaches the lake town of Schliersee. Off to the right, the waters gleam bright blue under a sky of the same color. The road westward then twists and turns upward until a massif of three peaks rises directly ahead of me. The pair on the left, table-topped, have had their summits sliced off by some heavenly cleaver. The peak on the right is the fair sister of the trio, a graceful triangular pinnacle of stone enrobed in a cloak of the deepest green.

I go around this threesome to enter a broad upland valley walled in by soft and gentle mountains. At a village named Bayrischzell, I stop and walk down to a coffee shop/bakery. A group of Bavarian burghers sits on a terrace outdoors, their tables groaning under individual servings of creamy cake cubes the size of cinder blocks. I look away from this latest excess to take in the view. The trio massif has its back to us in the distance, preceded by a long mountain meadow made white by a profusion of Queen Anne's lace. I raise my phone to take a picture, but a large fellow steps in and blocks the view. The back of his black T-shirt is adorned with a grinning death's head above the words GOOD EVENING BITCHES.

After this Bavarian sight, the road narrows and rises abruptly through a series of switchbacks until the Sudelfeld Pass is reached in the trees. By the roadside, a very large bratwurst of German bikers disport themselves in the sunlight, whipping their long hair like Spartans at Thermopylae. The ride down is surprisingly hair-raising. Before each switchback stands a sign with a motorcycle graphic and an announcement that rumble strips lie ahead. Apparently the highway patrols here are tired of fishing lifeless bikers out of the trees far below on the valley floor. I later learn that the Sudelfeld, although only 1,123 meters in elevation, is the Bavarian pass most favored by two-wheeled road warriors, given its level of difficulty.

Beyond a town called Wall, an astonishing perspective opens up. In the foreground lies a green valley punctuated with hillocks, to be followed by hills, then foothills, then emerald mountains backed by the soaring gray stone walls of the Austrian Alps. It is a jaw-dropping sight, a colossal 3-D Romantic engraving stretching for scores of kilometers. Such is its beauty that I forget to be scared.

Eventually I rejoin the valley of the River Inn. At a charming, over-decorated town called Oberaudorf, a smorgasbord of bikers sprawls at outdoor beer gardens swilling from tankards suitable for weightlifters. As in most Alpine towns, the hotels here sport unilingual English signs that proclaim BIKERS WELCOME! At Oberaudorf that message has been heeded.

The dread *UMLEITUNG* sign appears. Mercifully the detour message does not come accompanied by mysterious initials, as it sometimes does in France. The only other sign in view announces HEART ATTACK PAINTBALL, complete with a helpful directional arrow. I go the other way. Unexpectedly, the *Deutsche Alpenstrasse* suddenly umleitungs me all the way into Austria, another country—to Kufstein, the second largest city of Tyrol. A massive medieval fortress dominates the town, which seems otherwise to be a smokestack convention. Unwilling to desert my Bavarian dreamscape even for a few moments, I head to the autobahn for a quick hop back to Germany. It occurs to me what a relief it is that almost all the customs houses I've seen on this trip have been deserted, that I never have to wait at borders, that it is clear sailing all the way. When I was growing up, such effortless passage had been the norm between my native Canada and the United States. Now that has all changed, with endless backups caused by unsmiling and suspicious border guards. Europe has gone in the other direction, leaving the New World looking very much like what the Old used to be.

On the entrance ramp stands a figure with his thumb stuck out, the first hitchhiker I have seen thus far. He is irresistible, looking like Santa Claus on a budget holiday: white beard, red face, and green suspenders holding up tattered trousers. I have to stop. He gets in.

I introduce myself first, in English. He replies, "I'm Reinhard, the last of the hippies."

I appraise him. He could very well be the last one, as he appears to be in his late sixties, early seventies.

He explains that he has been all over the world, taking pride in his status as the last stoner out of Afghanistan before the Soviet invasion. Reinhard has a place to stay in his hometown of Graz, Austria, but he prefers life on the road, on a permanent magical mystery tour.

"Where are you going?" he asks.

"Berchtesgaden."

"Sounds good!"

The frontier flashes by. I give voice to my thoughts about the advantages of a borderless continent and the dismal developments in post-9/11 North America.

Reinhard smiles at me. His look tells me that he thinks he is talking to someone as mindlessly sunny as Voltaire's Candide.

"Just wait for the next crisis," he chides. "Then you'll see."

I take this to be typical European pessimism, until the migrant crisis of the following summer proves Reinhard absolutely right. The delicate borderless framework of the Schengen Agreement, approved in 1985 and fully implemented in 1995, strained to the breaking point in Europe as refugees headed northward overland from the Mediterranean. Then terror attacks in the fall and the spring put it in intensive care.

After about a half hour of guilty expressway pleasure, we rejoin the *Deutsche Alpenstrasse* at Bernau. Reinhard has given me an entertainingly opinionated overview of his homeland. What does he think of Tyrol? "Too Catholic." Salzburg? "Too bourgeois."

I mention that I plan on visiting Klagenfurt, in the southern region of Carinthia.

"Carinthia!" he exclaims. "Oh no, God no, don't go there. They're all a bunch of Fascists."

The villages in the Chiemgau region of Bavaria parade past, a succession of tiny gems nestled at the foot of the mountains. Reinhard's mention of Fascists reminds me of my misgivings about spending so much of this stage of my journey thinking about the Nazis. I tell him as much.

He remains silent for a long moment. "The Bavarians like life. They like to laugh and sing. They are my cousins," he says, before continuing. "In the north they are cold people, very hard." I am put in mind of the U-boat captain in the church whistling for his wife. "I will travel everywhere," Reinhold concludes, "everywhere but Saxony. In Saxony I would get beaten up, maybe even killed. Too many neo-Nazis, they hate hippies like me."

He lets this sink in.

"Are you serious?" I ask at last.

"Yes!"

His piercing blue gaze confirms his conviction.

We travel along in silence for a long moment. At a pretty village called Reit im Winkl, I pull over. I cannot resist the name. Reinhard and I agree to meet back at the car in half an hour. He fires up a spliff and then drifts farther into the parking lot.

On the town's main street, horse-drawn carriages festooned with flowers take visitors for leisurely meanders through the old quarter. In a square, a tall *Maibaum* (Maypole), painted the white and blue of Bavaria, stretches high into the sky. It has several dozen silhouetted figures attached to horizontal tabs, each depicting a traditional craft or trade. Reit im Winkl takes obvious pride in its past and would not like to see its Maypole stolen. That was a fairly common occurrence in the past: A neighboring village would steal a neighbor's pole then demand a ransom, usually beer and sausages. But sometimes the theft went well beyond the quaint. In 2004, a group of pranksters aboard a helicopter swiped the *Maibaum* planted on the peak of the fearsome Zugspitze. This, despite a directive from the park manager to his staff, urging them "to protect the pole as if it were their own eyeballs." As ransom, the thieves demanded four sandwiches, four train tickets, and an unspecified amount of beer.

I notice an announcement on a display board extolling the virtues of the *Hindenburghutte*. Wondering what a Hindenburg Hut is, I push open the doors of the tourist office.

A young woman tells me the Hut is a mountain hotel-restaurant with many amenities and activities, winter and summer, and that no, she does not know why it is named after Paul von Hindenburg, field marshal during World War I and president of Germany in the 1920s and 1930s. Maybe he came here once? I also learn that Reit im Winkl, thanks to a microclimate, is one of the snowiest places in all of Germany and that there is a four-kilometer-long natural toboggan run starting at the *Hindenburghutte*. I think fondly of one of my favorite authors, Robert Louis Stevenson, who loved tobogganing as much as his friend Arthur Conan Doyle loved skiing. Given the tourist treasure expended at snowy Reit, it is doubtful that its inhabitants indulge in the Bavarian ritual of *Aperschnalzen*, or competitive whipcracking. Contests usually take place in February and are thought to have originated in pagan times as a ceremony to whip away the snow. *Aper* is a Bavarian word for a snow-free place, while *schnalzen* means "flicking." The town fathers of Reit would have to discourage such economic self-destructiveness.

As for the town fathers, do they put up the Maypole? I tell the hostess that it appears to be a difficult task.

She looks me in the eye and says, "In the spring, when the time comes, the strongest young men of the village erect the pole."

I watch as her full lips form a pre-Freudian smile and she moves off to torment the next tourist.

A MELLOWED REINHARD and I plow through the trees and mountains on our way eastward. When we cross a low pass entertainingly called *Schwarzbachwachtsattel*, Berchtesgaden is not far off. I rouse my snoozing companion and tell him that we have almost arrived. Where does he stay on his travels?

"Cemeteries. Sometimes churches."

I happen to know something about the old cemetery in the center of Berchtesgaden. I tell Reinhard the sad story of Toni Kurz, the native of Berchtesgaden who dangled to death on the north face of the Eiger. He is buried there. So is Hitler's sister, Paula.

When we near the cemetery, which stands behind a Franciscan church, Reinhard signals for me to stop. He grabs his rucksack from the backseat, gets out of the car, and executes a wistful wave. With that, the last of the hippies rounds a corner and disappears from view.

Berchtesgaden turns out to be diverting. The first thing I notice at the cultural center is an exhibition devoted to the actress Romy Schneider, who spent her early school years here. To my relief, the only Nazi gewgaws on offer are books devoted to the town's dark past. There are no postcards of the Duke and Duchess of Windsor visiting here in 1937, or of Neville Chamberlain's ill-starred sojourn the following year. In the main square near the old cathedral and town hall, a striking mural painted in the 1920s honors the dead of World War I. It was repainted—deNazified—in the 1950s; its frozen action figures, soldiers and peasants, serve as the town's permanent antiwar billboard. In the arcades are plaques listing the names of the Berchtesgaden men who fell in both world wars. The number of names, in this region of a hundred thousand inhabitants, is truly horrifying. As if to underscore this sentiment, a sculpture exhibit nearby features standing skeleton figures, fashioned from black metallic scrap, aggressively pointing mean-looking machine guns at passersby. Bavarian excess, once again.

As a totem of a sinister past, Berchtesgaden differs from Garmisch-Partenkirchen. There, the Olympic Games served, despite the propaganda distortions connected to them, as a celebration of youth and, at base, an athletic competition. But Berchtesgaden played host to the heart and soul of the Hitlerian project. The Führer and his henchmen spent more time here than they did in Berlin, and the decisions made near this sleepy mountain town led to the deaths of millions. The region may now brand itself *Die Perle der Alpen* (The Pearl of the Alps), but many generations will have to come and go for its historical infamy to be erased.

Breakfast at my hotel is taken in a sunny room rendered sepulchral by pairs of elderly German husbands and wives not talking to each other. I spear several pig products while reading my guidebook to The Eagle's Nest, Hitler's aerie in the mountains. The cynosure of Nazism was not in the town of Berchtesgaden but in the province of the same name, at a place called Obersalzberg.

The road to Obersalzberg is steep and twisted, so much so that a waffle of Belgian bikers expends five frustrating minutes to overtake me completely. We climb 365 meters in three kilometers. The parking lot at our destination is a sea of German tourists. When I pull in beside one family, my French plates inspire baleful glares. Already queasy at being here, I try smiling at them to appeal to their better angels. It does not work.

The town of Obersalzberg no longer exists. In 1945, British Lancaster bombers and, subsequently, dynamite-laden American GIs, took care of it. In its heinous heyday, the settlement grew to scores of buildings, including Hitler's house, the Berghof; the homes of Martin Bormann, Hermann Göring, Rudolf Hess, and Albert Speer; plus an SS barracks, a hotel and bar, a kindergarten, a theater, a brothel—all the amenities necessary to make Obersalzberg a self-contained complex from which a drug-addled Hitler could govern without the nuisance of expert advice from the technocrats in Berlin. He could just kick back at the Berghof and listen for hours as Martin Bormann, his lapdog-turned-Svengali, lectured him on the niceties of terror, murder, war, and hatred.

In 1937, a decision was made to build another structure, this one eight hundred meters higher in elevation than the Nazi compound at Obersalzberg. Bormann supervised all aspects of the construction. The structure was sited on a rocky summit ridge known as the Kehlstein—hence its name, Kehlsteinhaus. (The English and French moniker for the place, The Eagle's Nest, was coined as a joke by a visiting French ambassador.) The whole project—tunnels, approach road, infrastructure, the chalet itself—took just thirteen months to complete, a staggering engineering feat celebrated in the visitors' center gift shop. Bormann, knowing the inefficiencies of Nazi slave-labor practices, paid the workmen handsomely, at more than twice the average day rate, and supplied them with good food, women, and decent lodgings. The place was officially inaugurated on 20 April 1939, Hitler's fiftieth birthday. The international press was invited to be overawed at the ribbon-cutting, but not the German media. Hitler kept the existence of his mountain *folie* (which cost, in today's currency, 150 million euros) a secret from his beloved *Volk*, not wishing to tarnish his carefully cultivated image as a man of the people.

The crush of tourists is such that we are issued time-stamped tickets for the bus ride up to the Kehlsteinhaus. I and the hostile German family from the parking lot have to cool our heels for about an hour before the moment of delivery arrives. I board the bus, well appointed with panoramic windows, and sit across the aisle from an English couple. Our driver is the late Bob Hoskins. The Englishman studies the stamped ticket in admiration and says, "They wouldn't do this in Italy."

His wife counters, "They wouldn't do it in England, either!"

She and I smile; he does not.

The recorded multilingual spiel informs us that we are to travel 6.6 kilometers up one of the most beautiful mountain roads in Europe. Steep and scary it most certainly is. At the mother of all hairpin turns, nervous laughter breaks out among the passengers. Prior to the banalization of air travel, the views out our windows were reserved for the gods. The depth of the abyss is amazing. I close my eyes tightly. *It's not that I'm afraid of heights*, I'm afraid of Nazis.

The coach reaches its destination and we walk into a large plaza seemingly suspended in space. We are then directed to a 120-meter-long tunnel cut into the mountain, illuminated by pompous sconces, before turning right into a domed stone chamber—part Pantheon, part *Raiders of the Lost Ark*. The brass doors of an elevator await. We are then whisked up a further 124 meters into the Kehlsteinhaus.

The interior of the aerie is something of an anticlimax. There are tables set out everywhere for diners. Even the famed, off-white octagonal room—designed to wow foreign dignitaries—looks more like a college dining hall nowadays. Hallways, Hitler's study, Eva Braun's hideaway—all are smothered in wooden tables awaiting steins and sauerkraut. Even with this screen of foodie extravagance, the visitor eventually notices that the chalet is stupendously impractical as a seat of government. There were no bedrooms, cabinet meetings were never held here, and Hitler, an acrophobe prone to altitude sickness, came up to the Kehlsteinhaus just over a dozen times, and then only for short visits, preferring the terra firma of his Berghof far below. In short, it was a colossal waste of money. During the war, the chalet became the personal precinct of Eva Braun, who enjoyed sunning herself on its many outdoor terraces. (American soldiers on leave in the postwar era did the same, as the house was a rest and recreation center for them until it was handed back to the Bavarian government in 1952.) In the only notable occurrence to have taken place here in wartime, the wedding reception of Braun's sister was held in the Kehlsteinhaus's octagonal room on 5 June 1944—the eve of D-day.

Outside, the aerie is an entirely different story. The views take in a circus of mountains in Austria and Germany as far as the eye can see. And the eye can see far—more than 150 kilometers on a clear day. Today is one such day. Can I be moved by this view, knowing the identity of the hideous owner of the Kehlsteinhaus? The mountains, I know, are blameless. I see the glacial lake of Königsee tucked in the valley thousands of meters below, a pearl of the Alps if ever there was one. Opposite, to the right, rises a mountain called Untersbergmassif, a limestone breadbox of menace. Just days earlier, it was the darling of the German-language sensationalist press. A spelunker in its Riesending Cave complex had been disabled by a rockfall a kilometer deep into the mountain and rescuers took almost ten days to extract the poor fellow. More benign are the Untersberg's associations with popular culture. It served as the arresting *Bergfilm* opening to *The Sound of Music*, with Julie Andrews warbling "The Hills Are Alive" in one of its mountain meadows (on the German side of the mountain, no less), and then as the escape route of the von Trapps in the film's closing sequence. More venerable are the local legends that have Holy Roman Emperor Frederick Barbarossa and/ or Charlemagne sleeping within the mountain.

Perhaps these associations can drown out Adolf. Perhaps not. I climb the hundred meters or so from the Kehlsteinhaus to a large iron cross planted atop the ridge. Although the Christian connections to this site are tenuous at best, the improved vista from this, the highest spot of the Kehlstein promontory, can inspire almost religious sentiment. Far, far away, puffy white clouds dance over the peaks, their shadows racing across rocky summits. At the green base of the circus of mountains, villages and towns can be made out, red and pink in the midday sun. The grandeur of the Alps is on display.

On heading to the elevator once back in the Kehlsteinhaus, I finally manage to find an exhibit that does not involve menus. To my dismay, it deals almost exclusively with the engineering prowess involved in constructing the chalet, opening the approach road, and getting water and electricity up the mountain, as if that were the only thing to contemplate at this place.

On the bus ride down, I don't want to attract derision by closing my eyes, so I read more from the guidebook. On its first page the author, Bernhard Frank, states baldly, "At a time of a resurgence of Neo-Nazism we want and must emphasize the tyranny of the Third Reich. The reader should on no account get the impression that the NS dictators on the Obersalzberg were the harmless and 'nice neighbours' of the local population." The explicit mention of Neo-Nazis puts me in mind of Reinhard's fear of visiting present-day Saxony, where harmless hippies like him have endured beatings. Yet the skirting of the obvious at the Kehlsteinhaus still rankles somewhat. Surely, the Bavarian government doesn't expect visitors to get their information on the site's Nazi past solely from a glossy guidebook purchased at a souvenir shop?

On my way back to the parking lot, I notice a handsome modern building off to the right, about a hundred meters distant. Directional signs point to the elongated two-story chalet, indicating that

the structure is the *Dokumentationszentrum Obersalzberg*. When I enter
by its glass doors, I realize that I have been wrong about Bavarian historical reticence, for this is a comprehensive museum about the Nazis
and their cruelties. Opened in 1999, the sixtieth anniversary of the
outbreak of war, the museum strikes me as a museum for Germans,
particularly Germans in high school, who doubtless take obligatory
class trips here to learn of their country's shameful past. Although
an English audioguide can be rented, the exhibits are exclusively in
German. My suspicions about its mission of political hygiene for the
young are confirmed when I later pull this from its website:

> The *Dokumentation Obersalzberg* fulfils its purpose with a
> permanent exhibition which is accompanied by special exhi-
> bitions, lectures and events as well as a comprehensive educa-
> tion programme. It serves to explain and discuss the National
> Socialist past. In this way it should be possible to counter old
> and new right-wing extremism which draws its appeal, espe-
> cially for young people, from the reactivation of ideological
> fictions and political slogans of National Socialism.

The deftly curated space opens with the travails of the locals. On
a video, an old woman relives "the circus" when Hitler came to the
Berghof in the early days. He arrived simply, with little security. (He
had come to Obersalzberg in the 1920s under the pseudonym of Herr
Wolf and wrote part of *Mein Kampf* here after his release from prison
for the failed Beer Hall Putsch.) "People lined the small country lanes,
hoping for a smile, a handshake," she remembers. "People wouldn't
wash their hands afterwards. Or they would collect gravel from where
he had trod. It was pathetic." The old-timer then goes on to detail

the expropriations brought about by Bormann in the mid-1930s when Obersalzberg became a giant building site. Her father was visited by Bormann and was told, "Either sell your farm or get sent to Dachau." His thirteen children prevailed upon him to sell.

From there the museum goes into a no-holds-barred presentation of Nazism, Hitler's dictatorship, and anti-Semitism, all accompanied by wrenching photographs of public hangings, trains headed to the death camps, maps, even a heartbreaking photo album of Auschwitz, open to a page showing the last moments of life for a group of women and children, milling about near a spinney of trees as if ready to picnic but in reality just instants from being ushered into the gas chamber. I am dumbstruck. There are no skeletons hiding in the German closet; they are all out there, like a punishing slap in the face. Other countries still hoard their skeletons—think of the Smithsonian *Enola Gay* controversy in the early 1990s—but Germany has chosen to own up to its past in the most public way possible. The Germans are grown-ups.

Toward the end of the exhibits stands the ultimate rogues' gallery. Photographic portraits of the men most responsible for the horrors of World War II and the Holocaust, accompanied by biographical notices detailing their misdeeds. The presentation of these bastards, on translucent glass panels, strikes me as a touch too tasteful, but that is the only discordant note in what has been a symphony of sickness. From there, a long passageway leads downward, lined by panels painstakingly presenting the events of the war chronologically. Interestingly, the curators make no attempt to disguise their disgust at the Allies' carpet-bombing campaign on German civilian targets in the closing years of the war, a campaign that many historians now consider a war crime. Apparently, what's good for the goose is good for the gander. The passageway then enters a labyrinth of underground bunkers, rooms, and corridors, a subterranean city hastily dug after the Battle of Stalingrad in 1943 intimated that the Nazi thousand-year Reich might have a much briefer shelf life. I do not stay long—a group of German tourists, all using Nordic walking poles as at Bad Wiessee, makes standing in the concrete bunker complex akin to passing time inside a popcorn-making machine.

Outside in the sunlight, I gun the Mégane downward, eager to get off the Nazi mountain. The last of Bavaria's excesses has proved the most distressing. I almost miss Neuschwanstein and Oberammergau.

9. Salzkammergut and the Grossglockner

———— ⊡ ————

SALZBURG IS THE MOST GLORIOUS salt lick in all of Europe. A city of passageways, yellow and pink pastel façades, then sudden squares of baroque splendor, the place inspires reverie even in the rain. I feel like buying a white wig. Ernst has rejoined me for this leg of my journey. We stroll the old town on the left bank of the River Salzach, its profusion of statuary, fountains, churches, mansions, and topiary-rich parks attributable to the wealth derived from the salt mines in the surrounding mountains—hence its name, Salzburg (Salt Fortress). Ruled for centuries by bishop-princes, who erected the gigantic medieval Hohensalzburg Castle on a hill overlooking the town, it was incorporated into the Habsburg holdings only in the early nineteenth century.

Architecture is not the city's only draw. Its musical heritage brings millions of visitors here every year. Salzburg was the birthplace and hometown of Wolfgang Amadeus Mozart, a fact that the city beats tourists over the head with. Mozart is everywhere in Salzburg, his face adorning every conceivable kind of knickknack. To walk the shopping streets is to slalom past life-size cardboard likenesses of him, propped in place before stores selling Mozart memorabilia. Costumed salesmen and saleswomen approach visitors with boxes of *Mozartkugeln*, dark chocolate balls with nougat and pistachio marzipan in their interior. Apparently these chocolates are a venerable tradition in the city, dating all the way back to 1890.

Then there are the von Trapps of musical and film fame. They serve as Salzburg's other mascot. A common sight here is a group of tourists, usually Japanese and American, being herded from one *Sound of Music* sight to the next. "This is where Liesl and Rolf kissed." "This is where Maria and the children sang, 'Do-Re-Mi.'" The group is then ushered onto a bus for a trip to the hinterland for more of the same, as Trappologist tour guides point out the inconsistencies between the real-life story and the movie. Even my guidebooks to Austria feel obliged to have sidebars relitigating the musical's distortions.

In the late afternoon we explore a less tony neighborhood on the left bank of the River Salzach. On passing a commuter rail station, where Salzburgers of modest means must go to travel home, away from the expensive center of town, we find ourselves in a weary crowd—the women wearing dirndl dresses, the men in dusty lederhosen and felt hats. No yodel is heard. These people are leaving the old city's land of tourist make-believe, where they pose as Alpine peasants in hotels, shops, restaurants, and horse-drawn carriages. Their shift is over, their smiles of *Herzlich Wilkommen* (a warm welcome) have vanished. They are a bedraggled lot, grimy and sweaty in the gray, muggy day.

Ernst declares that the producers of *The Sound of Music* were right to shoot their movie here. "The place is a movie set," he says, then indicates the commuters. "These guys are the extras."

Which is—and is not—true. For one thing, the city hosts a world-class music and theater festival in the summertime. Ever since its founding in 1920 by poet and dramatist Hugo von Hofmannsthal, theater and film director Max Reinhardt, and composer Richard Strauss, the five-week Salzburg Festival has remained a highlight of the European cultural calendar. In 2006, to celebrate Mozart's 250th birthday, it staged all twenty-two of his operatic works.

Salzburg is also home to several universities, which may account for the youthfulness of the people crowding the old streets. The city center, which was restored after suffering significant damage from repeated Allied bombing raids during World War II, remains one of Europe's most splendid baroque neighborhoods, seemingly all spires and domes. Its churches house extravagant profusions of painting and statuary. We enter the cathedral and see, to our surprise, several dozen people, kneeling alone and engaging in silent prayer.

"At least this is authentic," Ernst whispers in the candlelit dimness.

The sight of the faithful tempers our scorn for the city's commercialism. We take a pew in the back of the sanctuary and contemplate the elaborate stucco statuary and the colorful ceiling frescoes depicting the Passion of Christ. Even Zwinglian Ernst seems cowed into silence. On leaving the cathedral, we head toward the river, crossing a vast square called Residenzplatz. The reason for its name takes up one whole side of the square—the Salzburg Residenz, the former palace for the city's bishop-princes, soberly looks out over the expanse, its gray façade and three stories of windows giving no hint of its sumptuous interior, which now houses an art gallery. Mozart gave his first concert here, at age six.

We cross the Salzach and find our way to Steingasse. The baroque vanishes in favor of the medieval. This tiny, cobbled lane, once home to butchers, potters, and dyers (professions needing the waters of the nearby Salzach), also constituted the main trade route into and out of the city—a rather amazing reminder of how cramped urban life was in the Middle Ages. Today the lane is a quiet place, with children walking their bicycles into recessed doorways. A plaque indicates that Steingasse is the birthplace of Joseph Mohr, who in the early nineteenth century wrote the lyrics to the carol "Silent Night." Another building, at number 24, sports a red lantern and lettering that reads *LA MAISON DE PLAISIR*. This is the oldest operating brothel in Salzburg, dating back to Mozart's era.

We finish our tour near dusk at the Mirabell Gardens, a park with carefully trimmed topiary and formal flower beds laid out in the French fashion. Groups of statuary represent mythological figures— Aeneas, Paris, Pluto, Hercules, among them—and fountains abound. And, yes, the Mirabell's horse fountain is where Julie Andrews and her charges sing part of "Do-Re-Mi."

Dominating the park is the Mirabell Castle, a large yellow affair as big and baroque as the Salzburg Residenz. The original castle on this spot—it was entirely overhauled in the eighteenth century— was commissioned in 1606 by Prince-Archbishop Wolf Dietrich von Raitenau as a trysting spot for him and his mistress, Salome Alt, the beautiful daughter of a Salzburg merchant. When the pope refused to issue a dispensation allowing the smitten bishop to marry Alt, von Raitenau realized that, for the sake of propriety, she would have to be housed somewhere other than his official residence within the walls of Salzburg—hence Mirabell, which at that time stood outside the walls of the city. He must have spent a lot of time there: From the start of their relationship in 1593 to his death in 1617, Alt bore him fifteen to seventeen children. Historians disagree on the exact number. And, given my very recent travels, I am interested to learn that the wedding of Eva Braun's sister, on the eve of D-day, took place in the Mirabell's Marble Hall, still a place of choice for Salzburgers ready to tie the knot.

THE GRAYNESS PERSISTS the next day, muting our outing to the mountains of the Salzkammergut lake district. The region—Salzkammergut means "Estate of the Salt Chamber"—stretches out to the east of Salzburg and remains one of the prettiest in the Alps. Ernst does the navigation and, to his credit, exhibits no sign of Swiss scenery chauvinism as sights of exceptional beauty pass before us. We do a loop to the south to see what is reputed be the loveliest of all, the village of Hallstatt, on the glacial lake of that name. It is stunningly situated on a narrow spit of shoreline, at the foot of the soaring Dachstein Mountains. Its colorful old houses are reflected in the clear waters of the lake. Little wonder that UNESCO classed it a World Heritage Site in 1997.

Hallstatt has been around for thousands of years. Neolithic man discovered and mined the salt in its mountains, followed by hundreds of generations up to and including the present day. It is said to have the oldest salt mine in the world. For the last few hundred years, water rather than the pickax has been used in the process. A mixture of three parts salt and seven parts water is sent to be processed at a town forty kilometers distant via a "brine pipeline" originally constructed in 1595 from thirteen thousand hollowed-out trees. So the oldest mine meets the oldest pipeline, although today the pipes are plastic.

Even more important is Hallstatt's role in the study of the Late Bronze Age and Early Iron Age. In 1846, Johann George Ramsauer, the manager of the salt works, came across an ancient cemetery near

Hallstatt containing at least a thousand burials. For the next two decades, he devoted himself to the careful exhumation of each burial, cataloguing its remains and the artifacts—swords, brooches, statuettes, etc.—interred alongside their owners. In this prephotography age, he commissioned a watercolorist to execute faithful replications of the objects found.

A whole world opened up. It became obvious to historians that even as early as 500 or 600 BCE, the miners of Hallstatt—who were Celts—had been trading their salt as far north as the Baltic Sea and as far south as the Mediterranean. Luxury goods from the Greek colony of Massilia (present-day Marseille) were found in the burials, as were Etruscan objects. These revolutionary finds resulted in the village's giving its name to a two-hundred-year stretch of human history, the Hallstatt Culture. This classification goes from the eighth to the sixth centuries BCE, the time of transition from the Bronze Age to the Iron Age.

In its current incarnation, the village is a gingerbread and pastel gem dominated by a needlelike church clock tower. The place also hosts the largest number of Chinese tourists I have seen thus far in the Alps, brandishing their selfie sticks like swords. The reason for this lies in Hallstatt's unique status as a village that has been successfully cloned. In 2012, an exact replica of the place was opened near the large city of Huizhou, in the Guangdong province of southern China. Touring the Chinese Hallstatt, one hears the strains of *The Sound of Music,* on a continuous tape loop. The cloning was done in a cloak-and-dagger fashion—for years, Chinese architects and designers had extended stays in the Austrian village, taking pictures and executing painstaking drawings without telling the town's officials what they were doing. Paid for by a Chinese mining magnate, the whole effort—costing just under a billion dollars—was intended to create a linchpin for a surrounding Western-style housing project, an upscale place of greenery and comfort where wealthy Chinese could escape the gritty cities formed around rampant industrialization. For the Austrian Hallstatt, the resulting publicity hubbub has been a boon—Chinese tourism here has increased more than a thousandfold.

When the rain closes in, we race back to the car and drive to the spa town of Bad Ischl. In the nineteenth century, the summering Habsburg royalty in Bad Ischl made the towns of the Salzkammergut places to see and be seen for the courtiers and creators of effervescent Vienna. The storybook appearance of the countryside also makes it ideal for Romantic maundering. Even a partial list of habitués of the lake towns is impressive: Gustav Klimt, Anton Bruckner, Gustav Mahler, Johann Strauss, Hugo von Hofmannsthal, and Johannes Brahms. The number of great composers besotted by the place suggests that the hills here are, indeed, alive with the sound of music.

We plop down for a coffee at a terrace in the town's Kreuzplatz, a small square in front of what was once the Imperial and Royal Theater and is now home to a cultural center and a repertory cinema. Its small but grand colonnaded façade speaks to the town's past distinction. On one occasion in 1897, *Die Fledermaus* was performed here for visiting royals from Asia, under the direction of its composer, Johann Strauss.

We take in the view of the well-maintained townhouses. Ernst, always on the lookout for the unseemly, directs my attention to a sign opposite us that says something about the summertime activities here.

"This is what this town is all about," he says triumphantly. The sign reads:

DR. MARTIN FUCHSBAUER

DERMATOLOGIE

VENEROLOGIE

AESTHETIC CHIRURGIE

ENTRANCE IN BACK OF THE BUILDING

I do not want to hazard a guess as to why the good doctor's patients have to go in by the back door.

Then again, Bad Ischl has long had an association with Venus and her etymological offspring, the venereal. In the early nineteenth century, an archduchess of Austria, despairing of her fertility, came to the spa town to take the waters and receive treatment. In the fullness of time, she gave birth to three sons whom she called her "Salt Princes." One of these boys grew up to become Emperor Franz Josef, the longest reigning Habsburg monarch and an obedient servant of Venus. When the time came for him to mate, the in-breeder's digest was consulted and his Bavarian aunt arrived in Bad Ischl to present him her marriageable daughter, Helene. Unwisely, the well-meaning aunt also included her younger daughter, fifteen-year-old Elisabeth of Bavaria, in her traveling entourage. When Franz Josef first beheld his beautiful first cousin, he fell madly in love. Poor Helene was shoved aside and five days later Elisabeth found herself engaged to be married. This Elisabeth is the famed Sisi, whose statue on the shore of Lake Geneva I admired at the outset of this journey. I crossed many passes and language barriers—French to Italian to German to Italian, then back to German—before arriving here in Bad Ischl, where Sisi is still celebrated. I'm intrigued to see how her life is remembered here, rather than her death, as in Geneva.

As we walk into the town center, I muse on Sisi's unfortunate end.

Ernst cuts me off. "Her assassin did her a favor," he says. "She led her life as a work of art. What's more artful than a dramatic death?"

"So you're saying she wanted to be assassinated?"

"No, of course not," Ernst replies.

We continue through the streets in silence.

At last Ernst examines me through his round glasses and says, "Why do you think she is remembered?"

"Because of her beauty."

"No, no, no! It's because her death was seen as the end of an era."

I'm about to dispute this when the Café Sissy comes into view to silence me. It is near a grand hotel that welcomed all the important visitors to Bad Ischl on their visits to the emperor and empress. A stone plaque on its façade lists their names with martinet precision. First come the names of the monarchs of Europe, then those of Austro-Hungarian nobility, followed by a roll call of commoners. The last name etched on this third list is Samuel Langhorne Clemens.

We peruse the menu posted on the wall. The choices that jump out at me are Sissy's Secret (mixed grill for one), Sissy's Special (mixed grill for two), Chef-Toast Sissy (turkey fillet on toast with cocktail sauce, onion rings, tomatoes, and salt), and Kaiser Franz-Josef Teller (fillets of pork in mushroom sauce).

"We are not eating here," Ernst says with a certain finality. I hate to say it, but I agree with him.

Instead we wander through the ornate lobbies of the hotel. There are little medallions bearing the letters *K.u.K.* on the walls, the same type of medallion I noticed on Bad Ischl's lamp standards. But the real attractions are the portraits and busts of Sisi, showing her to be a fair creature with dark, deep-set eyes and a cascade of long, flowing chestnut hair. This leads us to a discussion on the correct spelling of her nickname. Ernst favors the frilly Sissy, which is only to be expected, given his proven disdain for the woman, while I opt for the simpler Sisi, the one adopted by most histories of the period.

Just as Mozart is the mascot of Salzburg, Sisi appears to play the same role in Bad Ischl—which is curious, since she loathed the place. Within a few years of her wedding, she stayed away as much as she could, traveling the Mediterranean, Hungary (which she loved), and western Europe—anywhere she could escape the constraints of Habsburg formality. She had been brought up in a freewheeling manner by her eccentric parents—she also spent a lot of time with her cousin Ludwig, the Bavarian dreamer of Neuschwanstein—and was totally unprepared for the rigid discipline demanded of her. Her powerful mother-in-law despised her and tried to keep her in her place, and her husband, though impetuous at the outset of his lightning courtship of her, proved to have the spontaneity of a rock. Sisi did her dynastic duties by producing a few children early on, but her sole son, Crown Prince Rudolf, eventually ended up killing himself in a shocking murder–suicide pact with his mistress at Mayerling, a hunting lodge in the Vienna Woods. Sisi donned mourning clothes and never took them off. Franz Josef got the message. He took up with a Viennese actress named Katharina Schratt, who bore an uncanny resemblance to Sisi in her youth. The empress, perhaps relieved that her husband had turned his attentions elsewhere, helped set up Schratt in a villa in Bad Ischl.

The next morning, as we walk up a tree-lined drive to the Kaiservilla, Franz Josef's hunting lodge, I see them again, the letters *K.u.K.*, on a gateway. I ask Ernst about the mysterious abbreviation. He explains that it was the moniker for the Austro-Hungarian Empire, a stand-in universally used, somewhat like present-day *USA* and *UK*. *Kaiserlich und Königlich*

(Imperial and Royal) signified that Franz Josef was kaiser (or emperor) of Austria and king of Hungary and several other places in his sprawling multiethnic domain. The *"und"* was often removed—especially in the eastern, more restive parts of the empire—leaving *K.K.*, which is pronounced "caca" and means exactly the same thing to children of many languages. In the 1930s, Austrian novelist Robert Musil, in his *Man Without Qualities*, has fun with the vanished state, calling it *Kakania*, which I leave to resourceful readers to translate for themselves.

The Kaiservilla is a yellow Italianate palace set on a large estate gardened in the English style. On entering, it becomes obvious that it was not just a hunting lodge in name only. The walls are hung with hundreds and hundreds of chamois horns, all bagged by the kaiser on his daily hunts. Each horn is labeled to show where the kill took place and on what date. Since the dogged Franz Josef spent sixty consecutive summers as emperor in Bad Ischl, that accounts for a lot of chamois. About forty-five thousand in total, we learn from a tour guide later on. She hastens to add that he shared the meat with the local population, a generosity not exhibited by Franz Ferdinand, his nephew, who became next in the line of succession after the Mayerling incident. The archduke did not share his kills, which, according to our guide, amounted to 270,000 animals in his lifetime. Famously, he himself was shot to death in Sarajevo, in 1914.

Only a part of the sprawling villa is open to public inspection, as the wing Sisi intermittently inhabited is now occupied by her great-grandson, Magister Markus Salvator Habsburg-Lothringen, and his family, who presumably do not want smartphones stuck in their faces all day long. Hence the obligatory guided tour, to keep us lowlifes from wandering into rooms and disturbing their highnesses. The hunting trophies overwhelm the corridors leading from one exquisite room to the next. The Red Salon, where Franz Josef received heads of state (including President Ulysses S. Grant, Prince Otto von Bismarck, and a whole raft of kings and tsars), is modest in size, fitting for the emperor's austere way of life—with the exception of his hunting obsession, of course. He was at his desk every morning at 4:15 a.m., conducting affairs of state. Dawn was time for the hunt. As he had no other hobbies, it is rumored that his reverence for routine led him to set a specific time for having sex with his wife, as a sort of Bureaucrat of the Bed. As for the bed he slept in every night, it was a simple iron army cot.

Sisi is remembered in a sitting room. The walls are covered with landscape paintings of her native Bavaria. A glass display shows the costly gifts showered on her by the crowned heads of Europe. Against one wall is a rather unbelievable sideboard, made of thirty types of wood, fashioned for eleven years by a hobbyist from Carinthia. Near it stands a gift from her beloved Magyars, a drinking horn, made from a Hungarian ox, that can hold eight liters of wine.

Not that Sisi would have indulged. Our tour guide tells us that she was a dietary control freak, to the point of anorexia, sometimes eating just one potato a day. At this point, Ernst shoots me an annoying I-told-you-so look. Sisi's exercise regimens were rigorous—she wore out her ladies-in-waiting with vigorous hikes in voluminous skirts up the mountains of the Salzkammergut. When not in full-blown depression, fits of vomiting and fever plagued her. Obsessed by her image in a pre-Photoshop age, she never sat for a photograph after her thirty-second birthday.

We are led at last into Franz Josef's study. On his desk is a bust of the teenage Sisi, devastatingly lovely. It was at this desk on 28 July 1914 that the emperor declared war on Serbia, setting off the falling dominoes that would lead to the cataclysm of the Great War. He signed three declarations—in German, French, and Latin. Occupying the desk now is a declaration issued the same day, entitled "To My Peoples!" This document had German, Hungarian, and Czech versions. It attempts to explain the decision to go to war, beginning:

> To my peoples! It was my fervent wish to consecrate the years which, by the grace of God, still remain to me, to the works of peace and to protect my peoples from the heavy sacrifices and burdens of war. Providence, in its wisdom, has otherwise decreed. The intrigues of a malevolent opponent compel me, in the defense of the honor of my Monarchy, for the protection of its dignity and its position as a power, for the security of its possessions, to grasp the sword after long years of peace.

His peoples and those of other countries eventually became disillusioned. By war's end, the Habsburgs, Hohenzollerns, Romanovs, and Ottomans had been consigned to the trash heap of history. If the events at Bad Wiessee can be said, arguably, to signal the end of Romanticism, then the signature at the Kaiservilla marks the end of the nineteenth century, with its princes, dukes, and kings engaging in hothouse diplomacy while their countries outgrew them.

Outside again, Ernst points out a statue of a foppish young man with his ear cocked. There are two hunting dogs at his feet. Although entitled *The Eavesdropper*, the artwork is clearly a tribute to the beaters that scared thousands of chamois into Franz Josef's gun sight. Ernst, the sage of St. Gallen, declares that this is clearly a homoerotic statue evoking the raunchy Viennese partying that took place in Bad Ischl for many summers. When I, who have read the documentation in the gift shop, inform him that the work was a gift to Sisi from Queen Victoria, he utters a loud Swiss "a-HA!" and walks off, his suspicions confirmed.

Our destination is a teahouse far into the estate, built for Sisi by Franz Josef so that she could moon about her misfortunes far from the duties of court. It is an English teahouse, now converted into a museum of photography. Much of it is an overly thorough presentation of early daguerreotype technology, but there is one room that attracts my attention. This features photographs of the royal family. One portrait shows an intelligent, troubled young woman looking into the camera. She is beautiful, complex. How could anyone handle being thrust into an arcane, codified world at the age of sixteen? Sisi stares out at the visitor.

TODAY WE WILL take the *salz* in Salzkammergut seriously. Time to visit a salt mine. We drive southeast of Bad Ischl through the thickly wooded mountains where the report of Franz Josef's hunting rifle once echoed. Due to bad planning, our route lies past Hallstatt once again, but neither of us really regrets seeing for a second time its church steeple and colorful houses reflected in the serene waters of the lake. We round the south shore and head for the village of Obertraun, a quiet, quaint place undisturbed, seemingly, by mass tourism. From there we will take the road upward to the Koppen Pass, a prospect that does not daunt me, as its elevation is less than a thousand meters.

This is when I learn that it is wise never to become overconfident in the Alps. Although the Koppen is a low pass, the road builders seem to have thought that crossing it should be done as quickly as possible. There is only one hairpin; the rest is a steep, steep climb. Beyond a place called Südanfahrt, there is a long stretch of narrow roadway with a ridiculous 23 percent gradient. Perspiration beads on my brow, as I can barely see over the hood of the car. Ernst laughs nervously, then starts when we are overtaken by a daredevil schnitzel of Austrian bikers. The Koppen Pass is at last reached, and we seem to have entered an area of pure wilderness, conifers and rockfaces and a river, the Traun, rushing far far below. But no, this is genteel Austria. A short descent and we arrive at the spa town of Bad Aussee, yet another summertime haunt of Vienna's brilliant fin-de-siècle luminaries. The town is said to be the geographical midpoint of Austria, a distinction dubiously commemorated in 2005 by the construction of the Mercedes Bridge at the confluence of two footbridges spanning twin tributaries of the River Traun. The Mercedes of the bridge is indeed Mercedes-Benz, and a gigantic three-pointed-star logo of the car company stretches a whopping twenty-seven meters horizontally over the river. The corporate intrusion is made all the more incongruous because the inhabitants of this town of sixteenth-century houses remain among the few Austrians to wear unaffectedly the *Tracht*— that is, traditional Austrian dress. Unlike the exhausted suburban Salzburgers fleeing the tourist make-believe, many women of Bad Aussee proudly wear the tight bodices and full skirts of the dirndl as they stroll the town doing errands.

We head north and upward along a road almost smothered by woodlands to the tiny outpost of Altaussee, an Alpine Shangri-La once frequented by Sigmund Freud and Theodor Herzl. Our goal is not the village but a mountain to the west called Sandling. To the north rises the moody eminence of Mount Loser, often scaled by the visiting Viennese. The local nickname for the height is "Loser Ear" because of the ear-shaped rocky summit. Today it is home to the largest solar power plant in the Alps. Beyond it rises the Totes Gebirge massif, once the hiding place of deserters from Hitler's Wehrmacht. By the spring of 1944, word had gotten out to draft dodgers and deserters in Germany and Austria that the remote region was a "safe house," thanks to its being nearly inaccessible. Local sympathizers, however, knew their mountains and regularly brought these men food and supplies. At war's end, thirty-five deserters were discovered there.

In the visitor center at Sandling, we are instructed to don white robes and pants, somewhat like karate gear or hazmat suits without the headgear. Over our shoes we adjust slip-ons. Miraculously, we are the only tourists here, and our amiable young guide makes a joke about not having to raise his voice.

Soon we are in a dimly lit gallery, perhaps three meters tall and two meters wide. We are surrounded by rock and crystal, purple and black. In places, some planking secures the rockface, as the salt behemoth of Sandling rises a millimeter or so in elevation every year. The guide informs us that we are to walk about two kilometers into the center of the mountain. As we do this, we are treated to a recitation of facts and figures: Sandling has been mined for more than seven thousand years; 60 percent of the mountain is composed of salt, evaporite residue of the great oceans that covered this area millions of years ago; the salt works, the largest in Austria, are still in operation, producing 80 tons a day, of which 13 percent is table salt, 23 percent industrial salt, and the rest, road salt. As at Hallstatt, most of Sandling's salt comes from what the guide calls the "wet method," which requires a high-pressure stream of water to dissolve the salt and eventually bring it to the surface as brine. The water is then boiled off, leaving only salt. As for the "dry method"—or, more properly, the room-and-pillar method—the salt is removed in a checkerboard pattern to leave permanent, solid salt pillars for mine roof support. About half of the salt is removed. At Sandling, this method is used sparingly.

Ernst asks us to stop for a moment. Even in the wan light, I can see that his face is greenish. He fishes out a handkerchief and mops his damp brow. Both the guide and I stare at him—Ernst is a claustrophobe! In a weak voice, he says that he's okay and we can continue. As I walk behind him, visions of revenge dance in my head. The tables have been turned since he grabbed my shoulders during the ascent of the Ebensalp in Appenzell. I rehearse in my head the things I can say to terrify him: "Jeéz, I hope there won't be an earthquake, or we'll all be goners." "Ernst, can you just imagine how many millions and millions of tons of rock surround us?" "Wow, there sure isn't a lot of room in here. I wonder if it gets narrower farther on?" But as I entertain these thoughts, I find myself growing more and more uneasy. I realize that I am scaring myself. I banish the thoughts and the chance for revenge passes.

Surprisingly, the mine brightens and opens up the farther in we go. The gallery leads into a roomy chamber where a fully ornamented Christian chapel stands to one side. It is dedicated to St. Barbara, patroness of artillerymen and anyone, like a miner, who handles explosives. The young woman, thought to be of the third-century Near East, was possessed of such great beauty that her father locked her in a tower to prevent an onslaught of suitors. When Barbara confessed to her pagan father that she had become a Christian during her captivity, he tried to kill her but was foiled, as she was miraculously transported to the mountains. Her father then denounced her to the authorities, who found her and tortured her. Because she would not recant her faith, her father was summoned by the prefect to lop off her head. This he gladly did, only to die himself on his homebound journey after being struck by a lightning bolt, a natural explosive force. Thus, Barbara is revered by anyone who likes to blow things up.

Further entertainment comes when we leave St. Barbara's stone cavern and descend to a lower gallery. This is not done via a stairway; rather, we sit on a long, smooth slide made of blonde wood and hurtle downward. The slide is about twenty meters long, so we pick up momentum and feel the rush of air in our ears. During the tour, we do this twice, flashing through stone caverns at speed. Eventually we arrive at a chamber covered in photographs. This is where more than ten thousand looted works of art were stored by the Nazis, destined to adorn the Führermuseum to be constructed in Linz, Austria, near Hitler's birthplace. The low humidity and temperature in the heart of the mountain, plus its remoteness, made it an ideal place to stash a cache (Neuschwanstein was another place used for this purpose). The photos tell a story of breathtaking cultural theft: Standing stacked in this chamber seventy years ago were works by Dürer, Rembrandt, Brueghel, Rubens, Van Eyck, Michelangelo, and hundreds of others.

The first week of May 1945 ranks as the wildest in the history of Altaussee. In the distant mountains, deserters from the German army were hiding out, fed by the villagers. The village itself housed the fleeing heads of governments of the various pro-Nazi regimes set up in eastern Europe. Altaussee had been designated as the best place to hide out, lost high up in the Alps. And the architects of the Holocaust, including Adolf Eichmann, sought refuge in the remote Austrian village, a sad irony for a place that a few decades earlier had welcomed Theodor Herzl, the founder of Zionism. But American soldiers were on the move, quickly making their way through the Salzkammergut. The atmosphere in Altaussee was, as can only be imagined, febrile in the extreme.

In the midst of all this uncertainty, the miners of the Sandling watched as eight large, heavy crates were moved into the chambers containing the artworks. Each was marked, in German, with the words, TAKE CARE: MARBLE. DO NOT DROP. Disbelieving eyebrows shot up; there had to be something else in there. After several days, two curious miners, Hermann König and Alois Raudaschl, pried open one box and found five hundred kilograms of explosives, perhaps unexploded American ordnance retrieved from the bombed-out cities of Austria. Whatever its nature, the eight crates of explosive matériel were powerful enough to destroy the entire cache of stolen art.

Which was precisely the intent of August Eigruber, the Nazi governor of the region. It is unclear whether he was obeying or disobeying an order of the soon-to-be-dead Führer, but his determination to wipe out this precious legacy of the European past is not in question. The locals thought otherwise. In the most fantastical part of the story, Alois Raudaschl, evidently a man of stupendous bravery, stole secretly through Altaussee to meet up with the monstrous Ernst Kaltenbrunner, head of the Austrian Gestapo. The Nazi grandee, destined for execution at Nuremberg the following year, was one of the many vicious war criminals holed up in the village. Kaltenbrunner outranked Eigruber, and, without the latter's knowledge, approved Raudaschl's last-ditch plan. In the dead of night of May 3–4, the miners hauled the crates out of the mountain. They also hid some of the art in remote galleries of the mine and even stashed some in their homes. We know this, our guide informs us, because long after the events of that dramatic night, a missing panel of Van Eyck's priceless *Ghent Altarpiece* was discovered in the kitchen of a local man. Apparently he took one of the figures depicted on the panel to be a miner, so he kept it and used it as a surface on which to cut his daily bread.

The clandestine removals completed, the miners then set charges at all the entrances to the galleries. In the early morning of 4 May 1945, they detonated them. St. Barbara worked her magic—the treasure trove was now inaccessible.

"Until the Monuments Men came, like in the movie," I say, referring to the recent George Clooney film.

This remark provokes something akin to a sneer on our young guide's handsome features. On our way back to daylight, he gives us a master class on all the things *The Monuments Men* got wrong. They did not even come to Sandling to see what the actual place looked like. The filmed tale is ridiculously warped, resembling in no way the true story, giving the Americans almost all the credit for securing the art. The guide heatedly goes on and on, intense in his passion to debunk a movie.

At last we emerge from the last gallery into the reception center. Color returns to Ernst's face. Our hazmat sliding gear is thrown into a bin and we sign the visitors' book. When the guide sees my place of residence—Providence, Rhode Island—he seems to regret the vehemence of his lecture on *The Monuments Men*.

"It is true that you Americans," he says to me, "saved our European civilization."

Ernst scowls. I hand the guide a lavish tip.

MOVIES OCCUPY the last afternoon of our excursion in the Salzkammergut. And why shouldn't they? This Austrian lake district cries out for a cinematographer. Lushly forested mountains and sparkling blue bodies of water combine to please the eye no matter which way you turn. First up is the Attersee, the largest lake of the Salzkammergut. Narrow and long, the lake is dominated on the eastern horizon by a karst limestone behemoth. Apparently the locals share my opinion of heights: The eminence is called Höllengebirge (mountains of hell). Standing opposite on the western shore, in the village of Unterach am Attersee, I recognize the perspective immediately. Unterach was the stand-in for Bad Aussee in Visconti's *The Damned*, and it was here, cinematically at least, that The Night of the Long Knives occurred. I inspect the inn of the orgy, the wharf where the SS made landfall. . . . Thankfully, all seems forgotten now, a hiccup of this charming village's long vocation of seducing the sensitive. Gustav Klimt immortalized it in several paintings.

Next up is Mondsee, a lake bounded on its southern shore by a stern row of mountains. The scenery is made for the fabulist, as in Ian Fleming's *Thunderball*, when Ernst Stavro Blofeld announces to his fellow villains of SPECTRE: "Thanks in part to our German section, the recovery of Himmler's jewels from the Mondsee was successfully accomplished in total secrecy, and the stones disposed of by our Turkish section in Beirut." More benign is the town of Mondsee's association with *The Sound of Music*, or, as it was ungallantly referred to by its male lead, Christopher Plummer, "The Sound of Mucus." Plummer's and Julie Andrews's characters were wed in requisite Hollywood splendor in Mondsee's picturesque cathedral, amidst the customary explosion of Austrian baroque. I ask Ernst if he wants to visit the church. He shakes his head vigorously, and I agree—we both had our fill of baroque in Salzburg.

I slip onto the autobahn for the long drive back to Switzerland. I'm bringing Ernst back to St. Gallen, then going to southern Austria. A silence falls between us. Yet there is something that must be addressed.

"No matter how she died," I say at last, "Sisi would always be remembered."

He snorts. "Sissy is remembered because she was assassinated."

"No. She was the Hedy Lamarr of the nineteenth century."

"Who?"

I explain that the Austrian-born movie star was the template for society ladies going under the knife in the 1940s.

"Remember that sign for the cosmetic surgeon we saw in Bad Ischl?"

Another snort. "Women do not go to him to make themselves look like Sissy. They go because they've got gonorrhea."

He has a point, I hate to say once more.

"Lamarr was a genius," I venture, "just like Sisi." I tell him that the screen beauty invented a technology that would later usher in wi-fi and Blu-ray. "And she once lived in the house used as the von Trapp family mansion in *The Sound of Music*."

Knowing there is no Trappologist in the vicinity, I add this bit of unconfirmed apocrypha for emphasis.

To no effect. "Stephen," Ernst says, "you're making no sense."

"Remember Romy Schneider?"

"Yes. . . . And your point?"

I explain that the actress, another Austrian beauty, portrayed Sisi in a very popular three-part German-language biopic. And that she reprised the role for Visconti in *Ludwig*.

"Romy reintroduced Sisi to popular culture," I conclude.

Ernst turns in his seat to look at me directly. The mountains fly past.

"Look, if I say that Sissy would have been remembered even if she hadn't been killed," he says with deliberation, "would you promise to shut up about her?"

I laugh—and keep the promise.

ZELL AM SEE, home to the most annoyed drivers in Austria: As I cruise around looking for a hotel, I am serenaded by a symphony of honk-

ing horns. This impatience may be attributable to the locals' frustration
with the hundreds of thousands of visitors who flock to the place every
year. Located in the southern part of the state of Salzburg, Zell deserves
such year-round worship. Tall mountains surround a small pristine lake,
its waters made even more limpid by the prohibition of motorized boats.
The lake's German name—Zeller—is poignant for me: My immigrant
Irish father, who passed away just months earlier, spent his working life at
a Canadian company of the same name. I look out over the lovely expanse
and think of my dad.

Evening brings solace. At a pizzeria, I fall into conversation
with two couples, one from Copenhagen, the other from Antwerp.
To my amazement, they voice their disdain for Dutch campers. I
ask the Dutch-speaking Belgians why their countrymen do not
take to the roads with campers.

"Because we're not cheap," the husband replies simply.

But surely that is just a stereotype? Every culture singles out
another for cheapness.

"We Danes are supposed to be cheap," the wife from Copenhagen
allows.

"And are you?"

"He is," she says, pointing to her husband.

When the laughter dies down, our Swedish waiter tells us the Austrians have a satirical song about Dutch campers. He thinks the cook
can sing it for us.

He returns, saying the cook is not in the mood.

We break up and I head out for a stroll. Soon I am on the lakeshore in Elisabethpark, named for the ubiquitous Sisi. Ernst is
no longer with me, so I can mention her. The park is crowded,
with many of the women wearing veils and the men sporting dark

beards. I later learn that Zell promotes itself heavily in the Gulf states.

Attention turns now to the Zellersee, where the Magic Lake show is taking place. Consisting of dozens of fountains, laser projections, synchronized lighting, and special effects, the show is a pop-culture extravaganza. In short order, we see projected on the water scenes from concerts and films as music blares and lights flash. There's Idina Menzel singing "Let It Go" from *Frozen*, then Freddie Mercury. The latter, who I previously thought no one could upstage, looks tame compared to the next performer, Austria's own Conchita Wurst. Winner of the Eurovision song contest earlier in the year, the bearded drag queen belts out a pop standard as the crowd on the shore looks on agog. I wonder what the tourists from the Gulf think of this taste of Europe. And then I think of poor Sisi, shoved aside by this new Queen of Austria. To add insult to injury, Wurst hails from the Salzkammergut.

The following morning promises a somber beginning. Prior to leaving for Europe, I was advised by an Austrian friend that anyone writing about the Alps had to visit Kaprun, a neighboring ski resort that delivered the worst shock to the country since World War II. On the morning of 11 November 2000, the opening day of the skiing season, a fire on a funicular train running upward through a mountain tunnel claimed the lives of 155 people. Most met a grotesque end, incinerated as they climbed out of the train and up the tunnel (the fire started in the rear of the train), placing themselves in what basically became a fiery flue of toxic smoke and blazing heat. The dozen passengers to survive had been in the last car of the train. A volunteer fireman on a skiing holiday wisely instructed his terrified companions that they should skirt the inferno and walk *down* the tunnel to safety.

The mouth of the tunnel can still be clearly seen in the side of the mountain, but no train has operated since that dreadful morning. A construction crane stands idly off to one side, as if the decision to dismantle or rebuild has yet to be made. Debris from the approach track lies on the valley floor like a collapsed roller coaster. Skiers now take a modern aerial lift to the mountaintop, where the snow and ice of Kitzsteinhorn Glacier await. I know that today will bring its share of the white stuff, so I elect instead to look for a memorial to the victims.

It is not hard to find. Off to one side of a parking lot stands a severe modern building of dull gray stone. Shoebox shaped, it has the particularity of possessing scores and scores of vertical niches carved into its two long sides, running from the roofline to the foundation. The plaza before the entrance is forbidding, with gray granite flagstones leading to a blind wall, relieved only by a simple metallic door. I depress the door handle and step inside. The visitor is immediately confronted with a dark marble slab inscribed in German, English, Japanese, Slovenian, and Polish, honoring the victims of the disaster. As I round this imposing stela, a long rectangular chamber comes into view, suffused with subdued yellow, red, and white light. Each of the 155 niches contains colored glass and a white translucent plaque on which the victim's name and date of birth are listed. They range from people in their first decade of life to those in their sixth, but most are in their twenties and thirties. Recurring last names show that entire families were wiped out. In each niche, their kin have placed votive offerings and heartbreaking photos. I go from niche to niche, looking at the smiling faces. One holds a gold medal beside a triumphant grin: a nineteen-year-old German, Sandra Schmitt, women's moguls champion.

It is sometimes thought that the Alps have been tamed, domesticated, engineered into innocuous scenery. Kaprun reminds us that this is simply not true. The mountains remain dangerous. We do not agree with medieval man that demons and dragons inhabit the heights, but we must agree with him that those same heights can be perilous. Every year, skiers, snowboarders, climbers, bikers, motorists, even hikers, lose their lives in the majesty of these mountains. A catastrophe of the magnitude of Kaprun is very rare, thankfully, but it should tell us that of all places on Earth, the Alps are among the worst to run out of luck.

AS WITH ALL THRILLS ALPINE, you start amid the trees in a seemingly benign valley bordered on both sides by gentle green mountains. At a village called Fusch, in the valley next to Kaprun's, the signs appear: *GROSSGLOCKNER-HOCHALPENSTRASSE* (Grossglockner High Alpine Road). If Austrian sign painters get paid by the letter, then their only rivals in affluence would be the Welsh. The road I am about to take is one of the glories of the Alps, built in the 1930s to connect the Austrian states of Salzburg and Carinthia. Aside from this utilitarian purpose, it also serves as one of the most spectacular drives in this rugged region of spectacular drives. The route stretches for forty-eight kilometers, climbs more than two thousand meters, and offers a close-up view of Austria's tallest summit, the Grossglockner.

A toll booth appears. At thirty-four euros, the toll seems as steep as the road. Everywhere there are signs, in a plethora of languages, asking bikers, in essence, not to be stupid. The climb begins in earnest after the booth, and I vow to keep track of the number of hairpin turns. This proves impossible, as I am distracted by the scenery; then I notice that each switchback is helpfully numbered, with its name and altitude.

Sometimes these turns come in dizzying succession, but oftentimes the road describes a straightaway lazily hugging a cliff face. The larches become scrawny then vanish altogether, at which point, for reasons that escape me, the sturdy wooden guardrails are replaced by stones the size of everyday bricks, placed too far apart to brake anyone's momentum unless he or she is extremely lucky. The mountains on the other side of the gorge exhibit extremely pointed peaks, like witches' hats. This must be the so-called Hexenküche (the Witches' Kitchen). They are covered with large expanses of snow, which are, disconcertingly, at eye level. We are no longer looking up at the summits, we are looking across at them.

My side of the valley runs out and I approach a pass. I decide to stop for lunch. I could have paused at any number of restaurants and shops—the Grossglockner road has these sorts of establishments every couple of kilometers, giving new meaning to the British notion of a high street. My choice is the Edelweissspitze, a.k.a. Bikers' Point. The vista is astonishing; we can now see the snowy ranges to the east, thirty-seven mountains towering more than three thousand meters and nineteen glacier fields. It's as if the whole world is a bedlam of snow and ice. The whiteness stretches on forever. I am about to cross the main central range of the Alps. I had read that the eastern Alps were lower than the western ones, but I now realize that a thousand-meter deficit does not make that much of a difference. The view here is as terrifying as the perspective atop the Aiguille du Midi in Chamonix. We are at an elevation of 2,572 meters.

The wind picks up with sudden violence. I bend into it and head to the restaurant chalet at the other end of the parking lot. I pass a sea of Harleys. The latest to arrive is a large goulash of Hungarian bikers, each rider accompanied by a girlfriend on the back of the seat. They take off their helmets and whip their hair in the wind. Behind them, a procession of about two dozen vintage Trabants is crawling up the approach route. Most tow a trailer painted in psychedelic colors and possess a driver sporting a bushy beard. This countercultural embassy from Berlin honks its hokey East German horns and rounds the bend. I dearly hope that Reinhard, my hippie hitching friend, crosses paths with these like-minded souls.

Lunch is eaten to the sound of yodeling blaring out of a speaker system. It is not at all like the edgy singsong of the male choir of Meiringen, in Switzerland; rather, it seems more like a saccharine mash-up. Ernst's observation about Austrian yodeling seems to be borne out: It is indeed more syrupy and cloying than its Swiss counterpart. As for carrying news of health, the flocks, and religious events across great distances, this mellifluous Austrian yodel features just one word— *Arizona*—repeated over and over again, so its social purpose seems murky. Does the yodeler like iced tea in a can? Navajos?

The Grossglockner road is the marquee attraction of Hohe Tauern National Park, one of Europe's largest nature reserves. On the way southward from the Edelweissspitze, it does not disappoint. Far below the eternal snows, glittering lakes can be glimpsed on the valley floor. Clusters of alpenrose cling bravely to the steep slopes plummeting downward from the roadway. At hairpin number 20, a truly deranged flock of sheep teeters on a rockface, perhaps grazing on minerals. Then, to my delight, a marmot skitters across the road ahead of me, my first sighting of the adorable Alpine creature. A small furry rodent the size of a large cat—and looking like a cross between a beaver and a child's stuffed animal—the marmot has been successfully reintroduced into the Hohe Tauern nature reserve, in much the same way that the ibex was reintroduced into Italy's Gran Paradiso Park. The animal, sibling to the groundhog, is a social being, usually living in a burrow with several adults and pups. During the winter it hibernates, waking every week or so and then falling back into a deep sleep during which its body temperature falls significantly to conserve energy.

Vegetarians getting by in the high altitudes on a diet of lichens, grass, flowers, and berries, marmots are also known for their curious whistle. They emit high whistling sounds, in quick succession, when they sense danger, as a warning to their fellows. Here in the Alps, this whistle is the rodent equivalent of the yodel. I slow to a creep just in case the bounding marmot was accompanied by friends, but in a few minutes I am satisfied that he was a loner.

I am confronted by a tunnel. This marks the Hochtor Pass. I enter its three hundred meters of darkness and come out to a new perspective. Whole new ranges of rock heave into view. Now I face the Schober massif, a serrated wall of peaks inhospitable in the extreme. The road immediately begins descending steeply, so much so that a trio of cyclists whizzes past me at great speed. The scree of shattered rocks eventually gives way to green upland meadows dotted with livestock lounging in the summer sun. I have time to wave at the animals, as I am stuck behind a Latvian determined not to take his luxury sedan out of first gear. At last a spur road splits off to the west, leading to the main attraction of the drive. The Latvian must be uninformed—or uninterested—for he continues on the main road southward.

The *Gletscherstrasse* (Road of the Glaciers) ascends inexorably, past rushing waterfalls and through avalanche galleries. It gamely hugs the side of a steep valley wall. Past a bend near a place called Schöneck, the Grossglockner at last comes into view. At nearly 3,800 meters in altitude, Austria's premier peak is magnificent, a towering triangle of geological gigantism. At its foot, the Pasterze Glacier, an eight-kilometer-long chaos of ice, catches the light and seems to eddy alongside the mountain. The road then begins a series of harrowing hairpins masking and then revealing the view of the Grossglockner. When, after several kilometers, the route straightens out, the motorist meets the unexpected: a multistory parking lot into which he has no choice but to enter. It marks a dead end. The structure faces a broad pedestrian plaza—there will be no drive-by pictures from a speeding car.

This is the *Kaiser-Franz-Josefs-Höhe*, a plaza for admiring the spectacle opposite and far below. The Grossglockner today is garlanded by a necklace of wispy clouds several hundred meters beneath its summit. It is a remarkable mountain, an enormous pyramid of whiteness. After Mont Blanc, the peak is the second in the Alps in topographic prominence. One has to climb 2,423 meters from its base to the summit, which was first done in 1799 by climbers inspired by the achievement of Jacques Balmat and Michel-Gabriel Paccard at Mont Blanc.

In the plaza itself sits the most thought-provoking monument I have seen this summer—a ten-meter-long bronze boat installed by Austrian artist Johann Weyringer, said to evoke a legend of sailing the seas here in a very distant past. The sculpture stands as an invitation to wonder at the implications of geological time. These massive mountains were once not here, and this part of the globe was covered by an ocean. Looking out at the Grossglockner—so large, so sky-filling, so damned *there*—I find it difficult to grasp the immense stretches of time involved in the creation and destruction of mountains. As at the Iseran Pass and the Insubric Line, I find these lengths of time to be unfathomable, literally.

Thoughts of danger crowd out those of time as I take the scary high road down to its conclusion. Signs appear in four languages: Mine reads CONTROL THE BRAKES. As I have yet to see such signage in the Alps, this does not inspire confidence. Alas, the road builders were not kidding. The slope becomes very steep and the hairpins come fast and furious. I have to train my eyes on the road, so I am spared glimpsing the abyss, although fear turns to surprise at one turn as I see below me four people taking in the hay on what appears to be a field with a forty-five-degree slope. At last, the road becomes well behaved and I arrive at the charming village of Heiligenblut. The spiky stone steeple of its fifteenth-century pilgrimage church is a postcard icon of Austria: If you line up your viewfinder correctly, the steeple can seem to be pointing at the summit of the Grossglockner. The reason for the church's status as a pilgrimage destination lies in its possession of a vial of Christ's blood (*Heiligenblut* means Holy Blood), brought here from Constantinople by some knight errant in the tenth century. The knight did not intend to donate the vial, but getting caught in an avalanche on his way up to the Hochtor Pass took him out of the decision-making process. He is buried in the crypt.

10. The Dolomites and the Stelvio Pass

———— ⊡ ————

Trent (or *Trento*, in Italian) sits to the south of the Alps, a lovely old center bathed by the waters of the River Adige. Its situation at the juncture of the Latin and Germanic peoples has made the city's history an elaborate game of chess. The forested foothills to the north bristle with fortresses, like so many knights, bishops, and castles in the gambits of greed and ambition played between empires and kingdoms. Yet it was the bishops who left the most lasting mark on the city's reputation, at least in the history of thought.

In the mid-sixteenth century, Trent hosted a meeting of Catholic grandees to grapple with doctrinal matters. It had been a bad half-century for the Church. Luther, Zwingli, Calvin, Cranmer, and many others had been calling out for reform, or, worse yet, had been setting up their own churches. For eighteen years, the Council of Trent wrestled with the questions posed by the Protestant Reformation. The bishops at last came up with their answers, which, to spare us Catholic arcana, may be summarized as follows: "No! No! No! No! And no!" Thus Trent became the poster child for a profoundly reactionary

movement known primly to history as the Counter-Reformation. The
Latin adjective for the city—Tridentine—eventually came to mean
the hidebound and intolerant in matters of Catholic dogma and ritual, particularly after the Second Vatican Council of the early 1960s
belatedly recognized the Enlightenment and dragged the Church
toward modernity. But the Tridentine crowd still clings to that distant
council at the foot of the Alps, the most prominent of the lot being the
actor Mel Gibson. He is to Tridentine Catholicism what Tom Cruise
is to Scientology.

Twenty-first-century Trent is a pleasant, progressive place, con-
sistently ranked as one of the more agreeable Italian cities in which to
live. Yet it cannot shake its ties to a reactionary past, not even in the
city's most astounding cultural treasure. The Castello del Buonconsiglio, dominating the heart of the old town, is a marvelous medieval
and Renaissance castle, gigantic in size with elegant loggias and crenellated wall walks in abundance. The Buonconsiglio, once home to the
bishop-princes who ruled Trent and its rich vineyards and silk factories, speaks of great power held and exercised. Its lasting masterpiece,
located in the castle's *Torre Aquila* (Eagle Tower), is a series of frescoes
commissioned by Bishop-Prince George of Liechtenstein and completed in the year 1400 by an unknown artist. The paintings represent
the months of the year (March is missing) and present a compelling
picture of medieval life. The nobles are always at play—courting,
hunting, jousting, having snowball fights—while the peasants are
always at work. The figures of the nobles are also twice as large as
those of the peasants. And, what is even more interesting, members of
the two classes *never* interact.

Aside from their implicit social commentary, the frescoes show
stunning attention to detail. The tools of the peasantry—rake,

scythe, winepress—are faithfully portrayed, as are the billowing robes of the lords and ladies. This was Bishop George's feudal dream world, the world he wanted to see in 1400, the world that no longer existed. Notably absent from the artworks are portrayals of the rising middle class of the late medieval period—the wealthy merchants and the affluent skilled tradesmen (only one is shown, a blacksmith). Thus the Torre Aquila's beautiful series constitutes a reactionary statement. Bishop George apparently did not like the changed world in which he lived. And that world repaid the favor—in 1407, the middle and moneyed classes of Trent rose in revolt, deposed the bishop, and attempted to set up a republic.

Ignoring reality sometimes carries a cost.

THE DOLOMITES are the next range of Alpine mountains to be visited—the peaks that I have most eagerly wanted to see. Located in northeastern Italy, the range, once called the Venetian Alps, has long been famous for its eerie beauty, its huge stone outcroppings changing color depending on the time of day. Its renown also lies in the richness of the folklore it has inspired.

The gateway to the Dolomites is Bolzano, a historic city about sixty kilometers north of Trent. I should perhaps use its German name, Bozen, as some shopkeepers greet one in German first, Italian second. As this is not Switzerland, all the signage is bilingual.

An explanation is in order. This region of Italy, Alto Adige, is also called South Tyrol (*Südtirol*), as it was once part of the Austro-Hungarian Empire. This all changed with World War I, when Italy, the only combatant in the conflict looking for territorial gains (aside from France fighting to take back Alsace and Lorraine), attacked the

Alpine possessions of Austria. At the end of the war, the Austro-Hungarian Empire was broken up, and Italy, which had fought alongside France and Britain, was awarded much of what is now northeastern Italy. The Italian-speakers in these regions were delighted; the German-speakers, not so much.

I am joined by Ed, another old friend from our Paris journalist days together in the 1980s. As editor there of an English-language monthly, Ed leaned on me as his principal staff writer. He assigned me to what we called "the starlet beat," interviewing and profiling up-and-coming French film actresses whose photos were invariably splashed across the magazine's cover. Less glamorous but somehow more gratifying was his insistence that I write reviews of new restaurants and bars opening in Paris. Now a labor lawyer with a practice in Manhattan, Ed insisted on accompanying me to the Dolomites. Why, I do not know—and he will not tell me. Our last exchange of text messages as he waited for his flight to Milan at JFK concluded with his informing me: "You'll find out when I get there." "There," apparently, does not mean Bolzano, as Ed fends off my curiosity with a smile and a repeated, "You'll see, you'll see."

We stroll the old streets during the evening shopping rush. We hear a lot of German spoken and see an Italian merchant wearing lederhosen.

"This place is a trip," Ed declares.

Eventually, we take a Dickensian passageway from the main street and end up at a wine bar with a sole customer. He is Sergio, an elderly fellow named after a Spaniard his father knew. The Spanish Sergio flew in the Luftwaffe in World War II and was killed in action. After a few getting-to-know-you exchanges, Ed asks our Sergio if he feels more Austrian than Italian. His answer is categorical: "Austrian! We are all Austrians here!"

He goes on to say that his father fought in the Habsburg army in World War I and was proud of his record of killing Italians. When I mention that I will soon be visiting Caporetto, scene of the worst Italian defeat of that war, Sergio raises his fist in something approaching ecstasy. "My uncle was there. We *crushed* them."

Clearly, Sergio is no ordinary Italian. When Ed asks what he would like to happen, he outlines three options: (1) more autonomy within Italy; (2) the creation of a new country, the Republic of Tyrol; (3) his favorite, absorption into the Republic of Austria. Ed, ever the litigator, gingerly suggests that this might be unrealistic. Surely, too much time has passed. Is this just a dream of his generation?

"No, my sons feel exactly the same way," he says hotly. "We will never give up."

In honor of Sergio, later in the evening we order Wiener schnitzel. As this is Austria run by the Italians, it turns out to be the best I have tasted this summer.

The following morning brings further dreaming. We hike through the vineyards out of town to Runkelstein Castle (Castel Roncolo in Italian, Schloss Runkelstein in German), an impressive medieval fortress on a spur of rock dominating the valley. Like Trent's Buonconsiglio, Runkelstein is famous for its frescoes. And for their abundance—the castle houses the largest collection of secular frescoes in Europe. They represent a dream world not so much different from that of Bishop George's.

The frescoes were commissioned by Niklaus and Franz Vintler, two rich merchant brothers of Bolzano who purchased the castle in 1385. That sale was highly unusual—commoners at the time had no right to live in such splendid and fortified residences. But the Vint-lers had friends in high places, so they moved into Runkelstein with their families. At once the social climbing began in earnest. A famil-ial, and purely fictional, coat of arms was ginned up and painted on the wall. Then came the frescoes, depicting aristocratic pursuits—hunting, jousting, etc.—and starring none other than the Vintler brothers. They, and presumably family members, people many of these evocations of the life of the nobility—even though, in reality, they were excluded from such occupations. The cycle concludes in a final room dedicated to such classic medieval tales as "Tristan and Isolde" and "King Arthur and the Knights of the Round Table." The Vintlers doubtless wanted to show that they were familiar with the literary canon of the nobility. Like Sergio in Bozen and Bishop George in Trent, they were dreamers.

The most famous resident of Bolzano/Bozen can be considered the great-granddaddy of all these delusional Alpine strivers. He is the Iceman, a.k.a. Ötzi, the mummified Copper Age corpse found in 1991 by a couple of intrepid German hikers in the tall Ötztal Alps between Italy and Austria. He lived somewhere between 3350 and 3150 BCE and died around the age of forty-five, from an arrow wound to his right shoulder loosed by an assailant standing below and behind him. Then he was probably clubbed in the head. The body, along with tools, weapons, and clothing, was stumbled upon 5,300 years later, exposed by a retreating glacier. He is the oldest natural mummy ever found. And his state of preservation and that of his belongings con-stitute a treasure trove for scientists interested in DNA analysis, paleo diets (his last meal was chamois), blood types, Neolithic toolmaking, gut bacteria, tattoos, prehistoric diseases, and many other aspects of what was going on five millennia ago. Hardly a year has gone by since his discovery without a new revelation provided by analysis of the corpse. Some have likened him to a "snapshot" of our distant past.

Shortly after the sensational find was announced, a clever Austrian journalist dubbed him Ötzi, mixing Ötztal with yeti. The name stuck, and the murder victim was hustled off to Innsbruck for batteries of tests and X-rays. But the Italians smelled a rat. A new border survey was quickly ordered, and the location of the sensational discovery was determined to have been about 100 meters inside of Italy. After protracted negotiations and some sullen Austrian muttering, Ötzi moved from Innsbruck to Bolzano in 1998, to be housed as the centerpiece of a nineteenth-century bank building converted into the South Tyrol Museum of Archaeology.

The place is fascinating. Ed and I seem to be competing with each other to point out the most interesting artifacts: the Iceman's longbow, backpack, quiver, arrows, and provisions pouch. Ötzi's axe is particularly impressive. Its sixty-one-centimeter-long haft is made of polished yew, and the ten-centimeter-long blade, trapezoidal in shape, is made of almost pure copper. Clearly, this was a superior tool, perhaps indicative of the Iceman's high social standing. Accompanying text informs us that the axe could chop down a yew tree in thirty-five minutes, without needing sharpening during that time.

"Now, *that's* cool!"

Ed points me to a bearskin cap he is admiring.

"No, this is better."

I point to Ötzi's goat-hide leggings.

At last we come to the man himself, who can be seen through a window of his climate-controlled resting place. He is a contorted, recumbent figure, dark brown in color, with the sheen one sees on Peking ducks hanging in any given Chinatown. Ötzi has upwards of sixty charcoal tattoos, mostly lines and crosses. Researchers were stunned to find the tattooed areas corresponded to skin acupuncture lines, a pain-relieving technique that would not be developed for another two thousand years in far-off Asia.

In separate exhibits, we learn that the fellow was lactose intolerant, suffered from arteriosclerosis and Lyme disease, and exhibited diastema, which the museum's accompanying text helpfully defines as having a gap between his front teeth, "like the singer Madonna." We round a corner and come face-to-face with a replica of the Iceman in life, fashioned by two Dutch artists using the latest in scientific findings. He stands at five-foot-five and weighs about 110 pounds. Wearing just a loincloth, leggings, and shoes, he holds a stave in his right hand and stares at us from over his left shoulder. His graying hair and beard are scraggly, but his eyes are clear and piercing. His face is deeply furrowed. I confess to Ed my worry about conveying his appearance in this narrative.

He thinks for a minute and says, "Just say he looks like Kris Kristofferson."

WE LEAVE TOWN and head for the mountains. Within minutes, we are in Val Gardena, a verdant valley whose horizons are dotted with spectacular outcroppings of rock. These then are the Dolomites, what the Swiss architect Le Corbusier called "the most impressive buildings in the world." Folded, creased, fissured, punctuated by stovepipe towers, the massifs stand higgledy-piggledy on the pastures and woodlands, as though placed there randomly by some gargantuan toddler. As at Grossglockner, the unfathomable scale of geological time comes to mind: 250 million years ago these discrete formations were coral reefs submerged in a great ocean. Composed primarily of the mineral dolomite (named for French geologist Déodat de Dolomieu), which can be white, tan, gray, or pink, the huge outcroppings are famous for their kaleidoscopic nature, changing hues according to the weather or the moment of the day. The Dolomites have long been a landscape of the imagination.

We pass the town of Urtijëi (Ortisei in Italian, St. Ulrich in Gröden in German). If not Italian or German, then in which language is the town's name? The answer lies in the surprising fact that the Val Gardena is one of the five valleys in the Dolomites where the inhabitants speak Ladin, a direct descendant of the Latin spoken by the legionaries of old Rome. There are Ladin-speakers in two other Alpine provinces of Italy (Trentino and Belluno), and there is a profusion of distinctly different dialects within the language group—so much so that the inhabitant of one valley might not understand someone from another. Such was the hermetic power of the Alps, to isolate neighbors from one another. A similar situation obtained in Switzerland, where the varieties of Swiss German are remarkable for their dissimilarities. They might yodel across great distances to one another, but it is not clear that all of the message would be understood.

To take an example, the simple question of "How old are you?" can be rendered in Ladin, depending on the dialect, as "*Tan d'ani es'a?*" or "*Cotenc egn èste pa?*" or "*Quainch agn asto?*" or "*Kotanc agn asto?*" or "*Canti ani gias po?*" or "*Cuantì ani jas po?*" Clearly, we are a long way from Cicero here. (Ladin should not be confused with Ladino, the old Spanish spoken by the Jewish Andalusian diaspora.) As for the sound of the language, we ask an employee at a tourist office to give us a blast of Ladin. He obliges, and we listen—and understand nothing. As far as we know, he may have been reciting the Lord's Prayer—or insulting us. Back in the car, Ed and I work together to find a way to describe spoken Ladin and finally have to settle for: a Portuguese living in Germany trying to speak Italian. There are "shh" sounds, as in Portuguese, and guttural sounds, as in German, but the musicality and open vowels resemble Italian.

We stop in the town of Selva di Val Gardena.* As its name indicates, the town is surrounded by forests, which has made it a center of woodworking for centuries. Outside a sculpture workshop belonging to one Helmuth Runggaldier, we pause in front of a large bas-relief pine-wood rendering of Padre Pio, the twentieth-century Italian miracle-worker revered as a saint or rejected as a fraud by millions of Catholics worldwide. I am fearing an Oberammergau-like obsession with devotional art, until I spy a group of nineteenth-century firemen and a Pinocchio whose long nose points directly at a buxom woman in distress. Inside, the showroom houses a convention of devils and demons, exuberantly executed and luridly painted.

I ask Signor Runggaldier why there are so many devils in his shop.

"Because there are so many devils in the mountains here," he replies calmly.

"How about ogres?" Ed ventures.

"What is that?"

"They eat children."

The sculptor thinks for a moment, then allows, "Probably."

We're taking our leave when he finds out where I'm from. He takes my hand in both of his and says with conviction, "There is a lot of pine in Canada."

---

* Henceforth, all toponyms in the Dolomites will be given in Italian, to avoid confusion. As an example: The name of this town in German is Wolkenstein.

The Val Gardena comes to an end. We begin to climb to the first of the passes to clear today. The Dolomites pop up around every turn, sometimes flat and table-topped, sometimes looking like a pipe organ. Conifers stand in great clusters at the feet of the stone giants. The valley we have left behind looks tiny, as if we were looking at it through the wrong end of a telescope.

We reach the Sella Pass and get out of the car to gape. All around is a deep green lawn of moss and grass. The mountains of the Sella group, really three irregular rocks standing two kilometers long and hundreds of meters tall, resemble a symphony in stone. And the panorama at the pass comes close to taking in 360 degrees. Many of the massifs stand independent of each other, so the view varies between unearthly monoliths of rock and green valleys and woodlands far, far below. The play of light and shadow is remarkable. We are treated to a multicolored prospect of pink, gray, and rust, while the occasional white cloud obscures a summit like a celestial toupee. I have never seen anything like it.

Ed walks closer to the orientation table and squints up at the Sella. He seems to be looking for something.

"Stevie, come over here." He has a big grin on his face. As I approach, he points to one of the organ pipes of stone and says, "See that one? I climbed it."

"You what?!"

"I climbed it. See that ridge? That's where we bivouacked."

As I listen, astounded, he tells me that in our Paris days he was an accomplished rock climber. He would often take off for a week or two—that, I remember—and head to the Pyrenees or the Alps. That, I did not know. He is a muscular, barrel-chested guy, even now in his fifties, so such a hobby does not seem out of the question.

"Why did you do it?" I ask.

"I used to run. I got tired of the horizontal."

But my surprise runs deep, akin to finding out one's sister spends her spare time running marathons. Ed tells me of his adventures in the Dolomites and I at last understand the reason he was so eager to join me here this summer. This is his rock nostalgia tour.

"These mountains are memories for me," he says.

I think of this later at our hotel. The Alps, particularly the Dolomites, are unforgettable, so powerful is their effect on the imaginative. Try as we might to put them in perspective, the awe (and fear) they occasion lingers long after leaving them. As for the locals, I suspect that nary a one takes the presence of these behemoths for granted. The Swiss waitress at Vevey, I recall, confessed to loving them.

The road down from the Sella Pass is a spectacular journey around rocky prominences glowing in the sunlight. The Dolomites are God's gift to man: Small wonder that UNESCO threw up its collective hands in 2009 and declared the whole region to be a World Heritage Site. We descend into a charming valley town called Alba di Canazei and break for lunch at the Caffè Symphony—apparently I am not the first to find these mountains somehow symphonic. We sit on its terrace nibbling at salads when a truly impressive international procession rumbles past. Ed and I count at least six dozen Mercedes convertibles from the 1950s and 1960s, the automotive showstopper of this summer in the Alps. The elderly male drivers' faces are set in concentration, while their wives wave gaily at us.

The Pordoi Pass awaits, the highest of the paved Dolomite passes (2,239 meters). To reach it, one must traverse a serpentine of switchbacks yielding a series of jaw-dropping views. There seems to be a stony goliath in every direction, now standing straight, now leaning over, depending on the gradient of the roadway. The villages in the green valleys at the foot of the mountains grow smaller and small, until they are rosy dots. We pass several groups of iron-legged cyclists, inching their way to the top. At the pass, we take the proffered iPads and snap pictures of the triumphant climbers in front of a large stone bas-relief stela depicting Fausto Coppi, Italy's premier cyclist of the mid-twentieth century and a national hero whose premature death at forty, from malaria, plunged the country into mourning. The Pordoi is one of the many passes crossed in the *Maratona dles Dolomites* (Dolomites Marathon), one of bicycle-mad Italy's most-watched races. A single-day affair in early July involving up to ten thousand riders, amateur and pro, the Maratona is part carnival, part stress test. Thousands of spectators line the road and scream as the great peloton of cyclists lumbers up to the pass, then coasts at great speed downward, like a murmuration of starlings, the many individual riders standing out for a moment then melding into the mass on the hairpin turns. Aside from the Tour de France and the Giro d'Italia, this race remains one of the most remarkable of the European cycling season.

On the way down, we are confronted by a prodigious rock stretching at least three kilometers long and reaching thousands of meters in the air. Its right extremity is a fist of rock and snow, illuminated a brilliant white by an errant sunbeam. Its left side traces an almost feminine curve.

"Looks like a ship," Ed remarks. "What's the kind with a stern like that?"

"Galley?"

"No, like the ones Columbus had."

"Caravels?"

"Yes, that's it. It's a stone caravel. Do you see it?"

I nod, impressed. At his insistence, we take a long and sinuous detour to stand at the foot of the Marmolada, the so-called Queen of the Dolomites, a ridge with five very tall peaks. The westernmost, at 3,343 meters in elevation, is the region's tallest. On a clear day, the imposing outcropping can be seen from the canals of Venice, some one hundred kilometers to the south. There is a certain nobility to its towering menace, but the overall effect is one of brute force. The Marmolada displays a disturbing number of sheer cliffs. Ed points to a pilasterlike feature climbing the main rockface and informs me that this, too, he clawed his way up twenty-five years ago.

The shadows lengthen and we make our way to Cortina d'Ampezzo. Our resolve to go there directly falters when we come across a magical expanse of water, the Lago Bai de Dones. A small lake surrounded by a dizzying palisade of stone, including the strange *Cinque Torre* (Five Towers) formation of tortured rock, Bai de Dones has invited mythmaking since time immemorial. Indeed, as have all the Dolomites, the richest wellspring of fantastical folklore in the Alps, with its mix of Celtic, Roman, Germanic, and Romance traditions. Here, on this lake, lived an anguane, a cloven-footed female water nymph who, according to which legend you prefer, helped infertile women become pregnant or seduced male wayfarers. In truth, hundreds of anguane stories can be found throughout northeastern Italy, and not only in the Dolomites—testament to the region's lively pagan past. According to popular tradition, the anguane stopped mixing with humankind after—what else?—the Council of Trent.

MAGICAL, MUSICAL, MYSTICAL—after just a short time in the Dolomites, all of these descriptive words spring to mind. There is absolutely no mystery to why these mountains fire the imagination. They are unearthly, almost lunar. Violent irruptions of rock glowing pale in the moonlight, they inhabit the narratives told by the Ladin peoples in the past.

There is the princess of the moon, who came to marry a prince of these mountains. In her trousseau she brought to earth a brilliant moon flower, the edelweiss, to brighten the severity of the brooding peaks. But soon she fell ill, disheartened by the darkness of the mountains at night, so unlike those of the moon. The prince, in despair, took to wandering the forests of the kingdom. There he came across a Salwan, a cave-dwelling dwarf leader whose scattered people possessed magical powers. On hearing of the prince's plight, the Salwan summoned his fellow dwarves together, and the next night they set to work. Standing on the jagged peaks, groups of Salwans captured the moonlight and wove it into a magical, glowing cloth, which they then draped over the mountains. This is why the Dolomites are also called the Pale Mountains. The moon princess, on seeing this transformation, was overjoyed, and her homesickness vanished.

Then there is the alpenglow, the roseate blush that suffuses summits just before sunrise and just after sunset. The phenomenon can be seen throughout the Alps, but in the Dolomites the show is particularly stunning. Ladin legend has a dwarf king, Laurin, inhabiting a hollow mountain surrounded by a profusion of rosebushes. When, after a series of misadventures, King Laurin loses his realm, he angrily turns all the roses into stone, uttering a spell by which they were never to be seen again by night or by day. In his haste, he forgot about dawn and dusk—neither day nor night—which is why the stone roses show their true colors at those two times. The Dolomite massif where Laurin lived is called, in German, Rosengarten.

There are many other legends haunting the Dolomites: maidens turned to stone, witches doing mischief in the woods, sorcerers hurling rainbows into lakes, and a host of other supernatural occurrences. Perhaps the most intriguing concerns the kingdom of the Fanes, a realm unknown to history yet very much alive in multiple folktales. A warrior people led by a Boadicea-like princess named Dolasilla, the Fanes conquered the Dolomites in some distant past, aided at different times by different allies—marmots, eagles, and a cohort of one-armed men. According to tradition, they will return one day in a promised time, and life in the Ladin valleys will return to the way it was lived long ago. Until then, the Fanes remain present in many place names in the region.

All of which makes for fascinating musing as we walk the streets of Cortina d'Ampezzo. Known more now for its jet-set ski clientele and for its starring role in *For Your Eyes Only*, a 1981 James Bond movie, the town is magnificently encircled by jagged mountains, a scene that cannot but inspire lingering thoughts of ancient secrets and fabulous creatures. The view must have inflamed the childhood imagination of Dolomites native Dino Buzzati, whose *Tartar Steppe* brilliantly evokes the menace of the Alps.

We head into those mountains after a few days of Ed's rock nostalgia tour, up a road that instantly becomes ridiculously steep. The muscle Mégane handles the slope effortlessly, which elicits a whistle of appreciation from Ed. The trees give way to an open prospect dominated by a dreamlike lake surrounded by mountains. Named for an impish sprite who convinced her giant father to become a mountain so that she could obtain a magic mirror from a fairy, Lake Misurina spreads out in pristine clarity, its necklace of elegant shoreline hotels testament to the locale's status as a beauty spot of the first order.

Misurina, by the way, met her end when she grew frightened and fell to her death from her father-turned-mountain; his tears, in the form of streams and waterfalls, created the lake in which she lies submerged with the magic mirror.

Ed and I leave the car to stroll along the lakeshore. I buy a few tubs of marmot oil in a souvenir shop, apparently a panacea for all that can ail a body. He busies himself with postcards. The morning is as near to perfect as possible. The scene is so benign and summery today that it is hard to imagine how harsh the winter can be here. The lake was the scene of the 1956 speed-skating races of the Winter Olympics (Cortina d'Ampezzo was the host city), the last time those events were held on natural ice.

Alas, the prospect to the northwest, where we are headed, is one of gathering dark clouds. Undeterred, we head straight for them, for awaiting us is the most famous formation in the Dolomites. The *Tre Cime* (Three Peaks) *di Lavaredo* are a demonstrably weird quirk of geology: three independent monoliths stretching thousands of meters in the air from a sloping gravel scree. They are quite separate, and alone, with nary a trace of vegetation. It's as though some prehistoric Poseidon planted his trident here, and the three tines have emerged from the sea floor to make this arresting display. The middle and tallest eminence, the Cima Grande, ranks as one of the six great north faces of the Alps. From its base, there is an overhang stretching more than 210 meters, followed by a sheer vertical with almost no purchase for the climber. The Cima Grande is not for the mountaineer; it is the wall par excellence for the rock climber. I have not seen such a terrific display of the vertical since beholding the Petit Dru at the Mer de Glace. Even the Nordwand of the Eiger is not as vertical as what we are gazing at now. On this face there can be no spider of ice, or snowfield, or glacier. The Cima Grande is too steep.

Midway along the footpath at the base of the Tre Cime, there is a lovely white chapel adorned by two memorials. One commemorates a local climber, the unofficial custodian of the site, who died at the age of a hundred years and ten days. The other honors Heigl Rosl, an Austrian who fell from the face on 25 August 2008 at the age of forty-five. As I examine the latter, Ed squints, then points his finger at the westernmost peak. I am ready to listen to another retailing of his past exploits, when he says, "There are two people up there! Over on the right, about mid-way up."

It's my turn to squint. I scan the unforgiving gray wall, starting at the bottom and slowly rising skyward. Suddenly, there is a swatch of green and blue, and another. Two climbers, like insects, cling to the rock, each one in turn inching upward. It is a study in foolhardiness and heroism, a demonstration of the lengths to which people will go to conquer these inhospitable, monstrous eminences of rock.

Hail begins to fall. We scurry with scores of others to the distant Rifugio Lavaredo, a restaurant-inn on a scenic prominence. To get there, we have to traverse a fantastical boulder field, some of the house-sized rocks sheared in half from the impact of their plummet to reveal a riot of mineral color. The great mountaineer Gaston Rébuffat, in his memoir *Starlight and Storm*, records witnessing a tremendous rockfall from the face of the Cima Grande. These huge boulders could very well be the remnants of that event sixty years ago.

The Rifugio Lavaredo is so crowded with German, Austrian, and German-speaking Italian tourists and hikers that remaining indoors gives one the distinct impression of being on a rush-hour U-Bahn. Ed and I take shelter outside under the eaves. The hailstones fall like ping-pong balls on the picnic tables of the outdoor terrace. Ed points once again and says, "They're coming down. Must be hell up there."

I follow his finger and see the two insects descending the rockface at an impressive speed. They must be soaked—and bruised.

Mercifully, the hail stops.

ED'S WEEKLONG BREAK in Europe is nearing its end, but we have one more destination to explore together. Accordingly, we get into the Mégane to make tracks. This we do by descending through the trees, northward, to the Puster Valley, a major east–west transport artery since the days before Antiquity. Ötzi may have walked here. The valley also has the distinction of being a watershed: Its eastern rivers flow into the Danube and the Black Sea; its western ones, into the Adige and the Adriatic. The westward drive along the valley floor feels like a return to the Tyrol. The valley dwellers are overwhelmingly German-speakers, and, if there is an Italianate building in the villages we pass, neither of us sees it.

Just north of here, the Brenner Pass, one of the busiest Alpine passes and by far the lowest in the area, sits astride the border between Italy and Austria. The approach road is an elevated expressway. On hills rising from the valley floor, once-mighty castles stare impotently at the autostrada viaducts bringing the rush of traffic practically to their doorsteps. I am eager to see the Brenner, as it has played an important role in trade and war for thousands of years. Prehistoric man crossed this pass, as did the Romans, the Holy Roman Emperor Frederick Barbarossa, and the great armies of the Habsburgs, but when we reach the pass, it is not a letdown, it is a crash-and-burn. The pass teems with strip malls and outlet shops with such mysterious names as Marc O'Polo. The border checkpoint, now rendered unnecessary because of the Schengen Agreement, has been transformed into a shop peddling luxury goods. The only thing of remote interest is a line of trucks awaiting their turn to load their containers onto flatbed railroad cars for the long journey to voracious Milan and points south.

We planned on staying the night in Vipiteno (Sterzing, in German), just south of the pass in Italy, but the outer town turns out to be a huddle of factories and logistics centers shivering under the expressway bridges. A few kilometers to the south lies the town of Bressanone (Brixen, in German), the birthplace of the greatest mountaineer of all time, Reinhold Messner. The first to summit all fourteen eight-thousand-meter peaks of the Himalayas and the first to summit Everest solo without using supplemental oxygen are just two of the many awe-inspiring distinctions Messner can claim in climbing circles. And, like our friend Sergio in Bolzano, the great man identifies himself as a South Tyroler first and as an Italian second. Judging our time to be short, we decide to skip Bressanone and continue westward, to the city of Merano.

This entails crossing the Jaufen Pass (Passo di Monte Giovo). I have never heard of this pass, so I assume it to be unremarkable. I will never learn. The ascent from Vipiteno is promising, a broad, kindly road leading gradually upward through trees and meadows. Once the tree line is passed, the road narrows, but not alarmingly so, and the views open up. Behind us, the Eisack Valley, where Vipiteno is located, spreads out as a distant patchwork of green and auburn and, far beyond to the east, the first peaks of the Dolomites can be glimpsed. It is a glorious golden summer evening, and Ed and I fall into silent contemplation.

The Jaufen Pass is crested, amid slopes covered in moss and lichen rendered less severe by the gentle light of the early evening. The mood of subdued elation gives way to befuddlement, then concern. The road downward narrows dangerously, and the first in a series of lunatic switchbacks comes up at us suddenly. Soon I am forced to play the stick shift as if I'm in a video arcade. The vertical drops are brutal, the guardrails flimsy—when they are there at all. To the north, beyond the valley floor far, far below, rise the forbidding snowcapped peaks of the Ötztal Alps, where Ötzi lay undisturbed for millennia. The descent is such that even Ed—no acrophobe, as his rock-climber days prove—clears his throat nervously whenever I take a hairpin at too fast a clip. And this happens frequently, as the gradient is very steep. The Jaufen Pass is punishing me for my insouciance as I approached it.

At last we reach the village of San Leonardo in the Passeier Valley and its wonderfully level ground. For Tyroleans, San Leonardo is sacred turf, as it was the birthplace and home of Andreas Hofer, whose rebellions against the Bavarians and Napoleon's troops temporarily wrested control of the region from allies of the French. He was eventually captured and taken to Mantua in chains. Napoleon, according to apocryphal accounts, personally ordered his viceroy there to "give him [Hofer] a fair trial and then shoot him." He instantly became a martyr to the cause of resisting Napoleon in German-speaking Europe. Hofer is to the Tyrol what William Tell is to Switzerland; the only difference is that we know Hofer actually existed. A folk song about Hofer's trial and execution, *Zu Mantua in Banden* (At Mantua Bound), is today the official anthem of the Austrian state of Tyrol. It is not hard to imagine what Sergio and perhaps Reinhold Messner think of the hometown of Andreas Hofer now being a part of Italy.

The spa city of Merano is reached within a few minutes. I note the *K.u.K.* (*Kaiserlich und Königlich*) sign on a couple of buildings. Apparently, Merano was another haunt of Sisi, who came here to take the waters and relieve her neuroses. Grand nineteenth-century buildings are everywhere, as are establishments offering special spa treatments. Both Ezra Pound and Franz Kafka availed themselves of Merano's facilities. I find the place confusing and drive around aimlessly. After the third pass before the train station, beside which a small park celebrates Andreas Hofer, Ed yells out, "There's a hotel!" I pull over and he jumps out. "I'll see if there are rooms," he says, impatiently.

There are, and the innkeeper's son, Manfred, immediately invites us out to drinks when he learns I'm from Canada. Apparently, his road to Damascus occurred in Vancouver. And it really was a road. When I tell him that the Austrians of Italy are the rudest, most impatient drivers I have encountered this summer, he concurs and says, "I had to go abroad to learn how to relax at the wheel." We speculate that the mix of Germanic and Latin temperaments might be toxic. Manfred informs us that the mix is by no means a given. Although Merano is half-Germanophone and half-Italophone, the surrounding countryside is overwhelmingly German-speaking. "People here are either bilingual or stupid," he says gravely, "and most of them are stupid."

THE ROAD WESTWARD from Merano through the Val Venosta (Vinschgau, to its German-speaking inhabitants) initially traverses apple orchards and vineyards, proof that this Alpine valley is blessed with a mild climate. They soon give way to Tyrolean villages with needle spires on their churches and a profusion of blooms in their flower boxes. The town of Schlanders boasts the tallest church tower in South Tyrol, its pencil-like red spire rising ninety-two meters into the sky. These upcountry villages are a favorite destination of German holidaymakers intent on hiking in a sylvan setting surrounded by towering mountains. The Val Venosta does not disappoint.

At a holiday village called Trafoi, gifted with a magnificent panorama of the surrounding snow-topped peaks, signs appear for the Stelvio Pass. This pass I have heard of and fear. It is the second highest paved pass of the Alps, just twelve meters lower than the Iseran Pass in Savoy. The approach to it is fearsome: forty-seven hairpin turns clinging for dear life to the side of a mountain. The presenters of the BBC's *Top Gear*, the popular automotive show, deemed the Stelvio to be the greatest drive in the world.

I gear up around the twentieth switchback. The guardrail is a sturdy stone wall, knee-high. Just as well, as there are horrifying views of rocks poised to hurtle down the slopes and crush humanity. At one point we pull over and get out of the car. Across the way is a solid wall of stone and cloud. But it is the view downward, from where we have come, that amazes. The roadway and switchbacks seem strewn over the steep green mountain slope like a long length of black string uncoiled. And whoever uncoiled it looped back and forth, back and forth, almost obsessively, so that no straightaway lasts long; the hooklike switchback is king. The dizzying vista stretches on for miles.

The thinning air is heady, so I let down the windows to feel the breeze. The extremely tortuous approach road to the Stelvio puts me in mind of James Bond. If Rousseau and Mary Shelley made the Alps titillating and Romantic, then the film version of Ian Fleming's character made them sexy. Of the twenty-four Bond movies, fully a third, by my count, have used the Alps as a location, as an accessory to danger and seduction. This is only natural, for mountains are the terrain of choice for those cursed with an anthropomorphic imagination, which is to say, all of us. There are phallic pinnacles, breast-shaped hills and mountains—and even valleys, when viewed from a great height, can be suggestive. The Dolomites' lore of legend owes a lot to their arresting shapes. Add to these formations a sense of the perilous, of the sublime, of letting-go, and you have a recipe for the primal. One doesn't need a dirty mind to think of sex when looking at the Alps; one needs only a subconscious, an id.

Not that such thoughts are entertaining me as I round yet another excruciating bend. I am focused on keeping the asphalt under us. But the rapid gear-shifting does seem Aston Martinish, like something Sean Connery or Daniel Craig would do, so the difficulty of the task replaces thoughts of sex with those of masculine glamour. I regret that my itinerary this summer will not take me to the peak of Piz Gloria in the Bernese Alps, where a museum devoted to Bond adorns a revolving restaurant used in *On Her Majesty's Secret Service* as the locale for the nefarious doings of Ernst Stavro Blofeld.

When we arrive at the pass, slightly carsick, surprise comes in the form of a finish line made with inflated blue tubes. The road beyond it is closed to automotive traffic. The mystery of the absence of oncoming traffic on our way up is resolved: A bicycle rally is taking place. The riders toil up the final few meters on a journey that took them from Bormio, in Lombardy, up to this remote height. The participants are boisterous, talkative, theatrical, gesticulating—in a word, Italian. It took a 2,400-meter climb from Alto Adige/Südtirol finally to feel back in Italy. At lunch, the Wiener schnitzel of Bolzano is replaced by blessed polenta.

But not for long. The small eminence above the pass is called the *Dreisprachenspitze* (The Peak of Three Languages). Before World War I, this was the meeting point of Italy, Switzerland, and Austria-Hungary. The last has vanished, but, as we have seen, the German language is alive and well in northern Italy. And, of course, Italian thrives in Lombardy. That leaves just Switzerland, or, more precisely, the canton of Graubünden (or

Grisons), where the Alps are up to their usual linguistic tricks. There, one of the languages spoken is Romansh.

ROMANSH, yet another legacy of the Roman legions, is a distant cousin of Provençal, Occitan, and French. In truth, the plural *cousins* should be used, for Romansh consists of five entirely distinct dialects whose speakers are unintelligible to each other. To remedy that, a standardized Romansh—*Rumantsch Grischun*—was created in the 1980s, only to be met with fierce opposition from the dialect speakers who felt their identity threatened. Still, the tongue is a national language of Switzerland, of equal rank with Swiss German, French, and Italian, even though Romansh-speakers make up only half of one percent of the Swiss population. Even in their home canton of Graubünden, Romansh-speakers constitute just one-fifth of the population, ahead of the Italian-speakers there but far behind the Swiss-German–speakers. In an already confusing country with regard to languages, Graubünden takes the palm for linguistic complexity: It is the only Swiss canton to be officially trilingual. Graubünden/Grisons is the exemplar for the human havoc wreaked by tall mountains.

Ed and I finish our meal and get ready to leave Italy. The rally is over, the road is open. The way down from the Stelvio on this side is as tortuous as the approach to it from Alto Adige. We navigate about a half-dozen switchbacks in the snow until reaching a plateau and a crossroads. To the left, the road to Bormio, Italy; to the right, the road to Switzerland. We go right and pass the international frontier. Almost immediately I regret our choice, for the guardrails on the dozens of hairpins on the descent are flimsy planks of wood horizontally attached to drunken posts. Replacing the wooden planks with toilet paper would be just about as efficacious in deflecting a wayward vehicle.

I calm my petty automotive despair by making a small detour. The town of Müstair, near the Swiss–Italian border, sits in a high pasture surrounded by Alps. It is the easternmost village in Switzerland, a pretty, linear, Romansh-speaking settlement famous for the Benedictine nunnery of St. John. The convent complex is ancient, said to have been founded in 775 by Charlemagne, out of gratitude for surviving a snowstorm when crossing the Alps. The main church is thus a Carolingian monument, with other buildings added throughout the Middle Ages. But its true claim to fame—one that merited its inclusion as a UNESCO World Heritage Site—lies in its frescoes, the largest ensemble of medieval frescoes anywhere. Unlike the medieval art at Trent's Castello del Buonconsiglio, which is Gothic and secular, St. John's frescoes are Carolingian (ninth century) and Romanesque (eleventh century)—as well as entirely religious in nature.

Entering the grand old church is akin to stepping inside a pious kaleidoscope. Every available wall surface contains figurative art—we are definitely not in a mosque. We crane our necks as the tour guide enumerates the scenes exuberantly depicted: events from the life of Jesus, a chilling Last Judgment, and a wealth of biblical stories. Behind the high altar, Salome dances before a banqueting King Herod as a servant displays on a platter the head of the convent's patron, John the Baptist. Ed rightfully remarks that since there are so many stories and legends depicted here, the convent really should be in the Dolomites. Somewhat bedazzled, we leave the church and exit through the gift shop. I pick up a packet of Sister Clara Cavigelli's aniseed biscuits, which we munch on the way back to the road leading down to the valley known as the Engadine.

That road, sinuous and steep, soon leads us into a wilderness. This swath of mountain, forest, and lake is Switzerland's only national park, created in 1914. In a country so fashioned by the hand of man, the park reminds us of what Switzerland was like before the dawn of tourism, the rise of industry, and the encroachment of the agrarian and pastoral. At a turnout where we stop to admire a panoramic view, we are delighted to see a marmot scrambling across a gently sloping rockface. Display boards tell of other creatures thriving here: chamois, ibex, and eagle.

The final kilometers of the descent compete with the Italian side of the Stelvio for the number of giddy hairpins. At last we reach the valley town of Zernez, where yet another bike rally is just ending. I drive across a bridge spanning a fast-flowing river: It is the Inn, my old friend from Innsbruck. Engadine means "Valley of the Inn People" in Romansh. And that bewitching language can be heard in the streets and café terraces of Zernez. I try to get in the swing as the waitress approaches our table. "*Allegra!*" I cry out, using the Romansh word for "hello." She looks bored and replies, in English, "We don't serve cocktails."

We drive upstream for the final stage of our journey. Villages with such intriguing names as S-chanf, Cinuos-chel, and Zuoz file past. The last is a particularly picturesque village, its old houses exhibiting the colorful sgraffito plasterwork typical of the Engadine. Façades and entranceways are embellished with figurative and geometric decorations, lending the Romansh settlement an Italianate air. These age-old places—many date at least from the ninth century—have kept up traditions that seem to predate Christianity. One is an Alpine whipping day, the *Chalandmarz* (First Day of March), when boys roam the streets with cowbells and then later lash the ground to drive away evil spirits and awaken the fairies of spring.

The Engadine's most famous destination, St. Moritz, is a lakeside jewel of grand hotels and luxury shops and the granddaddy (or perhaps dowager) of Alpine winter tourism and sport. In 1864, local hotelier Johannes Badrutt changed the course of Alpine history by inviting four well-heeled English tourists who had summered in St. Moritz to come and visit in the winter. Badrutt would foot the bill. That foursome of intrepid Britons came and loved what they saw: stunning scenery, pristine snow, and a frozen lake under sunny skies (St. Moritz enjoys three hundred days of sunshine annually). The genie was out of the bottle. Within a generation, hordes of wealthy foreign tourists flocked to the resort, and the boom in winter sports had begun. Grand hotels sprang up to meet the demand and ski slopes were created and groomed. Polo games were staged on the lake, sleigh rides tinkled through the streets, and string quartets played in hotel lobbies. The Alps would never be the same.

What Monte Carlo is to the Med, St. Moritz is to the Alps. Throughout the twentieth century, the resort grew in importance and was emulated elsewhere, as at Megève in Savoy. In 1928 and 1948, St. Moritz hosted the Winter Olympics, elegant affairs staged for the moneyed leisure class. Interestingly, the town was going to team up with neighboring Davos to bid for the 2022 Winter Games, but the cost of infrastructure improvements and the like led to the bid being withdrawn, showing that the present-day Olympics have become such a monster that even two of the most exclusive resorts in the world cannot afford to host them.

And exclusive it is. In a fruitless search for a cheap hotel, Ed and I drive through a pounding rainstorm up hilly boulevards of relentless upscale merchandise. En route, we pass St. Moritz's famed (in St. Moritz, anyway) leaning medieval church tower, which tourist brochures invariably state is more askew than its iconic cousin in Pisa. At last we settle on two hostelries, which then engage in a most un-European war of price-cutting for our business. It is definitely the off-season.

Soaked from our walk, we take dinner at Pavarotti and Friends, a terroir Italian establishment hung with ham and bursting with bottles. The owner is the spitting image of the late, great Italian tenor. The resemblance is uncanny. Like Pavarotti, he is a native of Emilia-Romagna, settled in St. Moritz for twenty years, but we cannot tease out of him an admission that he is related to the singer. Expectation quashes nosiness when the Pavarotti doppelgänger recognizes Ed, following his wine choice, as a fellow bon vivant and tells us he "will take care of us." A plate of mind-boggling salumeria arrives at our table, followed by plates of steaming pappardelle laced with white truffle shavings. The effect is narcotic. The Wiener schnitzel of Bolzano fades into memory, and the lard line becomes mercifully elastic. Ed and I fall into gustatory thralldom, barely able to pay attention to the flat screen where the World Cup final is taking place. We finally rouse ourselves to sporting awareness after a shared tiramisu and a *caffè corretto* or three—that is, a shot of espresso laced with grappa. We don't need to be totally sober as the Germany–Argentina final reaches its inevitable conclusion, the game of soccer having been immortally defined by the English footballer Gary Lineker: "Football is a simple game. Twenty-two men chase a ball for ninety minutes and at the end, the Germans always win."

The rain lets up the next morning. A few short kilometers west of St. Moritz, past shimmering blue lakes, lies the village of Sils Maria. It is exquisitely situated, attracting tourists from the time when tourism was not the mainstay of the Engadine. Hermann Hesse came here, as did, famously, Friedrich Nietzsche. The latter summered in Sils for much of the 1880s, untroubled by whipped horses, as he was in Turin, though supposedly he was pelted with pebbles by local schoolchildren as he moodily walked the lakeshore. Nietzsche wrote much of *Thus Spoke Zarathustra* in the village, claiming that the book's promotion of the eternal recurrence of things—a philosophical notion positing, very broadly, that there is nothing new under the sun—occurred to him when regarding a "pyramidal block of stone" to the west of Sils Maria. Indeed, that fearsome block of the Alps is clearly visible from the door of Nietzsche's house, now a museum, in the village. Alas, as this is Monday, the *Nietzsche-Haus* is closed to the public.

I am doubly disappointed, as the view from Nietzsche's writing desk, aside from taking in the Alpine block of stone, also affords a glimpse of a little chalet behind some trees. That chalet's claim to fame lies in a vacationing young Dutch girl who stayed there in the 1930s— Anne Frank. Her father, an avid photographer, documented their stays there, with Anne playing beneath the window once pensively looked through by Nietzsche. Both were, in different ways, victims of the Nazis. Anne was deported and killed in a death camp, and Nietzsche's exalted thought was perverted by them to become virulent racism. The juxtaposition is as arresting as that in the salt-mountain village of Altaussee in the Salzkammergut, when, with a generation separating them, Theodor Herzl and Adolf Eichmann stayed. Local lore in Sils has it that, upon the opening of the museum, an elderly woman of the village entered it on a whim and saw, to her great surprise, pictures of a childhood friend with whom she had played in the 1930s. It had to be explained to her who that friend was: Anne Frank.

Latterly, the place has become known through *Clouds of Sils Maria*, a French film, starring Juliette Binoche and Kristen Stewart, about the cruelty of aging for an actress and the vagaries of opportunity for her younger counterparts. The clouds in the title refer to the Maloja Snake, a meteorological phenomenon observed in the autumn, when warm air from the neighboring Italian lake district crests the low Maloja Pass (which is alongside Nietzsche's "pyramidal block of stone"), turns into mist at the higher elevation, then descends into the Engadine and its lakes to follow their serpentine contours to well beyond St. Moritz.

Back in the car, Ed and I marvel at the multiple stories of this week, legendary and lived, in these mountains. Pagan, Christian, fairylike, plutocratic, tragic—they all seem connected to the unearthly landscape. These are the human stories of the Alps, each one trying in its own way to make sense of what, until recently, could not be explained. But the communities living in the Alps are not geologists, they are observers of their surroundings and creators of their languages and of their worlds. Their imagination has tried to account for these gigantic stone monsters. That effort is noble but doomed to failure. The Alps cannot be encompassed, tamed, understood—they surpass our powers and always will.

11. Plöcken and Vršič Passes

————— ▫ —————

The last stage of my Alpine summer has its beginnings in a reunion with two rocky acquaintances. To the north of the town where I have spent the night—Lienz, Austria—rise the forbidding heights of the Grossglockner; to the south of town stand the Dolomites, here a screen of tall mountains corrugated by ravines and divided into sharp, hostile rockfaces. Locally, their zombie apocalypse appearance has never escaped notice: they are known in Lienz as "the Fiends."

My reason for starting here is to score the trifecta in one day. I want to go from the Germanic through the Latin and end in the Slavic. My travels have convinced me that the Alps, so magnificent in their rocky majesty, are also subversive, almost underground agents (a strange thing to say about mountains) in creating and crafting human geography. We cannot truly understand geological time, but we can get our heads around our shared human past and present. The cleavages and partitions—the lard line, the linguistic divide, among others—are fostered by the spectacular topography placed square in the middle of Europe.

I follow the River Drava out of town. As Lienz is located in a tiny enclave of Tyrol, I cross almost immediately into the Austrian state of Carinthia, the one that hitchhiker Reinhard characterized as being peopled by Fascists. Unlike Tyrol, which looks longingly southward toward its lost province of South Tyrol in Italy, Carinthia turns its back on the south, where the Slavs of the Balkans live. Some of these Slavs have crossed the Alps to settle in Carinthia, which has caused friction with nativist Austrians. This, combined with economic distress in the 1980s, led to the rise of a far-right party headed by a colorful provocateur, Jörg Haider. Twice governor of Carinthia, the xenophobic Haider was in the habit of saying nice things about the Nazis and bad things about the Jews. Much of the rest of Europe recoiled in horror from his antics. That all came to an end on 11 October 2008, when Haider, after a booze-fueled evening at a gay club, drunkenly crashed his car on a bridge, dying in a blazing inferno near Klagenfurt, Carinthia's capital. Thirty thousand people showed up for his funeral, and a bridge spanning the Drava was named after him. I have decided not to stay in Carinthia.

Instead, I'm heading for the Plöcken Pass and Italy—more specifically, the region of Friuli-Venezia Giulia. The Friuli part of that tripartite region has a distinctive language, which is spoken alongside mainstream Italian. Once again, the Alps wreak havoc with communication.

The ascent begins in a village called Oberdrauburg. The drive up, while steep and studded with switchbacks so pitched one has the impression of driving in a velodrome, holds no terrors for me. Trees are everywhere, crowding the roadway, hiding the horrifying views, although every now and then a limestone monolith appears in the distance, stretching far into the blue. Two Austrian bikers, a mini-schnitzel whose leather jackets display a NASCAR-like multitude of brand advertisements, pass me at tremendous speed, then take the bend ahead, their knees a mere inch from the asphalt. Why do these soon-to-be-seriously-injured young men like to lean so much? And why can't they understand the don't-be-stupid road signs? A sign in German with an exclamation mark announces a rough ride in one hundred meters—and it is not kidding. For the first time in my Alpine summer, the road surface takes on a New-Hampshire-in-the-spring aspect, with frost heaves torturing the pavement. The consequent juddering is hard on the shocks and the coccyx.

At last I reach the pass. No sign, no bikers, only a restaurant resolutely on the piggy side of the lard line. I ponder this as I begin the easy descent through the trees. Why the discretion? After all, the pass marks an important invisible boundary between the Germanic and the Latin. Eventually I come out on level ground—a high valley floor with three villages: Laas, Kötschach, and Mauthen. All of the signage is in German. I scratch my head: Is Friuli another Alto Adige, a place where German-speaking Italians vent their frustration at not belonging to Austria? Enlightenment finally comes in one road sign that reads: PLÖCKENPASS ITALIEN 14.

I was mistaken, I am still in Austria! After scrutinizing my road map, I realize that the height I just cleared, in the Gailtaler Alps, is called the Gailberg Saddle. Ahead of me, to the south, rise the Carnic Alps, which is the frontier of Italy and Austria and thus the location of the international pass. Yet another sign informs me that there is a World War I museum in this high valley, evoking in my mind the frightening, bloody past of these mountains. The Carnic Alps and the Dolomites, unbelievably, formed part of the

Italian Front of the Great War, fought here between Italians and the multiethnic armies of the Austro-Hungarian Empire. Whereas the Western Front consisted mostly of a dreadful slog in the wet plains of Flanders and northern France, the Italian Front was a high-wire act of natural danger added to that supplied by the opposing army's artillery. It comes as something of a shock when I see that the Dolomites' Tre Cime di Lavaredo (the Three Peaks visited with Ed in a hailstorm) and the summit ridge of the mighty Marmolada formed part of the no-man's-land of this front. This was beyond madness, clinging to mountainsides in the depth of winter and taking potshots at a similarly shivering enemy, all the while enduring the usual perils. On 11 December 1916, known to history as White Friday, several thousand soldiers died in avalanches. Tradition usually cites ten thousand deaths, though this is now disputed. What is not disputed is that far more of the Great War soldiers perished by being buried in the snow than by being gassed. As the annual snows retreat, corpses of these unfortunates are still being found in the mountains.

The Italians entered the war in 1915, after toying with the idea of fighting with Germany and Austria, with whom they had formed the Triple Alliance in 1882. Instead, they picked the Triple Entente (France, Britain, Russia), after being promised territorial gains at the expense of the Austrians in the secret Treaty of London. The Entente promised the Italians the moon, so eager was it to keep them on its side. Rome wanted all of the Dalmatian (Adriatic) coast down to Albania. There were pockets of Italian-speakers in what is now Slovenia and Croatia, but hardly enough to justify annexation to the Kingdom of Italy. After the war, the French and the English reneged on most of the provisions of the Treaty of London, particularly those relating to the Dalmatian coast, causing widespread furor in Italy and spurring its interwar expansionism in Africa.

As for Austria-Hungary and its war goals, the empire just wanted to hang on to its possessions south of the Alps, particularly the city of Trieste, which had been its major port for more than two hundred years.

When Italy attacked the Austrians in May of 1915, the tenor of the war was expressed by Gabriele d'Annunzio, a novelist and journalist known for his carnal enthusiasms and nationalist exultations as the self-styled "poet of slaughter." He became Italy's chief propagandist of the war effort, writing on the first day of the first offensive, "We are fighting with arms, we are waging our war, the blood is spurting from the veins of Italy! . . . The slaughter begins, the destruction begins. One of our people has died at sea, another on land. All these people, who yesterday thronged in the streets and squares, loudly demanding war, are full of veins, full of blood; and that blood begins to flow. . . . We have no other value but that of our blood to be shed." D'Annunzio would get his way: By war's end, 689,000 Italian soldiers were dead, about one million were seriously disabled, and an estimated six hundred thousand Italian civilians died due to harsh conditions created by the war. Most of the Italian and Austro-Hungarian military deaths occurred in the Alps.

I grip the wheel tightly in expectation as I near the approach road to the Plöcken Pass, once the Alpine no-man's-land of World War I. If the Gailberg Saddle was tough, then the higher pass will undoubtedly be an ordeal. But no, to my surprise, the road upward is a breeze, its only demerit being the horrific rockface in front of me, which I will somehow have to drive around. After a dozen or so disorienting switchbacks, the road heads into a long avalanche gallery that then becomes a tunnel. When I emerge from this—blam!—I'm at the border and I cross the invisible language line, from the German to the

Italian. Plöcken Pass becomes the Passo di Monte Croce Carnico. I pull over beside my friends, about forty motorcycles gleaming in the sunshine. The men lounge on a restaurant terrace, a sea of black leather.

The descent from the pass is mercifully free of other drivers. As I head downward, I experience and approve of an Italian innovation: hairpin tunnels. The Italians, by common agreement, are the best Alpine road and rail engineers. Switzerland's marvelous transportation infrastructure owes a lot not only to Alfred Nobel's dynamite but also to the Italian engineers and workers who crafted many of its tunnels and viaducts. The roadway off this mountain, its tunnels numerous, seems specifically created to calm the fears of the acrophobe. *But it's not that I'm afraid of heights.* . . .

When I arrive on the valley floor, the houses are more colorful—orange, even red—than their Austrian counterparts. Is it my imagination or is the color beige in Italy brighter than elsewhere? As the billboards flash by, I realize that there is a new Anglicism that has conquered the Continent. In the nineteenth century, it was the water closet, the WC, demanded by persnickety English tourists. Now it is Outlet, never translated into the local language, as in Outlet Shops, Outlet Village, and Factory Outlet.

"*Dottore! Dottore!*"

I look up and see an old man wagging his finger at me. I am in the main piazza of Tolmezzo (in Friulian: Tumeiç), fishing for change to feed the meter. I glance at my watch. Noon. Parking is free at lunchtime. I thank the gentleman and head under the old arcades to a restaurant terrace bedecked with checkered tablecloths. As the *insalata caprese*—yet another imitator of the Italian tricolor—is placed before me, I sigh with contentment. No heavy creamy dressing on this side of the lard line. I lift my fork to my mouth and watch a large flock of pigeons flap its way up and over the bright piazza.

At a roundabout on the outskirts of town, some militaristic group has planted in the central circle a fighter jet. The aircraft is secured to a slanted pedestal, so that it points almost straight up at the sky. Doubtless there is a military installation in the surroundings—Tolmezzo and its neighbors long housed the famed Italian Alpini Battalions. Beyond the fighter jet, on the horizon, is a stone behemoth doing a passable imitation of the Rock of Gibraltar. This then is the range known as the Julian Alps, named after Julius Caesar, who in 50 BCE founded what would become the town of Cividale del Friuli in the shadow of the mountains.

There is a narrow valley running between the Julian and Carnic Alps. I head eastward, the mountains marching on both sides of me, one after the other, green on their lower slopes, harsh limestone gray on their summits. The valley, unfortunately, is a victim of Alpine infrastructure. Not only is the highway, with its long viaducts, disruptive of the scenery, but so too is the autostrada, with its own viaducts and tunnels. The two roadways snake around each other, like a French braid, both of them successfully avoiding the railway tracks and bridges.

The region is known as the Slavia Friulana, a part of Friuli long influenced by the Slavs of nearby Slovenia, who settled here as early as the eighth century. But wait, it gets more confusing. I pull into the charming border town of Tarvisio. The signage is in four languages: Italian, German, Slovene, and Friulian (a cousin of Ladin). Thus we have, respectively, Tarvisio, Tarvis, Trbiž, and, mercifully, Tarvis again. The town also shares the distinction, along with the neighboring municipalities of Arnoldstein, Austria, and Kranjska Gora, Slovenia, of forming a tri-point not only of national borders but also of culture and language. This is where the German, Latin, and Slavic meet, at a watershed of idiom and dialect. On the last leg of my journey, I have finally found a language line as complex as a cobweb. The Alps have contrived to give me a memorable send-off.

Once I have crossed the border, everything becomes unintelligible. Slovenian is written with the Latin alphabet, but that does not help in any way at all. Any non-Hungarian-speaker visiting Budapest will know what I mean. The cognates are just not there. Is this building in front of me a beauty parlor or the Ministry of Foreign Affairs? Even the farms look different. Again and again I see curious hayracks in the fields, elongated wooden structures that look like what we used to call monkey bars or jungle gyms, protected from the rain by a long, metallic, pitched roof in the shape of a chevron. In between the horizontal wooden bars, hay has been packed tightly to dry in the breeze.

Today's destination, the village of Kranjska Gora, is Slovenia's most popular ski resort. This being high summer, the place does not suffer from overcrowding, although one particular demographic— heavily pregnant Slovene women—seems to have a weakness for the locale. Walking its streets becomes an exercise in dodging bellies. At last I settle into a terrace and realize that I am in Slavland. I hear men at the next table kibitzing. Their voices are low and musical, but when a punch line is delivered, the laughter is soprano, falsetto even, emitted in a Gatling-gun burst. I have heard this vocal tic before, in the company of Russian friends in the United States. Still, it is somewhat pleasant not to understand what people around you are saying: You can imagine them discussing geopolitics or the time–space continuum, whereas in fact they're talking about last night's episode of *The Mindy Project*.

At dinner, I ask the waiter about the weird hayracks that caught my attention on the drive into the village. He draws himself up and announces that they are what is called a *kozolec*, a source of Slovene pride and somewhat of a national symbol. He is quite solemn when imparting this information. I think of other national symbols—America's bald eagle, Britain's bulldog, France's rooster—and decide that the Slovene variant is decidedly less belligerent. What can be more laid-back than drying hay? I later learn that one of Slovenia's animal mascots is the honeybee. The place is an oasis of civilization.

The following morning, the way out of town to the *Ruska cesta*—the Russian Road—is pitifully signposted. At a roundabout, I see a bratwurst roaring off to the right, at about ten o'clock directionally. Motorcyles = Mountain Driving! I put the car into fifth and try to keep them in view. Of course I can't—they are flying at barely subsonic speed over the asphalt—but the road begins to rise, and a majestic and terrifying wall of rock lowers before me. The Julian Alps. At last a sign confirms that this is, yes, the *Ruska cesta*. The mountain road—correct that, the *insane* mountain road—through the Julian range, joining Kranjska Gora and the town of Bovec via the Vršič Pass, was built during World War I by POWs from the armies of Tsar Nicholas. It was a major undertaking—fifty kilometers long with fifty switchbacks—and provided a strategic way of supplying the Austro-Hungarians locked in a struggle with the Italians farther south. However intelligent its plan and execution, that doesn't make the road less dangerous—especially when it was being built. Fairly early on, at switchback number 8, I encounter the *Ruska kapelica*, a lovely wooden Russian Orthodox chapel. (The Slovenes are Catholic.) Its tan wooden slats overlap, somewhat in the manner of shingling, giving the sanctuary a strange animation. Its raison d'être, however, is anything but lovely—it was erected to honor the memory of 110 Russian laborers swept to their deaths by an avalanche in 1916.

The road onward and upward pleases me. The driver is cosseted on both sides by pine trees. Each hairpin bend, numbered with its elevation as on the Grossglockner road, has a helpful cobblestone surface, so that when the car starts behaving seismically, one knows it is time to grip the wheel and get in gear for the approach. Every now and then the greenery thins, exposing a heart-stopping perspective of the valley floor far below. Yet somehow I am no longer fearful. After a summer of jittery viscera in high places, this, the last pass on my journey, fails to plunge me into panic. *It's not that I was afraid of heights*, I tell myself, it's just that I was oversensitive. Yes, that must be it. Hundreds and hundreds of hairpins have finally straightened me out.

I begin to have second thoughts about my smug self-assessment when switchback number 16 reveals a horrorshow of stone opposite me. I pull over, slightly queasy. This is Mount Prisojnik, a colossal rockpile several kilometers long and stretching 2,547 meters into the sky. It cannot be ignored. I go over to the multilingual signboards posted at the belvedere from which the massive wall can best be viewed. One of Prisojnik's distinguishing features resides on its right shoulder, a large, circular peephole through which sunlight can be seen. It is known locally as "The Front Window." The other feature impresses even more. Down perhaps three hundred meters from the window and over to the left, the rockface is actually a face. Tricks of light and ledges have fashioned the likeness of a young girl's face. She is called "The Pagan Girl," supposedly a youthful giantess who helped travelers through the pass and then was changed into stone by wrathful furies.

As I read the stories told on the signboards, car doors slam behind me and loud voices, which at a distance sound as if they're speaking English, resolve into another West Germanic tongue as they come closer. My heart sinks, for I know what this means. Soon the merry Dutch are upon me, yawping in excitement and jostling me as they trace with their fingers some of the items pictured on the signboard. This gesture, of course, obscures the pictures, much like what happens to a subway wall map when fingered by out-of-towners. When one of their party obliviously places herself directly in front of me, so that I can no longer read the text or see the mountain properly, I admit defeat and turn back to my car. Just as I suspected, they are campers. But I am not angry; I consider theirs to be a farewell gesture to me on behalf of all of their countrymen I have slandered this summer.

When the tree line flashes by and the pass is reached, I am chagrined to find that there is nowhere to park. Not for lack of parking spaces—there are scores of them along the roadway's shoulders—but not one single space is free. We are in a Slovenian Valhalla peopled by hikers, bikers, and many, many cyclists. It is a sunny summer Sunday and everyone has come to the Russian Road. Among the cyclists are some heroic weirdos. On the way up, I passed someone operating one of those recumbent tricycles, moving so slowly that he might not reach the pass till Christmas. On the way down, I will see an older gentleman cruising smartly uphill with Nordic walking poles and inline Rollerblades that look rather like cross-country skis. My hat is off to all of them. Then of course there are the bikers. This pass seems to bring out the worst in them. I suppose it is a healthier way for men to release their energies than going to war. Europe tried that for several thousand years; now there are BIKERS WELCOME! signs everywhere.

My reading has warned me that the descent from the Vršič Pass is hair-raising. My reading told the truth. Good-bye to the cobbled hairpins, hello to curves so sharp you feel as if your car is perpendicular to the ground, as if you're executing the maneuver of a crazed biker. And the views: Fireman, save my child! The trees on the south side of the pass road are maddeningly modest, leaving yawning perspectives over the void. The level ground of the valley seems to be miles and miles beneath the roadway. All of this is enhanced by the absence of guardrails. I tell myself that this is yet another farewell. The Vršič Pass is warning me not to get too cocky.

At last I reach the valley of the River Soča. The roadway crosses and recrosses the frothy river penned in by tall mountains. At a turnout, I spy a sea of cars bearing Austrian, Slovene, and Italian plates. I stop for a look. There they all are, whooping with delight as their inflatable rafts rock in the foaming white water of the Soča. Far better for these three nationalities to be at play together today, considering what they were engaged in a hundred years ago.

Let me explain. I follow the River Soča and reach the village of Kobarid. To students of agony and debacle, they are better known by their Italian names: the River Isonzo and Caporetto.

AMONG ALL THE DUNDERHEADS to have excelled in stupidity in their command of armies during World War I, the gold medal must be attributed to Luigi Cadorna, the supreme chief of the Italian army. A vain and vicious martinet who disdained politicians and distrusted his troops, Cadorna believed that martial valor came from fear. On his watch, severe justice was meted out to those perceived to be derelict in their duties. Historians still debate whether Cadorna revived the ancient Roman practice of decimation, whereby every tenth man in a unit would be executed for some collective failing. What is not disputed is the depth of the general's savagery: The Italian army shot 750 of its own, a number that dwarfs the total for all the other belligerent armies combined. Machine guns were set up *behind* the Italian Front trenches, to shoot in the back those deemed to be dawdling about going over the top into no-man's-land. Cadorna was not one to share the blame for his disgraceful prosecution of the war; prior to the final insult of Caporetto, he had sacked 217 generals, 255 colonels, and 355 battalion commanders. And he had no compassion whatsoever for the Italians taken captive by the enemy. In the Great War, by gentlemen's agreement, each country would supply food to its soldiers held as POWs in hostile territory. Italy, alone among all the nations involved in the war, refused to send food for its captive soldiers. Cadorna declared that the knowledge that one would be fed was an inducement to desertion. He was the only commander to have arrived at this brilliant conclusion. Because of this policy, it is estimated that more than a hundred thousand Italian POWs died of starvation.

Were that all he did, Cadorna would not have earned his pride of place on the podium of murderous incompetence. But no. Neither a strategist nor a tactician, he ordered major offensives every three months or so. That, in itself, might not have constituted proof of pigheadedness, had not these offensives all occurred in the same place: the front at the River Isonzo. Cadorna oversaw not one, not three, not five, but *eleven* disastrous attacks along the Isonzo, with hundreds of thousands killed and even more injured in a repeated and usually futile attempt to gain a few kilometers. Touching stories have emerged of Austrian gunners imploring the men advancing toward them to turn around, as recounted in Mark Thompson's *The White War*. One has an Austrian officer crying out in Italian, "That's enough! Stop firing!" When the Italians complied, he called out, "You are brave men. Don't get yourselves killed like this."

By the fall of 1917, the effects of Cadorna's savage discipline and military blundering bore fruit: The Italian army was utterly demoralized, ready to desert at the drop of a hat. That hat-drop occurred on 24 October 1917 at Caporetto/Kobarid. At two in the morning, the valley filled with poison gas, causing panic among the Italian troops there who had masks that could protect them for a maximum of two hours. Thousands fled. An enormous artillery barrage—2,200 guns—shook the mountains four hours later. The Austro-Hungarians had been reinforced by hardened German divisions from the Western and Eastern Fronts, and the latter used their recently developed storm-trooper techniques—small special-operations squads that would infiltrate the enemy positions and attack unexpectedly from the rear. Within days, the entire Second Italian Army collapsed and a wholesale rout ensued. Men threw down their rifles, their commanders shot themselves, hundreds of thousands ran for their lives back into Friuli. When it was all over, two weeks later, the Italians had been pushed back a hundred kilometers and had dug in defensively on the right bank of the River Piave, near Venice. Twelve thousand of them had been killed, 30,000 wounded, 294,000 taken prisoner, and 350,000 disbanded, wandering the countryside aimlessly, in the hope of getting home. I remember what Sergio, the disgruntled Austro-Italian of Bolzano, said unfeelingly of his uncle's service fighting the Italians at Caporetto: "We *crushed* them!"

One German lieutenant, twenty-five-year-old Erwin Rommel, with a force of two hundred men under his command, had in just over two days infiltrated eighteen kilometers behind the lines, climbed three thousand meters, and taken captive 150 officers and 9,000 soldiers. In one instance, Rommel advanced alone, far ahead of his contingent, and accepted the surrender of around a thousand soldiers. To his astonishment, the Italians lifted him onto their shoulders and shouted *Evviva la Germania!*—Long Live Germany! Such was the devastating effect on morale that three years of Cadorna's blistering idiocy had produced. For his bravery, Rommel—the future "Desert Fox" of World War II—was awarded the Pour le Mérite, a.k.a. the Blue Max, one of Germany's highest military distinctions.

In Italy, *Caporetto* instantly became a byword for humiliating, catastrophic defeat, and it is still used metaphorically for everything from sporting events to political changes. The Slovene town of Kobarid wears its notoriety lightly, seemingly more interested in its new vocation as an outdoorsman's paradise. More Italianate in architecture than Slovenian—Italy lies just a few kilometers away—the village earned its place in world literature thanks to Ernest Hemingway, who wrote that Caporetto was "a little white town with a campanile in a valley. It was a clean little town and there was a fine fountain in the square." Never mind that Hemingway never set foot in the place, his *Farewell to Arms* immortalized the headlong flight westward of the Italian army through Friuli, which he witnessed as a volunteer ambulance driver.

Not that Kobarid ignores its place in history. It can hardly do so, as on a hilltop overlooking the town Mussolini erected an Italian ossuary for the remains of his country's fallen along the Isonzo Front. It is solemn and ugly. Many years later, the Slovenian government funded a museum about the battles waged along the banks of the river. In 1993, it won an award for best new museum in Europe—no small accomplishment, as Slovenia would not enter the European Union until 2004.

The museum merits the award. Located in a handsome three-story townhouse not too far from Hemingway's campanile, the exhibition rooms immerse the visitor in the wretched conditions of life in the mountains of the Isonzo Front. Dozens of artifacts and letters home and hundreds of pictures help re-create that reality. There is absolutely no triumphalism or chauvinism attached to the accompanying multilingual texts—they are more a clear-eyed description of events and conditions, with a touch of the elegiac. One picture stops me in my tracks—several Italian soldiers jammed into an ice tunnel, pointing their guns and mortars at holes hacked in the ice walls. This was madness.

I take the stairs to the top floor, passing a chapel-like niche adorned with a large framed photograph of Ernest Hemingway. The curators have obviously decided to play along, paying tribute to the man who never visited Kobarid. My smile fades when I enter the so-called Black Room, a photo gallery of horror, of the dead, of the mutilated. In a previous work on the Great War, *Back to the Front*, I called such photographs "war porn"; now I am not so sure, as this seems a fitting finale to the narrative told in the Kobarid Museum's succession of exhibition rooms. To my relief, an attendant comes to fetch me. I have reserved a screening of a multimedia presentation in English. (It is also offered in Slovenian, Italian, German, French, Spanish, Czech, and Hungarian and subtitled in Russian, Hebrew, and Croatian.) We have difficulty navigating our way out of a neighboring room, as a tour group defiantly blocks our way while examining a scale-model maquette of the mountainous front. The attendant sighs, exasperated, "The Italians! Always the same."

Eventually I am seated alone in the screening room, watching an admirably potted history of the Isonzo Front in general and the Battle of Caporetto (officially The Twelfth Battle of the Isonzo) in particular. Afterward, I regain the streets of Kobarid thinking of the Austrian,

Slovenian, and Italian whitewater rafters seen the day before. Europe has come a long way.

THE WHIMSICAL CITY of Ljubljana is the first stop on the final leg of my journey. My time and budget are running low, so I decide to skirt the high passes and explore the places in the shadows of the Alps. Well, sort of. I plan on giving myself a treat, in a city that has the mountains on a distant horizon.

Ljubljana is not that city. The capital of Slovenia nonetheless is itself a treat, with its playful decorative grace notes and an architectural repertoire ranging from medieval through baroque and Vienna secessionist (i.e., art nouveau) to postmodern. A bridge with a dragon at each of its four corners spans the narrow River Ljubljanica. The dragon is the symbol of the city—another fire-breather adorns the inevitable hilltop castle overlooking the old town. Snide local lore holds that the four dragons will wag their tails if the bridge is crossed by a virgin—of course, this has yet to happen.

On both banks of the river are restaurant and café terraces absolutely jammed with locals. At street corners and on bridges stand buskers, mummers, and magicians, all surrounded by rapturous crowds. I pause to hear a young woman with a guitar and an amazing voice, both rugged and smooth, a Slovene Adele. The animation in the old town takes me aback—this is, after all, a weeknight, yet it seems that the whole population has turned out to eat and drink, as if every warm summer night called for a carnival. I wander from the river and find myself in a quarter that is distinctly countercultural. Head shops, the scent of reefer, and carefully curated seedy cafés mix in with municipal art houses and squats devoted to keeping Ljubljana's bohemians happy. Foreign languages can now be heard, the young Reinhards of Europe having heard of the city's welcoming vibe.

I stop before a shop called Laibach. Laibach? The owner explains that this was an earlier name for Ljubljana. I tell him that I know of a band called Laibach. "Oh yes, they're still playing," he says. This information brings me back to the early 1990s, when I was the music editor at a magazine in New York. Laibach, an avant-garde Slovenian band, descended on the clubs of the city, and nobody knew what to make of them. Their sound, their look, their whole shtick—all were unmistakably Fascist. Were they, in fact, Fascists? The band members explained to the bewildered press that Fascism was part of European folklore, part of its DNA, and they were just expressing that tradition. Doubtless there are other Slovenian provocateurs lurking in this hip neighborhood.

Daybreak draws me back northward, Alpward, for a last day near the mountains. The Karawanks, a limestone range that is a continuation of the Carnic Alps, looms on the border of Austria and Slovenia. I head toward one of its glacial lakes, Slovenia's biggest tourist attraction. Like the lakes of the Salzkammergut, Lake Bled seems laid out by a draftsman concerned with perspective and perfection. It is almost too beautiful, its still waters changing color according to the time of day. A picturesque red-roofed medieval castle dominates from a hilltop on its western shore. In the middle of the lake, just off center, a wooded island rises up. Once the home of a temple of Živa, the Slavic goddess of love, it became Christianized in the distant past and the sanctuary became dedicated to the Blessed Virgin Mary. A Gothic chapel stands below a graceful baroque bell tower, which rises above the treetops and can be seen from any point on the lake. And, in the background, as always, my friends the Alps. It is time to bid them farewell.

The following day finds me in my final destination, the Italian port city of Trieste. I started by the banks of Lake Geneva, a good forty kilometers from the Alps, and I shall end on the shores of the Adriatic, similarly distant from the mountains. Although Trieste can hardly be said to be an Alpine city—a harsh limestone plateau called the Carso separates it from the Julian Alps—it might as well be, for its variegated population and history reflect those of the passes and valleys in which I have spent the summer. Besides, it is my birthday and Trieste has always been one of my four dream cities. The others—Paris, Istanbul, Aleppo—have all been seen in years past, leaving only this Adriatic gem on my list.

Trieste is, as I had hoped, exceedingly strange, an Italian city that looks Viennese, painted in a weird mustard color. For centuries, it was the port of the Habsburg Empire, one of the great cities of *Mitteleuropa* (the only one south of the Alps), its population a mixture of Austrians, Hungarians, Italians, and Slavs. Christians mixed with Jews and Muslims. There is a Serbian Orthodox Church in its old town, as well as remnants of Antiquity that pop up unexpectedly around corners and down alleyways.

The place was a melting pot, or a mosaic, but it became less so after the Italians took possession of the city after World War I. Memories of that conflict loom large in Trieste this summer, as it is the centennial of the funeral of Archduke Franz Ferdinand and his wife, Sophie, gunned down in Sarajevo and brought here amid appropriate solemn pomp. Large banners throughout the city show old photographs of the occasion, placed in the exact spot where the photographer stood one hundred years ago. In one, a crowd of young men looks out at the passing cortège, except for one fellow who stares directly at the viewfinder, impudent and very much alive. For some reason, this image moves me. Perhaps it is the knowledge that in a few short weeks he would doubtless be handed a uniform and a rifle and be marched off to an almost certain death in the Alps.

I sit at a café and whip out my notebook. No one bats an eye. Trieste is a writer's city par excellence, literary luminaries having flocked here for its unusual, unsettling atmosphere. One of the greatest was James Joyce, who taught English in Trieste in the first decades of the twentieth century, before moving to Zurich for his Fanny Urinia days. His past haunts are all signposted in the city, as they are in Dublin. In an incredible feat of memory over distance, Joyce wrote some of his greatest works—*Portrait of the Artist as a Young Man*, *Dubliners*, and much of *Ulysses*—in Trieste. Later, in *Finnegan's Wake*, he paid a skewed homage to his adopted home by punning: "And trieste, trieste ate I my liver!" Which a canny French reader can read as "*Triste, triste était mon livre!*" (Sad, sad was my book!)—especially one familiar with Paul Verlaine, one of whose poems is entitled *O triste, triste était mon âme* (O sad, sad was my soul). When not revolutionizing English-language literature, Joyce also contributed to its Italian counterpart. The sharp-eyed Irishman recognized the genius of a neurotic businessman and washed-up Triestine writer, Italo Svevo, and later made sure that his classic *Confessions of Zeno* found a publisher.

The litany of slightly insane brilliance is not limited to Joyce and Svevo. Giacomo Casanova, one of the greatest rogues and spies of the eighteenth century, concludes his endlessly entertaining memoirs in Trieste. Nineteenth-century explorer and sexual adventurer Richard Burton translated the *Kama Sutra*, *The Thousand and One Nights*, and a collection of erotic classical poems by Catullus while in the city.

Stendahl came this way, as did Rainer Maria Rilke, whose *Duino Elegies*, named for a castle just out of town, ranks as the poet's most important work. Filippo Marinetti inaugurated the futurist movement here. More recently, writer Jan Morris was fascinated by the city—her *Trieste and the Meaning of Nowhere* remains a touchstone to the city and its odd lack of identity. And it is no coincidence whatsoever that our greatest living travel writer, Claudio Magris, with his *Danubio* (Danube), is an Italian native of Trieste who has taught German literature at the university here.

If one walks farther into Trieste, one finds a pleasing hodgepodge, as befits its multiple nonidentities. Its cathedral is called San Giusto, as Justus was a Roman citizen of third-century Trieste martyred for his Christianity by being thrown into the Adriatic with weights attached to him. That sea can be seen from the hilltop sanctuary, which stands beside the city's citadel. The church contains columns from a Roman tomb and elements of the Romanesque, Byzantine, Gothic, and baroque. In the lower town, Trieste's Jews continue the city's devotion to the eclectic. Although their synagogue, one of Europe's most important, was completed as recently as 1912, the great gray stone building draws its architectural inspiration from the building style in vogue in fourth-century Roman Syria. So perhaps Trieste *is* an Alpine city after all: Its mixture of cultures, languages, faiths, and cuisines is wholly reminiscent of the passes I have crossed this summer. It's as if the human variety encountered—and created—in the center of Europe by the Alps has come to ground splendidly in seaside Trieste.

Nothing is straightforward here. Depending on which square you visit, the cobbled expanse is either pristine or filthy. At the Caffè San Marco, an art nouveau literary café in this caffeine-crazed city (Triestinos consume twice the amount of coffee as average Italians), red-lipped ladies who lunch sit alongside grizzled drunks downing grappa. In the back is a bookstore where university students stand at a window-side counter, their laptops open.

I head to the shore. This quarter of Trieste is resolutely Austrian, having been constructed in the eighteenth century under the orders of Empress Maria Theresa, the only woman to have ruled the Habsburg Empire. Grand buildings lead to grand squares. At one place, the uniformity is pierced by a small, rectangular harbor, known somehow as the Canal Grande, a stretch of water from which launches once departed to fetch the wealthy from their yachts. The area is Italy's finest seaside urbanism, bar none, but it is not a product of Italian genius.

I have switched cafés and closed the notebook for the last time. The Piazza Unità d'Italia stretches out before me. It is the largest square in Italy and the largest seafront square in Europe. It is so big, is there room for ghosts here? Yes. The sun is setting over the Adriatic, and a large group of visitors from a cruise ship follow their umbrella-wielding tour guide. It is an assault rifle of American tourists, reminding me that it is time to go home. I stretch languidly and order a last *caffè corretto*, knowing that my journey is over. In Trieste, this city of ghosts, a few dozen kilometers from the Alps, I think of the presences that have animated me and surprised me. Sisi, of course, but also Hannibal, Napoleon, Toni Kurz, Heidi, Sherlock Holmes, Edward Whymper, James Bond, Nietzsche, Rousseau, Joyce, and Frankenstein's monster.

I had not expected such a richness of the imaginary and the real. The Alps, before I spent this time in their fastnesses, was to me a rumpled blanket—a *very* rumpled blanket—over the heart of Europe. I did not know that they tell a story of humanity far beyond their bounds.

ACKNOWLEDGMENTS

SOME AUTHORS like to perpetuate the idea that writing is a heroic solitary endeavor. It ain't—there are people who help you out throughout the process.

In my case, this network of support spans an ocean. In Europe, I'd like to thank Heidi Ellison for her repeated hospitality in Paris. Likewise, Marie-Christine and Scott Blair warmly welcomed me into their Paris home for extended periods. And Elisabeth and Sandy Whitelaw were always there for me in the French capital with advice, food, and wine. Sadly, my very dear friend Sandy passed away in early 2015. A lover of, and an expert on, the Alps—he was on the British ski team at the 1956 Olympics in Cortina d'Ampezzo—Sandy will not be able, alas, to point out the errors in my book. He mastered many languages, so his help would have been invaluable in negotiating the linguistic minefield of a book on the Alps. I still hear his voice over my shoulder, but all of the mistakes in this narrative must be laid at my doorstep.

Also in Paris, my thanks to Pierre Masson, proprietor of the Librairie des Alpes, for his excellent advice. If you're in town, visit this gem of a bookstore—it's at 6, Rue de Seine in the sixth arrondissement, just behind the building housing the Académie française.

In Switzerland, my thanks of course to Ernst Herb, tour guide and travel companion extraordinaire. His friend, NoéMie Schwaller, became my friend and agreed to accompany me on that weird day in Heidiland. The following summer, she introduced me to her father, who shared some of his encyclopedic knowledge of the strange balancing act that is Switzerland. Thank you, Herr Schwaller. I am also deeply grateful to Paul Rechsteiner, who let Ernst and me stay in his St. Gallen flat while he was away in Bern. His job? He's a Swiss senator—which goes to show that not all politicians are cut from the same cloth. Elsewhere, Italian novelist and journalist Carlo Pizzati answered my queries with lengthy, funny, and immensely informative e-mails. *Grazie*, Carlo.

Closer to home, in Rhode Island, I want to thank my family—Eve, Rachel, and Jill—for their ever-bemused support of my obsessions. Also, a heartfelt thank you to Dana Holmgren, for her gentle and steady encouragement. A fellow writer in Providence, Phelps Clark, struck just the right balance between cheerleading and hectoring to keep me from my proclivity to procrastinate. He also made a valuable editorial suggestion that spared me a month or so of dithering. Phelps's friend, Tony Trocchi, a rock climber, did me a great favor by dipping into his extensive library and extracting a dozen of the best books and memoirs about mountaineering. And Spanish professor and avid mountaineer Francisco Fernandez de Alba was kind enough to read a draft of the manuscript before it was sent to my publishers.

In New York, thanks as ever to my old Paris pals Maia Wechsler and Edward Hernstadt for opening their Dumbo home to me whenever business took me to the city. And thanks, Ed, for keeping me company in the Dolomites and the Engadine. In Manhattan, long-time friend and fellow writer Eli Gottlieb provided the correct dose of despairing levity whenever the going got rough.

Thanks as ever to my unflappable literary agents in New York, Liz Darhansoff and Chuck Verrill. Last, a great measure of gratitude to my editor, Matt Weiland, for nurturing and feeding the Alpine bee in my bonnet. His editorial suggestions, alarming at first sight, turned a stumbling draft into a standing manuscript. Thank you, Matt.

Readers are encouraged to give me their feedback—even if they're just Dutch campers who want to express their outrage. Contact info can be found on my website: stephenosheaonline.com.

Index

Page numbers followed by *n* refer to material in footnotes.